NEVILLE COLEMAN has logged more than 10,(̩ ̣ ̣ ̣ in Australian seas under almost every possible set of circumstances and conditions. He is publisher of the magazine *Underwater: The Diver's Journal* and has written twenty-seven books on fish, shells, marine biology and diving, many of which are regarded as classic references. Neville is one of the best known and widely respected marine life authorities in Australia. He has led pioneering expeditions exploring Australia's underwater terrain and has discovered more than 200 new marine species.

An accomplished photographer, Neville is compiler of one of the world's largest photographic libraries dealing with marine subjects and lectures on underwater photography and on marine biology.

Books by the same author, listed in order of publication, 1974–1987:

Australian Marine Fishes in Colour	Reed
What Shell is That?	Lansdowne
Shell Collecting in Australia	Reed
Australian Fisherman's Fish Guide	Bay Books
A Look at Wildlife on the Great Barrier Reef	Bay Books
Australian Beachcomber	Collins
Field Guide to the Marine Life of S.E. Australia	Rigby
Field Guide to Australian Marine Life	Rigby
Shells Alive	Rigby
Scuba Diver's Introduction to Marine Biology	AMPI ▲▲
Observer's Book of Sea Shells	Methuen
Australian Sea Fishes South of 30 degrees	Doubleday
Australian Sea Fishes North of 30 degrees	Doubleday
Fishes of New South Wales	Doubleday
Fishes of Victoria	Doubleday
Harmful Fishes of Australia	Doubleday
Fisherman's Catchbook	Doubleday
Great Barrier Reef	ICP △△
Australian Great Barrier Reef (With Neil McLeod & J. Howest)	Dorr-McLeod Publishing
Nudibranchs of Australasia (with Richard Willan)	AMPI ▲▲
Beginner's Guide to Underwater Marine Biology	AMPI ▲▲
Discover Sea Shells	Hale & Iremonger
Discover Beachcombing	Hale & Iremonger
Poetry in Pictures Great Barrier Reef (with Mark O'Connor)	Hale & Iremonger
Shells in Australia	Reed
The Underwater Australia Dive Guide	Nelson
Australian Sea Life South of 30 degrees	Doubleday

▲▲ Australasian Marine Photographic Index
△△ Colour Library Books

The UNDERWATER AUSTRALIA Dive Guide

Neville Coleman

N E L S O N

This book is dedicated to all those who make the
Australian Diving Industry what it is today, and to all
those who will make it even better tomorrow.

Nelson Publishers
Thomas Nelson Australia
480 La Trobe Street Melbourne Victoria 3000

First published 1987
Copyright © Neville Coleman 1987

National Library of Australia
Cataloguing-in-Publication data:

Coleman, Neville,
The underwater Australia dive guide.

Bibliography.
Includes index.
ISBN 0 17 006919 2.

1. Diving, Submarine — Australia — Guide-books.
2. Australia — Description and travel — 1976- — Guide-books. 3. Scuba
diving — Australia — Guide-books. 4. Skin diving — Australia — Guide-
books. 5. Underwater exploration — Australia — Guide-books. I. Title.

797.2'3'0994

Designed by Karen Harbour
Typeset in 10.5/12 Garth Graphic by Trade Graphics Pty Ltd, Port Melbourne
Printed in Hong Kong

CONTENTS

PHOTOGRAPHIC DETAILS

Much of the photographic work within this book was accomplished with NIKON and NIKONOS cameras using Oceanic, PGI and Sonic Research Strobes on Ektachrome Professional and Kodachrome film.

AUTHOR'S NOTE:

All effort has been made to include as many establishments as possible and the opportunity was offered to all equally in regard to advertising and inclusion in the appendixes. No doubt in a publication of this scope there will be exclusions due to developments of which the author was not aware. I apologise for any oversights and assure those concerned that additions and corrections will be included in any subsequent editions.

I would appreciate hearing from anyone who has corrections or additions to this edition. These may be submitted in writing to Neville Coleman, Underwater Australia Dive Guide, PO Box 702, Springwood Qld 4127, or by phoning (07) 341 8931.

PHOTO CREDITS:

Roger Steene provided the photographs on pages 23, 28 and 153 of this book; Dave Worth the photograph on page 139. All other photographs were supplied by the AMPI and taken by the author.

ACKNOWLEDGEMENTS

All the photographs in this book (apart from four) were taken from the files of the Australasian Marine Photographic Index (AMPI). The Index contains colour transparencies of living animals and plants, cross-referenced against identified specimens housed in museums and scientific institutions. It also covers related marine activities.

As curator of the Index, I hope that one day the marine fauna and flora of Australia may be identified alive; there will then no longer be any necessity for large collections of animals to be made just for the purposes of identification. If we are to find methods of protecting our seas and husbanding the animals and plants that are in them, people must be made aware that they exist; it is for this purpose that the AMPI was created.

The following institutions have aided the AMPI to continue its programme of advancing the knowledge of living Australian marine organisms: the Australian Museum, the Museum of Victoria, the Queensland Museum, the West Australian Museum, and the Northern Territory Museum.

I would like to thank Nelson Publishers for commissioning me to write this book, which has given me the opportunity of sharing Underwater Australia with the world and, in doing so, of promoting the Australian Diving Industry.

Many people and businesses have assisted in the compilation of this book and I herewith acknowledge their help. They include the Tasmanian Tourist Commission, the South Australian Tourist Commission, the New South Wales Tourist Commission, the Victorian Tourist Commission, the Queensland Tourist and Travel Corporation, the Western Australian Tourist Commission and the Northern Territory Tourist Commission.

The NRMA and the RACQ were especially helpful with providing maps, accommodation catalogues and tourist directories, as were the various State National Parks and Wildlife Services, the Great Barrier Reef Marine Park Authority, and all the people and organisations who sent in material for the appendixes.

Those who have advertised in *The Underwater Australia Dive Guide* have had the foresight and faith to contribute towards its production and in doing so have enhanced both their businesses and the image of diving in Australia.

My heartfelt thanks go to Karen Handley, my research assistant, Elaine Legget, my typist, Chris Dvoracek, my editor, and Karen Harbour, my designer. Without their help my efforts, concepts, words and images would remain mine alone, together with their efforts they have become Australia's!

HOW TO USE THIS BOOK

Information about diving around Australia appears in this guide in a variety of forms: maps, tables, colour photos, directories, as well as narrative.

The reader may wish to browse through the book from beginning to end, or to consult the table of contents to locate chapters of specific interest. State-by-state chapters cover regional diving areas clockwise around the continent from Cape York Peninsula. A list of commercial services, a locator map and a table of general information is included for each area. Solid black squares are used in the tables of general information to show weather conditions, dive methods, marine life and many other details which apply in the area being described. Other chapters of the guide treat matters of general interest, such as underwater wildlife, marine hazards, medical services and instruction agencies.

To refer the reader to particular items of information, the guide concludes with a series of indexes to underwater flora and fauna (including cross-references to scientific and common names), to regional diving areas and to organisations named in the guide, as well as a general subject index. Italicized entries in the indexes show where to find relevant illustrations.

INTRODUCTION

'The challenge of tomorrow', I wonder how many people, divers and divers-to-be, can relate to those words. For most of us, diving beneath the sea is the ultimate challenge, and, hidden within the portals of our exterior selves lies an attraction to the excitement of the unknown.

Certainly the greatest challenge in my life was to overcome my fear of the underwater world and its inhabitants. It took me ten years of facing and experiencing all the sea had, before I could feel I belonged; not because I beat it, but because *I earned it*.

Yet never in my more than 10,000 logged dives beneath Australian seas completed over twenty-five years and under almost every condition and circumstance, have I faced a challenge as awesome as the one I face now: to produce a book on Underwater Australia that describes the best dive sites available, where both resident and overseas divers can enjoy the greatest diving Australia has to offer. Only 271 pages is all I have to outline, picture and display 20,000 kilometres of shoreline, hundreds of islands, thousands of offshore rocks and a million reefs. A formidable task by anybody's standards, yet one that deserves to be tackled despite its seeming impossibility.

In an effort to produce a usable result from so much available material I have had to control my exuberance and design a format that will give the diver an instant reference to each dive area. I refer to dive *areas*, because in this book there is not the space to describe individual dive *sites*.

Due to the differences in given diving localities within each state, in many cases it was necessary to amalgamate sites and localities into areas in order to give the best coverage of the Australian scene. Most areas have different climatic conditions and different localized conditions and for this reason each needs to be explained individually; some in fine detail, others in broader terms.

DIVING IN AUSTRALIA

The seas surrounding Australia have everything to offer; the known and the unknown. Around this island continent the diver is able to experience the entire range of tropical and temperate water diving. Unlike diving in other parts of the world, e.g. The Bahamas,

Solomon Islands, etc., diving in Australian waters is almost always adventure diving, *not* bathtub diving. To dive in Australian waters is always a challenge – rarely does the wind stop blowing – so that in most offshore diving ocean swells and surface wave chop are an integral part of the scene.

Most places (except the west coast of Tasmania) have, at various times of the year, periods when the wind does not blow and the seas are relatively calm; however, these periods are seasonal and must be understood as such.

Diving to me is not just a haphazard thing that is done on the spur of the moment. Indeed, if there is one Australian pastime that requires forethought, planning and a commonsense approach, then it's diving. Too many people in the past have not realized that although diving is an exciting, adventurous, exhilarating undertaking, if its rules of self-regulating common sense and training are not adhered to, undertaking diving may result in a quite different sort of undertaking!

THE HISTORY OF DIVING

The very history of diving in Australia has been one of invention and innovation. In the last fifteen years the sport of scuba diving has enjoyed tremendous growth and support, to the extent that it now attracts a major commitment by professional enterprise.

The majority of pioneers taught themselves to dive and either purchased what limited equipment was available, or built their own out of components already in use in other forms, e.g. fire extinguishers, oxygen bottles.

The initial interest in compressed air diving stemmed from participation in spearfishing and cray catching, as Self Contained Underwater Breathing Apparatus (SCUBA) enabled underwater hunters to go deeper and stay longer in search for their prey.

Modern diving in Australia appeared just after the Second World War. With the return of our servicemen and the integration of European settlers who had seen the Italian and French frogmen, the art of underwater hunting was introduced to Australia. However, they were not the first skindivers in Australia.

For more than one hundred years after its discovery, Australia had struggled along as a continent of separate states – each independent of the others, each drawing up its own laws and by-laws, each separated by distances equal to whole countries in Europe. The imports from other countries, particularly England, were large and, although some trade had begun in wool and produce, little money was made from export. Certainly in the marine field, the export of natural resources was almost negligible.

PEARL SHELL DIVING

It was not until 1861 that the beginnings of what was to become a flourishing trade in marine shells were discovered. In Nichol Bay in the north of Western Australia, an American sailor called Tays collected some pearl shells from beaches and mudflats of the intertidal zone. Although present in small numbers only, the quality of these shells was very high. The first pearl shells ultimately gave rise to a quest, which was to pioneer the vast lonely coastlines and islands of northern Australia. Before long the shells along the shoreline were depleted and local Aboriginals were employed (press ganged) to skindive for shells in shallow water. So it was that skindiving became the means by which Australia's first national export of marine resources developed.

By 1868 the pearling heyday had begun and a fishery was established from Torres Strait to Shark Bay in Western Australia. Before the Second World War the industry boomed and a number of Asian divers were brought in to work the pearl beds.

The principal diving dress of the day was an unwieldy helmet and corselet. The diver was fully encased in a dry canvas suit with heavy lead boots and a heavy copper helmet with glass faceplate. Connected to the helmet was a thick air hose through which the air was pumped to the diver from either a hand bellows or a mechanical pump. Each diver had a tender who looked after him and received a percentage of the diver's shells.

Carl Atkinson, one of northern Australia's pioneer salvage divers, built his own one man decompression chamber and saved the lives of over fifteen divers, many of them pearl shell divers.

Modern cultured pearl techniques developed in Japan and enhanced in north Western Australia support a multi-million dollar industry, with little of the inherent risks faced by today's hookah diving seed pearl shell gatherers.

Most divers were Aboriginals, Thursday Islanders, Japanese or Malays. The Asians were considered best suited to the work because of their willingness and their resistance to diver's disease, caused by working too deep for too long.

In those days there was no knowledge of the cause of the bends, it was just treated as an occupational hazard. There were few excuses for a diver not diving. Head colds, chest colds, arthritis and the bends were just everyday things to be put up with until their seriousness rendered the diver incapable of working. Ruptured ear drums, sinuses, or limited use of limbs are not as painful under pressure, so often the diver worked until he was paralysed, or died. If the diver did not dive the whole crew suffered, not just the diver. His tender earned no money, the crew were cut down on their quota, and the captain and owner also made less. The diver was the main link in the chain. If he found plenty of good shell, he was a hero – if he didn't dive for any reason, or he brought up no shell, he could well be ostracized or abused until he again went below and did well. Each pearling lugger and its divers would vie to be first at the grounds, first to get the best shell, and first to fill up and race it back to port to get the best prices.

There were many fatalities, little was known of decompression techniques, equipment often failed, storms arose while divers were on the bottom, and ropes and hoses parted due to the huge strain of continental drift diving. The hundreds of crumbling headstones in the divers' graveyards at Broome and Darwin today are grim reminders of the unknown toll that pearling took on human lives. These graves belong to the minority of victims whose bodies were found, or those who died where they could be transported to a burial ground.

Within fifty years the shallow water beds were fished out and it was necessary to dive deeper and deeper to obtain good shell. This increased the hazards to divers and scores were lost and bent diving the dangerous 80 metre (240 feet) grounds.

THE BEGINNING OF SCUBA

By the middle 1950s SCUBA sets were being sold in some sports store shops, together with a phonograph record that explained the few known rules of staying alive while scuba diving.

One of the pioneers of designing and developing underwater equipment in Australia was Jim Ager of Airdive Equipment (Victoria), who in 1954 (after several years of experimentation with oxygen rebreathing and air apparatus) formed Sea Bee Marine Sport and Diving. In the same year he registered the manufacturing side of the business as Airdive Equipment, taking out patents on a number of inventions. For over thirty years right up to the present day, Airdive Equipment has continued to produce an entire range of diving equipment; all designed, built and marketed from their Victorian base.

Equipment design advanced and the range expanded each year as more and more people took up the challenge of diving. Better masks, better fins, and better regulators appeared in sports stores but it wasn't until the late 1950s and early 1960s that the first part-time dive shops began to open in other states and that scuba sections were formed in spearfishing clubs.

Most spearfishing clubs did little to encourage the individual scuba diver and diving was often just something taken on after spearfishing competitions etc. Scuba training was provided by club committees in some cases, except where there was expertise available from people who had migrated from England or Europe, where the British Sub-Aqua Club had branches.

In Sydney in the early 1960s, clubs such as the British Sub-Aqua Club, which had a small but extremely keen contingent, offered scuba training for the price of a joining fee, but for most Australians the rules and regulations were far too strict and they did not stay long enough to complete the six month basic scuba course.

In New South Wales, the South Pacific Divers Club trained divers, as did the Underwater Research Group. So, in the beginnings of sport diving in Australia, most people were trained by part-time club members, and scuba fills were bought from part-time dive shops, air trailers, or home-made compressors.

There were few scuba diving training books available outside the USA, so Ben Cropp, an Australian who had had experience training overseas in America, produced a skindiving book which contained scuba diving techniques. However, the only *real* training guide was the British Sub-Aqua Club's Training Manual and this was to become Australia's first standard work on sport diving.

Although other clubs offered training, the British Sub-Aqua Club was the only club that trained its divers to the strict standards of their manual. Indeed, by the time each student had been through a third class divers course, e.g. three months to qualify as a snorkel diver and six months to qualify as a scuba diver (two nights per week and all weekend, no wetsuits allowed in any weather), they themselves could teach (but not qualify) up to that qualification.

Although some clubs were able to organise boat dives (usually through friends etc.) these were not common and most scuba diving was done from the shoreline. This type of diving was generally referred to as 'rockhopping', a term that developed from rock fishermen, was passed on to spearfishing (which in the early days of wearing sandshoes without fins, was real 'rockhopping'), and then down to the shoreline scuba diver.

Over a period of years each club developed its own local dive locations and would organise trips away (usually camping trips) on long weekends to try out other sites. Each new dive site discovered was a closely guarded secret, just as special cray holes, jew holes, loaded reefs and wreck locations were kept secret – until all the fish had been speared, the crays no longer existed, and the wrecks had had their fittings removed, been blown up for salvage, or been raided by competitive souveniring. This trend continued for another fifteen years. Most people entered the sea with one objective in mind: to take what they could and as much as they could as quickly as they could and then to 'get the hell out of it', before the sharks got them.

SHARKS

From its beginnings as a male-dominated sport descended from spearfishing, scuba diving's 'macho' image was developed and nurtured through the country's continuously reinforced paranoia about sharks. Fear of shark attack was the most significant reason why exploration beneath the sea was so late in coming to Australia and why in many cases amateurs did much of the early work part-time as a hobby.

Marine scientists were few and far between, and many of them were scared of sharks. Australia was infamous for its shark attacks on swimmers and spearfishermen and so little was known about sharks that each entry into the water weighed heavily on the minds of scuba divers.

Although there had been no attacks on scuba divers recorded (a fact which I took some measure of comfort in) the continuous media reports (always out of context), and the fears of the population in general, never let the scuba diver forget the seeming enormity of the risks involved. Some scuba divers carried all sorts of weapons for protection, from shark 'billies' developed along the lines of those shown and described in movies and books released through the Jacques Cousteau consortium, to 12 gauge shotgun 'smokies' and 303 shark-stopping impact 'guns'. Some divers would not dream of entering the water without this form of physical 'protection'.

Of course, by carrying these weapons around underwater, scuba divers became more or less reliant on physical defence and, in so doing, didn't fortify the mental defences that, in reality, are the most important. To test out the efficiency of their 'protective' weapons many scuba divers would spend their entire dives blowing to pieces anything bigger than a flathead (and in some cases even the flatheads got 'smokied').

My own fear of sharks was so great that once the 'gung ho' shark killing films of Ron Taylor and Ben Cropp were released, the stopping power of these awesome weapons influenced me to purchase one and to carry it on dives. The impression left by these films on me was quite significant and I, like most other people who watched the slaughter (except of course the spearfishing elite, who even then knew the real truth), saw these people as heroes. My dreams were full of visions of pioneering the depths with my trusty shark gun, blasting 'man-eating' grey nurses, whalers, and white pointers out of their territories to seek out the treasures (new species and unknown discoveries) that they guarded, and I was quite prepared to do it.

However, not being very brave, or experienced, I decided to try out my ultimate defence weapon on something less aggressive than a 3 metre bronze whaler (which at that stage I'd never even seen). Unfortunately, on the big day I first encountered a shark I was buddying with a visiting American scuba diver who was looking forward to seeing just how a 'big bronzed Anzac' handled sharks in dreaded Sydney Harbour.

So, threading our way down the bare-bodied beach at Camp Cove (inside South Head) we eventually entered the water just below the newly erected 'Shark Warning' sign. Visibility was around 5 metres (which is very good for Sydney Harbour) and off we went out into the channel looking for sharks. After seeing an authentic 'Shark Warning' sign, my American buddy was in a state of total excitement. Expecting at any moment to be dive-bombed by sharks, he swam a bit behind me. Little did we know at the time that the combined sound and continual exhalation of our exhaust bubbles would have sent any shark within a hundred metres beating a hasty retreat for the Heads.

Then, in the middle of the channel at 25 metres, my American buddy indicated that he wanted to surface and talk. Now I admit that I was scared of sharks, but surfacing in the middle of the South Harbour Channel on a Sunday afternoon wasn't my idea of survival. 'Smokies' aren't much use against speed boats and propellors at 2000 revs!

We found nothing out in the deep but on the way back into the shallows at Green Point spied a 2 metre wobbegong under a rock ledge.

Here it was, my big moment as a potential shark hunter. I extended the rubbers on my 303 'smokie' tipped hand spear, instinctively closed my eyes (some spearo!) and let fly on the wobby, right between the eyes. The expected explosion didn't happen (I had left the safety on). The surprised shark came out from under the ledge, shook its head, bowled both of us over, and took off like a rocket.

By the time I had cleared the water out of my flooded mask and looked around for my buddy the silt had settled, but he was nowhere to be seen. Carrying my disgraced 'smokie', I finned into the shallows to find my buddy sitting on a rock, fins still on, checking himself for bite marks.

Well, I don't mind telling you that he wasn't very impressed with his first dive with a 'gung ho' Australian 'underwater Anzac'; in fact he made a few remarks regarding the status of my parentage. He was quite convinced that I had set the shark on him on purpose. I didn't have the heart to tell him I'd left the safety on the 'smokie'.

Two things emerged from this experience. My buddy decided all Australian divers were mad, and I decided that in all probability if I couldn't 'bomb' a wobbegong lying on the bottom, I certainly couldn't 'bomb' a bronze whaler shark.

So much for the 'smokie'; I went back to taking my chances with the nudibranchs.

PRESENT DAY

The dive scene in Australia today is healthy and vigorous, although there is quite a bit of settling down to do in regard to pioneering new areas of business (facility ownership turnover runs in the vicinity of around 10 to 15 per cent throughout Australia).

Of course, like every other business, there are downtrends and uptrends. Diving is competing along with many other sports, but no other sport can offer participants the ultimate challenge that diving can.

We have the country: millions of hectares of diveable ocean, fantastic dive sites, thousands of reefs still unexplored, thousands of new species to discover, unique sea life unlike any in the world. A gigantic underwater playground where almost anybody can become their own underwater explorer and turn the fantasy of their imagination into a reality.

We have it all, but we must provide ourselves with an even more professional industry. Each person in the industry must try to improve, not only their individual image, services, outlook and product, but also the image of diving in Australia, so as to encourage increased participation.

We have the audience, that's been proved by the numbers of viewers that watch underwater shows.

Our pro facilities are being updated all the time (competition is one of the main levers towards bringing out innovative and imaginative thinking) and we are now a step beyond the past.

Things have stabilized, more or less, on the instruction agency side and the atmosphere is conducive to growth.

Businesses in the diving industry are taking a more assertive role, both in presenting their own products and in supporting their choice of consumer publications, realizing that presenting a quality image of the industry to the consumer will automatically enhance their own image and product.

Regular symposiums such as the 'Oceans' Film Festivals, the annual Heron Island Underwater Festival, and the Lord Howe Island Underwater Educational Seminars, go a long way towards bringing divers together and spreading the enthusiasm of those whose work, love and dedication help to make the industry what it is today.

THE FUTURE

Although the future of diving in Australia is assured, the diving industry is really only on the threshold; with enough positive, enthusiastic, professionally minded people, the sky is the limit. However, like anything worthwhile, we in the industry must not sacrifice long-term stability for short-term rewards. In the long run the integrity of people is what makes one business shine above another.

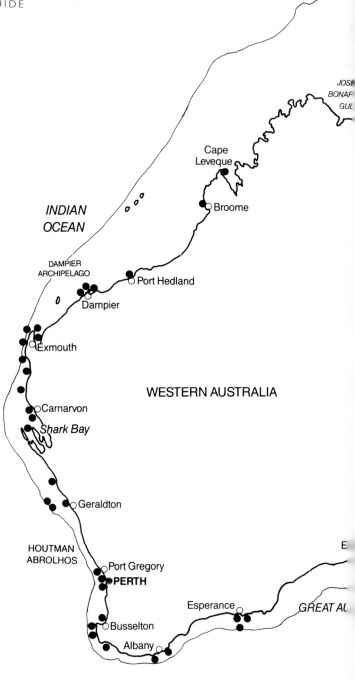

Areas marked with dots show where I have logged over 10,000 dives since 1963 as part of the Australasian Marine Photographic Index visual identification programme surveying Underwater Australia. To date over 10,000 species of animals and plants have been photographed and cross-referenced with corresponding identifying specimens, which have subsequently been donated to Australian Museums and Universities.

TORRES STRAIT

Thursday Island

ARWIN

GULF OF CARPENTARIA

Lizard Island

Cooktown

CORAL SEA

Cairns

Green Island

NORTHERN TERRITORY

PACIFIC OCEAN

Townsville

GREAT BARRIER REEF

Bowen

Mackay

QUEENSLAND

SWAIN REEFS

Rockhampton

Heron Island

Gladstone

Fraser Island

BRISBANE

SOUTH AUSTRALIA

Byron Bay

Coffs Harbour

Ceduna

NEW SOUTH WALES

Lord Howe Island

NUYTS ARCHIPELAGO

Port Stephens

BIGHT

Port Lincoln

ADELAIDE

SYDNEY

Kangaroo Island

Jervis Bay

TASMAN SEA

VICTORIA

Mt. Gambier

Port Fairy

MELBOURNE

Eden

Mallacoota

King Island

BASS STRAIT

Flinders Island

TASMANIA

HOBART

THE GREAT BARRIER REEF

Great Barrier Reef: three words that strike a chord with millions. What is it about this huge wondrous structure that draws people to it from all over the world?

Is it the multi-coloured tourist brochures with their dyed corals and dewy-eyed damsels? Is it the air-conditioned ultra-modern units with four sumptuous meals a day and all the booze you can drink? Or is it the chance of seeing one of nature's finest creations in all its glory; the chance to breathe the salty, untainted air, to revel under the clear night skies and to shiver as the winds whistle through the she-oaks? Who knows? But I, for one, would like to think it is the latter.

The Great Barrier Reef is an adventure; something in which all, from the youngest to the oldest, may share. It is wonderful just to sit on a white coral sand beach and watch as the receding tide eddies around the coral heads. Within minutes the surface is broken by one, ten, twenty and then countless hundreds of coral clumps that seemingly rise and break through the surface waters. Walking out into the shallows (adequately shod) and coming in close contact with these intricate structures gives an inkling of what the reefs can offer. But only an inkling, for although the calcareous architectures are beautiful, they cannot compare with the animals that construct them.

The reefs are created by lime-secreting plants and animals, algae and corals, that live in colonies along the Continental Shelf edge. There, conditions provide maximum sunlight penetration, moderately stable temperatures and good aeration, together with the nutrients and carbonate necessary for food and growth.

Basically, coral reefs are large mounds of solidified skeletonal debris covered by veneers of living coral. The shape and growth of a reef is controlled largely by the external elements and tidal currents. Living, reef-building corals generally occur in suitable areas from midtide level to over 120 metres.

Because of its dependence on varying climatic conditions, the

The Great Barrier Reef Marine Park is the largest Marine Park in the world, encompassing some 2500 reefs and some 900 islands and extending over 2000 kilometres from Gladstone in the south to Cape York Peninsula in the north.

reef is continually dying and regenerating itself. It has been shown that for some time after a natural disaster, such as a cyclone, the reef corals grow at almost twice their normal rate.

Communal groups of delicate, soft-bodied polyps combine salt water and their own body fluids to produce skeletons hard enough to pierce the hulls of ships: coral reefs. This throbbing mass of animals all live their lives in a predetermined pattern, a pattern which man is only on the threshold of understanding.

As our greatest underwater wonder, the Great Barrier Reef is also our greatest underwater responsibility. If we cannot evolve, invoke and implement a protection policy for the Great Barrier Reef, we can hardly expect to conserve Underwater Australia. Although it has taken quite a while to develop an adequate protection policy, a programme is now in full operation, with the Great Barrier Reef Marine Park Authority implementing the programme, and the Queensland National Parks and Wildlife Service carrying out the field work, policing the various sections and providing educational services. I am indebted to both of these organisations for the opportunity to reproduce the material which follows on the Great Barrier Reef region and the Great Barrier Reef Marine Park on pages 14 to 17 of this book.

THE GREAT BARRIER REEF REGION

The Great Barrier Reef region is an area of approximately 350 000 sq km extending along the Queensland coast from Torres Strait to off Bundaberg. The Great Barrier Reef Marine Park, the largest marine park in the world, has been declared over most of this area. The park contains more than 2500 reefs, banks and shoals. There are also over 900 continental and coral islands within its boundaries many of which are national parks. Many islands and coral cays support breeding colonies of migratory seabirds. Turtles, dugongs and whales also find refuge here. The fish, coral and other invertebrate communities represent one of the richest and most diverse faunas in the world. Because of these special qualities the Great Barrier Reef has been inscribed on the World Heritage List.

The Queensland National Parks and Wildlife Service is responsible for the day-to-day management of the Great Barrier Reef Marine Park on behalf of the Great Barrier Reef Marine Park Authority. The Service also manages the island national parks and state marine parks in the Great Barrier Reef region. Co-operation between State and Commonwealth Governments is ensuring complementary management for these areas.

Management
Marine Parks staff develop education programmes, run activities on reefs and islands and publish a variety of information for park users.

A visitor centre has been established on Heron Island, a popular dive destination. The centre provides educational material, and regular talks and slide shows are given for visitors. Marine Parks rangers are stationed on the island.

Underwater trails have been installed at some popular dive sites such as Green Island and Lady Elliott Island reef. Lady Elliott Island is a favourite destination for local and overseas divers. Other trails are planned for Magnetic Island, Hook, Hardy and John Brewer Reefs.

Marine Parks officers monitor the effects of recreational and commercial activities on reef and island ecosystems. Heavily used anchorages are identified and permanent moorings are installed to minimize damage to delicate corals. Inventories of seabird nesting colonies and island flora and fauna are being undertaken. This information is being used to develop management plans for many islands to ensure that visitor use is balanced with the need for conservation. The Service conducts underwater surveys and tagging programmes on coral trout in order to assess the effects of fishing on stocks of this prized table fish.

Several species of sea turtles are also the focus of a major research programme aimed at increasing our knowledge of these animals. Nesting female turtles can be seen on island beaches in the Capricornia and Far Northern Section of the Park from November to January.

The Queensland National Parks and Wildlife Service also has a programme to develop and upgrade facilities for day visitors and campers on some islands. Facilities include picnic tables, fresh water tanks and toilets.

Regular aerial and boat surveillance provides information on user activities as well as a visible presence in the Park. Although emphasis is on education of park users, Marine Parks staff are empowered to enforce regulations.

How you can care for the reef

Ultimately, the future of the reef resides with the users. The Great Barrier Reef Marine Park consists of a number of sections and zoning plans have been prepared progressively for each section. These plans allow for reasonable use while also separating conflicting activities. The island national parks are fully protected. Currently, divers may visit most reefs and islands. Only those areas which are Preservation Zones, Scientific Zones or are seasonally closed to protect breeding wildlife are off-limits to divers.

Before your visit, obtain a zoning plan for the reef and visitor information for the national parks you wish to visit. Commercial spearfishing and spearfishing with scuba or hookah are strictly prohibited in the park. Several groups of marine animals, plants and products are protected and may not be collected without a permit. Camping is allowed on many of the island national parks. However, as these islands are extremely popular with campers, you will need to apply for a camping permit well in advance (up to six months for some islands). For further information contact Queensland

National Parks and Wildlife Service Head Office in Brisbane or Regional Offices at Rockhampton, Townsville and Cairns.

THE GREAT BARRIER REEF MARINE PARK

The Great Barrier Reef region stretches over 2,000 km from its southernmost point near Bundaberg to the northern tip of Cape York Peninsula. Over 98 per cent of the region is included in the largest Marine Park in the world, the Great Barrier Reef Marine Park.

The responsibility for the establishment of the Marine Park and the development of management strategies has been vested in the Great Barrier Reef Marine Park Authority, a Commonwealth Government agency.

The Authority's goal in the development and care of the great Barrier Reef Marine Park is to provide for the wise use, appreciation and enjoyment of the Great Barrier Reef in perpetuity.

Diving as an Activity within the Marine Park

The Authority intends the area to be a multi-use park which provides opportunities for all reasonable uses, including diving, while still ensuring the long term survival of the Reef.

The only diving related activities totally prohibited are spearfishing with scuba and other underwater breathing equipment (except snorkel), use of powerheads while spearfishing and the taking of Queensland groper and potato cods larger than 1.2 m in length. Mining (except for approved scientific research purposes) and oil drilling are also prohibited.

Management Through Zoning

The main management tool used by the Authority is zoning.

Zoning plans are designed to ensure a balance between human needs and the need to conserve the Great Barrier Reef, and to separate conflicting uses. They allow multi-use of the Reef's resources but restrict or prohibit certain activities in specified areas.

Zoning plans are expected to be in operation for all sections of the Marine Park by 1988. The plans are developed with the help of extensive public input so that the needs and the knowledge of people who use the Reef can be taken into account. The Authority also uses research data and information from various government and commercial agencies in developing zoning plans.

The Zones

General Use Zones   The majority of the zoned part of the Marine Park is in one or other of the General Use Zones. These allow all or almost all commercial uses. There is no restriction on diving or other recreational activities although collecting may require a permit in some general use areas.

Marine National Park Zones   Marine National Park Zones of various types are more like land based National Parks. They provide areas for recreational use such as diving. Limited fishing is allowed in some areas.

Special Zones   Scientific Research Zones and Preservation Zones are small areas set aside from any normal use to preserve some areas of the Great Barrier Reef untouched.

Closure Areas   Some areas may be closed for a period for a particular purpose. Seasonal Closure Areas protect some bird and turtle nesting sites during the breeding season while Replenishment Areas allow fish stocks to build up on some reefs. Reef Appreciation Areas set aside parts of popular reefs for diving and other peaceful enjoyment.

Zoning Plans   Zoning plans and activities guides are available for zoned sections of the Marine Park. Make sure you have copies for the areas you are visiting or travel with a reputable tour operator who is using a zoning plan. Zoning plans are obtainable from the Great Barrier Reef Marine Park Authority in Townsville, or from the offices of Queensland National Parks and Wildlife Service in the regional centres.

Park Management

The sheer size and complexity of the Marine Park means that management is also a task of immense size and complexity.

The Queensland National Parks and Wildlife Service is responsible to the Authority for day-to-day management of the Marine Park. The management role of the Service includes implementation of interpretive programmes, monitoring (e.g. effects of visitor activities), surveillance (by aircraft and patrol vessels), and enforcement. The Queensland National Parks and Wildlife Service is also directly responsible for the management of the island national parks.

The major emphasis of management is on education. Increased awareness and understanding of the Marine Park will ensure that you, the users of the Marine Park, use and enjoy the Reef in ways which will conserve the beauty, diversity and abundance of life that makes the Great Barrier Reef such a magic world, particularly for you divers who have the chance to experience this underwater treasure at close quarters.

Further Information   If you wish to find out more about the Great Barrier Reef Marine Park, particularly the areas which you may wish to dive please contact:

Great Barrier Reef Marine Park Authority
PO Box 1379, Townsville Qld 4810

Queensland National Parks and Wildlife Service
PO Box 190, North Quay, Brisbane Qld 4000
(or Regional Offices)

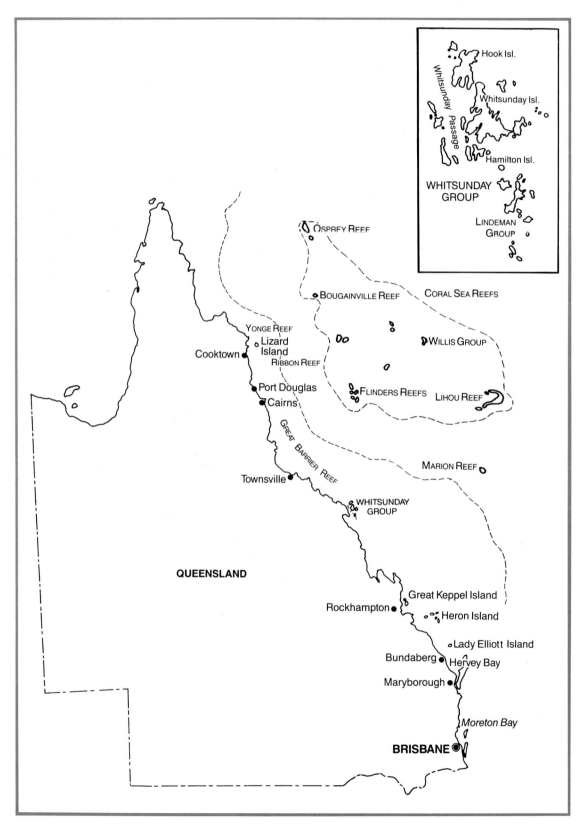

Hook Isl.

Whitsunday Isl.

Whitsunday Passage

Hamilton Isl.

WHITSUNDAY GROUP

LINDEMAN GROUP

OSPREY REEF

BOUGAINVILLE REEF

CORAL SEA REEFS

YONGE REEF

Lizard Island

Cooktown

RIBBON REEF

WILLIS GROUP

FLINDERS REEFS

LIHOU REEF

Port Douglas

Cairns

GREAT BARRIER REEF

MARION REEF

Townsville

WHITSUNDAY GROUP

QUEENSLAND

Great Keppel Island

Rockhampton

Heron Island

Lady Elliott Island

Bundaberg

Hervey Bay

Maryborough

Moreton Bay

BRISBANE

Diving
QUEENSLAND

The bicolor angelfish is a stunning specimen.

LIZARD ISLAND

The most northerly resort in Queensland, Lizard Island is accessible by air from Cairns or Cooktown, or by charter boat. One of the largest mainland islands on the Cape York Peninsula, it has a fringing coral reef and a sheltered lagoon.

Within its complex environs of reefs, including Palfrey Island and South Island, is some of the most exciting continental island diving in Australia. A boat is required to get to the best places and these include Mrs Watson's Beach (offshore), Granite Head, Mermaid Cove, North Point, South Island drop off and Bird Island drop off.

The lagoon is good for snorkelling, snorkel diving and scuba. Besides all the usual attractions there are some giant clams at the boat anchorage. Nearby North Direction Island, Eagle Island and Linnet Reef also have good diving, with many hundreds of species of fish and invertebrates, gardens of sea whips, hectares of black coral trees and blazing fields of soft corals.

The Lizard Island Research Station at Corner Beach is owned and operated by the Australian Museum.

GENERAL INFORMATION

Best times of the year:	■ Summer	■ Winter	■ Spring	□ Autumn
Typical weather:	■ Excellent	■	■	□
	□ Very good	□	□	■
	□ Average	□	□	□
	□ Fair	□	□	□
Accommodation available:	■ Camping	□ Hostel	■ Hotel	□ Motel
Airport:	■ Light aircraft	□ Jet	□ International	□ Helicopter

DIVE SITE GUIDE

Access:	□ Boat ramp	■ Charter boat	■ Air	
Dive methods:	■ Scuba	■ Hookah	■ Snorkel	■ Snorkel diving
Types of diving:	■ Boat	□ Jetty	■ Shore	
Description of dive site:	■ Island	■ Submerged reef	■ Shore	
	□ Wreck	■ Shallow water	■ Deep water	
Conditions at site:	■ Current	■ Swell	■ Wind chop	
	■ Tide changes	□ Boat traffic	■ Good visibility	
	■ Fair visibility	□ Poor visibility		
Dive time:	■ In-coming tide	■ Out-going tide		
	■ Spring tide	■ Neap tide	■ Slack tide	
Underwater terrain:	■ Drop offs	■ Gutters	■ Patch reefs	
	■ Sand & rubble	■ Rocky reef	■ Flat bottom	
	■ Low profile reef	■ Coral reef	■ Slope	
	□ Caves	□ Swim-throughs	□ Silty bottom	
Marine life:	□ Kelp	■ Sea grass	■ Sponges	■ Corals
	■ Sea whips	■ Sea fans	■ Black coral	■ Soft corals
	■ Anemones	■ Fan worms	■ Bryozoans	□ Brachiopods
	■ Crays	■ Crabs	■ Shells	■ Commensal shrimps
	■ Nudibranchs	■ Cuttles	□ Scallops	□ Abalone
	■ Sea stars	□ Basket stars	■ Sea urchins	■ Feather stars
	■ Ascidians	■ Sea snakes	■ Dolphins	■ Turtles
	■ Sharks	■ Fish	□ Numerous Fish	■ Abundant Fish
Experience level:	■ Pupil	■ Beginner	■ Intermediate	■ Advanced
Dive site rating:	■ Excellent	□ Very good	□ Fair	■ Photography
Management of resources:	■ Marine reserve	■ Protected species	□ Quotas	■ Collecting

Service: LIZARD ISLAND DIVE

Contact:
Lizard Island Dive
PMB 40, PO Cairns Qld 4870

Remarks: Although many dive charter boats only drop into Lizard Island for a look or a drink at the bar when coming from or going to more exotic dive locations, take it from me: try Lizard Island, it has some really nice diving.

The elegant hydrocoral is often seen in caves or beneath overhangs in areas with current or moderate water movement.

YONGE REEF – RIBBON REEFS

I suppose in all fairness I should write a complete screed on every reef on the Great Barrier Reef I've dived, but the superlatives would run out and I would be forced to repeat myself over and over again. To me they are *all* good dives. However, there are two northern reefs not too far away from each other that have a special place in my heart.

Yonge Reef is straight out to sea from Lizard Island. Inside the reef and in the pass there is some incredibly good diving, but outside, down over the front terraces where huge schools of giant trevally sweep in from nowhere and hammerhead sharks cruise by, is even better.

The deep azure blue depths beckon and 2 metre high pastel pink sea fans reach out into the currents, the coral formations go on forever

The pose struck by this specimen certainly helps explain its common name, noble feather star.

and purple-tinged mazes of elegant hydrocorals hang down from the roofs of submarine caverns while exotically coloured fish flit to and fro.

The Ribbon Reefs begin just below Cooktown at Ribbon number one and form a line of ten isolated elongated reef formations to make up the outer barrier. Fantastic diving can be had all along this relatively unknown formation. Blow holes, swim-throughs, tunnels, caves, overhangs and deep crevasses contain every marine creature imaginable – only bigger and better and more of them than you would ever dream of.

Number ten Ribbon Reef is the longest; over 20 kilometres in length, it terminates at Cormorant Pass, along with No Name Reef across the way. As well as being a good dive site in its own right, Cormorant Pass is famous for its resident school of tame potato cods. Potato cods were not recorded in Australian fauna lists until 1971, although known prior to that date. The first record was from the Dampier Archipelago in Western Australia, made during my initial photographic fauna survey of that area. The potato cods at Cormorant Pass school up to be hand fed and have grown in numbers over a period of years until now there are around twenty of them. Unique to their home territory, they are fully protected animals and Cormorant Pass is a zone B marine national park in the Great Barrier Reef Marine Park Cormorant Pass section. These potato cods have no fear of divers and when being fed in a group (which all big cods do when faced with competition), they often become quite pugnacious and greedy, and deal out a few bumps here and there to their providers. Big fish with big appetites, they are a thrill to swim with.

Nowhere else in Australia can you swim with so many big tame fish. It's been tried dozens of times in other places, and each time the fish have been speared or line caught by those who profit by the trust of others and kill for the thrill. Maybe one day we'll be able to live in peace with other animals. Until then, places like Cormorant Pass, Heron Island and Lord Howe Island will stand apart as examples of what can be achieved if enough people care.

Tame potato cods at the famous Cormorant Pass Cod Hole, Ribbon Reefs.

An outstanding dive
location, the Ribbon Reefs
have everything a diver
could wish for.

Charter Boats:

Esperance Star (12 divers)

Contact:
Seaboard Charters
PO Box 3, Peakhurst NSW 2210
Phone: (02) 534 3253, A/H (02) 53 8372;
or (070) 51 9436, A/H (070) 55 7235

Scheherazade (6 divers)

Contact:
Going Places Travel
26 Abbott Street, Cairns Qld 4870
Phone: (008) 079 014

Reef Explorer (12 divers)
Auriga Bay (12 divers)

Contact:
Reef Explorer Cruises
PO Box 1588, Cairns Qld 4870
Phone: (070) 51 4055, (070) 51 6360

Bali Hai 2 (8 divers)

Contact:
Bali Hai
PO Box 692, Cairns Qld 4870
Phone: (070) 54 5545

New Horizon (12 divers)

Contact:
New Horizon Tours

PO Box 360, Yeppoon Qld 4703
Phone: (079) 39 2307

Coralita (12 divers)

Contact:
Barrier Reef Cruises
PO Box 268, Yeppoon Qld 4703
Phone: (079) 39 1588

GENERAL INFORMATION

Best times of the year:	■ Summer	■ Winter	■ Spring	□ Autumn
Typical weather:	■ Excellent	■	■	□
	□ Very good	□	□	□
	□ Average	□	□	□
	□ Fair	□	□	■
Accommodation available:	□ Camping	□ Hostel	□ Hotel	□ Motel
Airport:	□ Light aircraft	□ Jet	□ International	□ Helicopter

DIVE SITE GUIDE

Access:	□ Boat ramp	■ Charter boat	□ Air	
Dive methods:	■ Scuba	■ Hookah	■ Snorkel	■ Snorkel diving
Types of diving:	■ Boat	□ Jetty	□ Shore	
Description of dive site:	□ Island	■ Submerged reef	□ Shore	
	□ Wreck	■ Shallow water	■ Deep water	
Conditions at site:	■ Current	■ Swell	■ Wind chop	
	■ Tide changes	□ Boat traffic	■ Good visibility	
	□ Fair visibility	□ Poor visibility		
Dive time:	■ In-coming tide	■ Out-going tide		
	■ Spring tide	■ Neap tide	■ Slack tide	
Underwater terrain:	■ Drop offs	■ Gutters	■ Patch reefs	
	■ Sand & rubble	□ Rocky reef	□ Flat bottom	
	□ Low profile reef	■ Coral reef	■ Slope	
	■ Caves	■ Swim-throughs	□ Silty bottom	
Marine life:	□ Kelp	□ Sea grass	■ Sponges	■ Corals
	■ Sea whips	■ Sea fans	□ Black coral	■ Soft corals
	■ Anemones	■ Fan worms	■ Bryozoans	□ Brachiopods
	■ Crays	■ Crabs	■ Shells	■ Commensal shrimps
	■ Nudibranchs	□ Cuttles	□ Scallops	□ Abalone
	■ Sea stars	□ Basket stars	■ Sea urchins	■ Feather stars
	■ Ascidians	■ Rays	■ Dolphins	■ Turtles
	■ Sharks	■ Fish	□ Numerous fish	■ Abundant fish
Experience level:	□ Pupil	■ Beginner	■ Intermediate	■ Advanced
Dive site rating:	■ Excellent	□ Very good	□ Fair	■ Photography
Management of resources:	■ Marine reserve	■ Protected species	□ Quotas	□ Collecting

This male blotched fairy basslet is just one of over 1000 species of fishes that inhabit the Coral Sea.

CORAL SEA REEFS

Venturing out from the protection of the Great Barrier Reef into the open waters of the Coral Sea to dive on the submerged peaks of sea mounts, some of which may be almost 300 kilometres from dry land, is what the true spirit of underwatering is all about. I can remember my first dive on Wal's Bommie near Samaurez Reef in the mid 1970s. I went over the side not knowing what to expect. At the stern of the boat I opened my eyes into a deep blue haze reflecting up from the depths. I 'pushed' up towards the bow, fighting the current and hanging on to my camera for all it was worth. My heart was pounding. I got halfway to the anchor line and there it was – a giant coral bommie (it must have been 20 metres or more across the top) standing up from the sea floor 50 metres below. I gazed in amazement and stopped finning. As I did so the scene melted away in front of my eyes, as though I'd been dreaming. The current was stronger than I thought. Next time I swam to the anchor rope before I stopped, and only then did I allow myself the pleasure of looking down.

I can remember thinking, 'every fish in the world must be right here'. I'd never seen so many fish in all my travels on the Australian Coastal Marine Expedition. I hauled myself down some 20 metres to the top of the anchor and just sat there in awe trying to believe what I was seeing. Clouds and clouds of fish; schools of butterfly fish in hundreds, fusileers, angels, snappers, wrasses, parrot fish, coral cod, fish going everywhere. Black coral sea whips, 4 metres at least in length, were hanging over the edge like giant fishing rods, and out in the blue, swimming in formation like living torpedoes, huge 'flotillas' of dog-toothed tuna. I sat and watched till my air

Sometimes seen on the outer reef drop offs at night, the pearly nautilus spends its daylight hours beyond depths of 150 metres.

ran out; my air had never seemed to run out so quickly, and I never took a picture. Since then I've dived many reefs in the coral sea but my favourites will always be Samaurez, Marion and Osprey.

If you ever get the chance – *go*! It's the experience of a lifetime.

Charter Boats:

Esperance Star (12 divers)

Contact:
Seaboard Charters
PO Box 3, Peakhurst NSW 2210
Phone: (02) 534 3253, A/H (02) 53 8372;
or (070) 51 9436, A/H (070) 55 7235

Scheherazade (6 divers)

Contact:
Going Places Travel
26 Abbott Street, Cairns Qld 4870
Phone: (008) 079 014

Reef Explorer (12 divers)
Auriga Bay (12 divers)

Few could resist the chance to take a dive under these conditions. The Coral Sea may not always be calm, but underwater, it's magic.

Contact:
Reef Explorer Cruises
PO Box 1588, Cairns Qld 4870
Phone: (070) 51 4055, (070) 51 6360

Bali Hai 2 (8 divers)

Contact:
Bali Hai
PO Box 692, Cairns Qld 4870
Phone: (070) 54 5545

New Horizons (12 divers)

Contact:
New Horizon Tours
PO Box 360, Yeppoon Qld 4703
Phone: (079) 39 2307

Coralita (12 divers)

Contact:
Barrier Reef Cruises
PO Box 268, Yeppoon Qld, 4703
Phone: (079) 39 1588

GENERAL INFORMATION

Best times of the year:	□ Summer	■ Winter	■ Spring	□ Autumn
Typical weather:	□ Excellent	■	■	□
	■ Very good	□	□	□
	□ Average	□	□	□
	□ Fair	□	□	■
Accommodation available:	□ Camping	□ Hostel	□ Hotel	□ Motel
Airport:	□ Light aircraft	□ Jet	□ International	□ Helicopter

DIVE SITE GUIDE

Access:	□ Boat ramp	■ Charter boat	□ Air	
Dive methods:	■ Scuba	■ Hookah	■ Snorkel	■ Snorkel diving
Types of diving:	■ Boat	□ Jetty	□ Shore	
Description of dive site:	■ Island	■ Submerged reef	□ Shore	
	■ Wreck	■ Shallow water	■ Deep water	
Conditions at site:	■ Current	■ Swell	■ Wind chop	
	■ Tide changes	□ Boat traffic	■ Good visibility	
	□ Fair visibility	□ Poor visibility		
Dive time:	■ In-coming tide	■ Out-going tide		
	■ Spring tide	■ Neap tide	■ Slack tide	
Underwater terrain:	■ Drop offs	■ Gutters	■ Patch reefs	
	■ Sand & rubble	□ Rocky reef	■ Flat bottom	
	■ Low profile reef	■ Coral reef	■ Slope	
	■ Caves	■ Swim-throughs	□ Silty bottom	
Marine life:	□ Kelp	□ Sea grass	■ Sponges	■ Corals
	■ Sea whips	■ Sea fans	■ Black coral	■ Soft corals
	■ Anemones	■ Fan worms	■ Bryozoans	□ Brachiopods
	■ Crays	■ Crabs	■ Shells	■ Commensal shrimps
	■ Nudibranchs	□ Cuttles	□ Scallops	□ Abalone
	■ Sea stars	■ Basket stars	■ Sea urchins	■ Feather stars
	■ Ascidians	■ Sea snakes	■ Dolphins	■ Turtles
	■ Sharks	■ Fish	□ Numerous fish	■ Abundant fish
Experience level:	□ Pupil	■ Beginner	■ Intermediate	■ Advanced
Dive site rating:	■ Excellent	□ Very good	□ Fair	■ Photography
Management of resources:	■ Marine reserve	■ Protected species	□ Quotas	□ Collecting

Crawling over the surface of its host soft coral, this undescribed species of ovulid cowry is a perfect subject for macro photography.

PORT DOUGLAS

Located 68 kilometres north of Cairns, Port Douglas is one of the oldest towns in north Queensland and is an operating base for many prawn trawlers working the Cape York Peninsula. It has slipway facilities and cold rooms. More recently it has stolen a little of the limelight from Cairns as a game fishing and charter boat port. Port Douglas also has a lot to offer the diver. Some of the best reefs and cays within the Cairns section of the Great Barrier Reef Marine Park occur only a little way to the north. Reefs like St Crispin, Pickersgill, Batt, Undine, Agincourt and Rudder offer fantastic diving and clear, clear water with diverse and interesting terrain and a multitude of fish and invertebrates.

Service:

PORT DOUGLAS SPORT & DIVE
PADI instruction, equipment sales, services, gear hire, air, local dive trips.

Contact:
Port Douglas Sport & Dive
Shop 3, Ashford Arcade, Port Douglas Qld 4871
Phone: (070) 98 5327

Service:

CORAL SEA DIVING SERVICES
NAUI/PADI instruction, accommodation, equipment, sales, service, gear hire, air, daily trips to the Great Barrier Reef, extended reef charters.

Contact:
Coral Sea Diving Services
Princess Wharf, Port Douglas Qld 4871
Phone: (070) 98 5254, A/H (070) 98 5710

Charter Boats: *M.V. Quicksilver* (20 divers)

Contact:
Low Isle Cruise
Port Douglas Qld 4871
Phone: (070) 98 5373
(Has day trips to Great Barrier Reef – Agincourt Reef – with transfers to 15 dive sites.)

GENERAL INFORMATION

Best times of the year: ☐ Summer   ■ Winter   ■ Spring   ☐ Autumn

Typical weather:
☐ Excellent   ■   ■   ☐
■ Very good   ☐   ☐   ☐
☐ Average   ☐   ☐   ☐
☐ Fair   ☐   ☐   ■

Accommodation available: ■ Camping   ☐ Hostel   ■ Hotel   ■ Motel

Airport: ☐ Light aircraft   ☐ Jet   ☐ International   ☐ Helicopter

DIVE SITE GUIDE

Access: ■ Boat ramp   ■ Charter boat   ■ Air

Dive methods: ■ Scuba   ■ Hookah   ■ Snorkel   ■ Snorkel diving

Types of diving: ■ Boat   ☐ Jetty   ☐ Shore

Description of dive site: ■ Island   ■ Submerged reef   ☐ Shore
☐ Wreck   ■ Shallow water   ■ Deep water

Conditions at site: ■ Current   ☐ Swell   ■ Wind chop
■ Tide changes   ☐ Boat traffic   ■ Good visibility
☐ Fair visibility   ☐ Poor visibility

Dive time: ■ In-coming tide   ■ Out-going tide
☐ Spring tide   ■ Neap tide   ■ Slack tide

Underwater terrain: ■ Drop offs   ■ Gutters   ■ Patch reefs
■ Sand & rubble   ☐ Rocky reef   ■ Flat bottom
■ Low profile reef   ■ Coral reef   ■ Slope
■ Caves   ☐ Swim-throughs   ☐ Silty bottom

Marine life:
☐ Kelp   ■ Sea grass   ■ Sponges   ■ Corals
☐ Sea whips   ■ Sea fans   ■ Black coral   ■ Soft corals
■ Anemones   ■ Fan worms   ■ Bryozoans   ☐ Brachiopods
■ Crays   ■ Crabs   ■ Shells   ■ Commensal shrimps

■ Nudibranchs   ■ Cuttles   ☐ Scallops   ☐ Abalone
■ Sea stars   ☐ Basket stars   ■ Sea urchins   ■ Feather stars
■ Ascidians   ■ Rays   ■ Dolphins   ■ Turtles
■ Sharks   ■ Fish   ☐ Numerous fish   ■ Abundant fish

Experience level: ■ Pupil   ■ Beginner   ■ Intermediate   ■ Advanced

Dive site rating: ■ Excellent   ☐ Very good   ☐ Fair   ■ Photography

Management of resources: ■ Marine reserve   ■ Protected species   ☐ Quotas   ☐ Collecting

Growing to around 70 mm,
the multi-pored sea star is
the smallest member of the
Linckia sea stars.

Remarks:

Port Douglas is as far as the sealed road goes and offers the last available air fills on the mainland. From here north the only real access to the almost unknown territory of Cape York's hundreds of reefs and islands is by charter boat (with the exception of Lizard Island which has a landing strip). A lot of the inshore reefs have very turbid water but during winter those away from the vicinity of large river outlets are quite diveable. Some have forests of black coral 2 metres high growing in depths of 20 to 40 metres.

When you think that we still do not have up-to-date fauna checklists for Sydney Harbour after 200 years of study, just imagine what's there to discover off the Cape.

CAIRNS

Inhabited by an easy going, cosmopolitan population of approximately 50,000, Cairns is situated on the banks of mangrove-fringed Trinity Bay. The capital of the far north coast, it hosts a modern international airport and excellent facilities, though visitors from larger southern cities may find things a little spread out. The inshore waters are not suitable for diving during summer.

In my early years I spent many a Christmas holiday camped in a wet leaky tent at Cairns, snorkelling the inshore rocks at Double Island off Ellis Beach (wearing a long sleeved tee shirt so the box jellies wouldn't get me). My first introduction to the real Great Barrier Reef was taking the day trips to Green Island, spending four hours snorkelling there and then catching the boat back to Cairns.

Sometimes I'd get a lift with fishermen who would drop me off at Michaelmas Cay or Arlington Reefs and pick me up on the way back that evening. Things have changed a lot in twenty-five years and today Cairns has the most modern pro facilities and a host of excellent charter vessels.

Service:

PRO DIVE
PADI instruction, complete dive shop service, equipment sales, gear hire including cameras, air 7 days a week, local dive trips on 23 berth cruiser. Fresh water diving by arrangement.

Contact:
Pro Dive
Marlin Jetty, Main Street, Cairns Qld 4870
Phone: (070) 51 9915

Service:

AUSDIVE
NAUI pro facility instruction, equipment, services, gear hire, air, day trips and weekend diving on the *M.V. Melawondi.*

Contact:
Ausdive
134 Sheridan Street, Cairns Qld 4870, *or*
5 Digger Street, Cairns Qld 4870 (pool)
Phone: (070) 51 4746

Service:

PETER BOUNTY'S DIVE CENTRE
PADI/NAUI instruction, equipment sales, service, gear hire, air, charter trips to the Great Barrier Reef.

Contact:
Peter Bounty's Dive Centre
PO Box 2401, Cairns Qld 4870
Phone: (070) 51 0294

Service:

PETER TIBBS DIVE CENTRE
NAUI pro facility instruction, equipment sales, gear hire, air 7 days a week, regular trips to the Great Barrier Reef.

An easily identified species, the long-nosed coralfish is a common resident of the reefs around Cairns.

Although the beautiful flatworm has been photographed at several locations over a period of years, it is still undescribed.

Contact:
Peter Tibbs Dive Centre
370 Sheridan Street, Cairns Qld 4870
Phone: (070) 51 2604

Service:

DEEP SEA DIVERS DEN
PADI facility, equipment sales, instruction, service, gear hire, local dives to the Great Barrier Reef.

Contact:
Deep Sea Divers Den
319 Draper Street, Cairns Qld 4870
Phone: (070) 51 2223

Service:

CAIRNS BARRIER REEF DIVERS
PADI instruction, equipment sales, service, gear hire, air, local charter trips to the Great Barrier Reef.

Contact:
Cairns Barrier Reef Divers
103 The Esplanade, Cairns Qld 4870
Phone: (070) 51 9655

Charter Boats:

Reef Explorer (12 divers)
Auriga Bay (12 divers)

Contact:
Reef Explorer Cruises
PO Box 1588, Cairns Qld 4870
Phone: (070) 51 4055, (070) 51 6360

Bali Hai 2 (8 divers)

Contact:
Bali Hai
PO Box 692, Cairns Qld 4870
Phone: (070) 54 5545

M.V. Teal
Barrier Reef cruises, regular departures, air conditioned, takes 50 passengers.

Contact:
Barrier Reef Cruises
Marlin Parade
PO 5995 MSO, Cairns Qld 4871
Phone: (070) 31 1116

GENERAL INFORMATION

Best times of the year:	☐ Summer	■ Winter	■ Spring	☐ Autumn
Typical weather:	☐ Excellent	■	■	☐
	■ Very good	☐	☐	☐
	☐ Average	☐	☐	☐
	☐ Fair	☐	☐	■
Accommodation available:	■ Camping	☐ Hostel	■ Hotel	■ Motel
Airport:	■ Light aircraft	■ Jet	■ International	■ Helicopter

DIVE SITE GUIDE

Access:	■ Boat ramp	■ Charter boat	■ Air	
Dive methods:	■ Scuba	■ Hookah	■ Snorkel	■ Snorkel diving
Types of diving:	■ Boat	☐ Jetty	☐ Shore	
Description of dive site:	■ Island	■ Submerged reef	☐ Shore	
	☐ Wreck	■ Shallow water	■ Deep water	
Conditions at site:	■ Current	☐ Swell	■ Wind chop	
	☐ Tide changes	☐ Boat traffic	■ Good visibility	
	☐ Fair visibility	☐ Poor visibility		
Dive time:	■ In-coming tide	■ Out-going tide		
	☐ Spring tide	■ Neap tide	■ Slack tide	
Underwater terrain:	■ Drop offs	■ Gutters	■ Patch reefs	
	■ Sand & rubble	☐ Rocky reef	■ Flat bottom	
	■ Low profile reef	■ Coral reef	☐ Slope	
	☐ Caves	☐ Swim-throughs	☐ Silty bottom	
Marine life:	☐ Kelp	☐ Sea grass	■ Sponges	■ Corals
	☐ Sea whips	■ Sea fans	☐ Black coral	■ Soft corals
	■ Anemones	■ Fan worms	■ Bryozoans	☐ Brachiopods
	■ Crays	■ Crabs	■ Shells	■ Commensal shrimps
	■ Nudibranchs	☐ Cuttles	☐ Scallops	☐ Abalone
	■ Sea stars	☐ Basket stars	■ Sea urchins	■ Feather stars
	■ Ascidians	■ Rays	■ Dolphins	■ Turtles
	■ Sharks	■ Fish	■ Numerous fish	☐ Abundant fish
Experience level:	■ Pupil	■ Beginner	■ Intermediate	☐ Advanced
Dive site rating:	■ Excellent	☐ Very good	☐ Fair	■ Photography
Management of resources:	■ Marine reserve	■ Protected species	☐ Quotas	☐ Collecting

Esperance Star (12 divers)

Contact:
Seaboard Charters
PO Box 3, Peakhurst NSW 2210
Phone: (02) 534 3253; A/H (02) 53 8372;
or (070) 51 9436, A/H (070) 55 7235

Scheherazade (6 divers)

Contact:
Going Places Travel
26 Abbott Street, Cairns Qld 4870
Phone: (008) 079 014

Remarks: The inshore waters may not have much going for them, but off-shore (off Cairns) the cays and reefs equal any in the world. I've dived on over 20 reefs in the area from Pickersgill Reef, just south of Cooktown, down to Sudbury Reef, a little below Cairns. They are all great dives, so wherever your charter skipper or day tripper captain takes you, you can be sure it will be excellent country.

TOWNSVILLE

A thriving international seaport beside Cleveland Bay, Townsville, with a population of around 87,000, is Queensland's third largest city. To the south of the city, at Cape Ferguson, is the world-famous Australian Institute of Marine Sciences, which has been responsible for producing a great deal of our knowledge of the Great Barrier Reef. Townsville is also the site of the Great Barrier Reef Wonder-world, one of the most ambitious and exciting educational aquariums in the world.

The Four Seasons Barrier Reef resort (a floating hotel) is anchored over John Brewer Reef and serviced by the 22 metre catamaran *M.V. Reef Link* and by helicopter. There is a dive facility at the resort.

Service: MIKE BALL WATERSPORTS
PADI instruction to all levels, equipment sales, service, gear hire, air 7 days a week, charters, 2–7 nights on *Watersport – Supersport;* dive charter boats take 26 divers.

Contact:
Mike Ball Watersports
252–256 Walker Street, Townsville Qld 4810
Phone: (077) 72 2583

On the way out to the various reefs off Townsville there is always the chance you'll meet up with friendly dolphins.

Service:

THE DIVE BELL
NAUI/PADI/FAUI instruction, equipment sales, all services, gear hire, air 5½ days a week, local dive trips, 2 day trips on weekends to the *Yongala* wreck and the Great Barrier Reef. Charter boat takes 24 passengers.

Contact:
The Dive Bell
Shop 4, 141 Ingham Road, West End, Townsville Qld 4810
Phone: (077) 71 3557

Service:

TOWNSVILLE SKINDIVING CENTRE
FAUI/PADI instruction, equipment sales, services, gear hire, air, local dive trips to the outer reef on *M.V. Sportdiver*, charters arranged.

Contact:
Townsville Skindiving Centre
77 Ingham Road, West End, Townsville Qld 4810
Phone: (077) 71 5997, A/H (077) 74 0730

Service:

SCUBA DOO DIVE & SPORTS
PADI instruction, equipment sales, service, gear hire, air 7 days a week, charter boat trips to the Great Barrier Reef.

Contact:
Scuba Doo Dive & Sports
22 Herbert Street, Bowen Qld 4805
Phone: (077) 86 2344

Charter Boats:

T.S.M.V. Divemaster (12 divers)

Contact:
T.S.M.V. Divemaster
PO Box 1450, Townsville Qld 4810
Phone: (077) 74 1363

Coral Princess (26 divers)

Contact:
Coral Princess Cruises
PO Box 2032, Townsville Qld 4810
Phone: (077) 72 4675, A/H (077) 72 5287

GENERAL INFORMATION

Best times of the year:	☐ Summer	■ Winter	■ Spring	☐ Autumn
Typical weather:	☐ Excellent	■	■	☐
	■ Very good	☐	☐	☐
	☐ Average	☐	☐	☐
	☐ Fair	☐	☐	■
Accommodation available:	■ Camping	■ Hostel	■ Hotel	■ Motel
Airport:	■ Light aircraft	■ Jet	■ International	■ Helicopter

DIVE SITE GUIDE

Access:	■ Boat ramp	■ Charter boat	■ Air	
Dive methods:	■ Scuba	■ Hookah	■ Snorkel	■ Snorkel diving
Types of diving:	■ Boat	☐ Jetty	☐ Shore	
Description of dive site:	■ Island	■ Submerged reef	☐ Shore	
	■ Wreck	■ Shallow water	■ Deep water	
Conditions at site:	■ Current	■ Swell	■ Wind chop	
	■ Tide changes	☐ Boat traffic	■ Good visibility	
	■ Fair visibility	☐ Poor visibility		
Dive time:	■ In-coming tide	■ Out-going tide		
	■ Spring tide	■ Neap tide	■ Slack tide	
Underwater terrain:	■ Drop offs	■ Gutters	■ Patch reefs	
	■ Sand & rubble	■ Rocky reef	■ Flat bottom	
	■ Low profile reef	■ Coral reef	■ Slope	
	☐ Caves	☐ Swim-throughs	☐ Silty bottom	
Marine life:	☐ Kelp	☐ Sea grass	■ Sponges	■ Corals
	■ Sea whips	■ Sea fans	■ Black coral	■ Soft corals
	■ Anemones	■ Fan worms	■ Bryozoans	☐ Brachiopods
	■ Crays	■ Crabs	■ Shells	■ Commensal shrimps
	■ Nudibranchs	☐ Cuttles	☐ Scallops	☐ Abalone
	■ Sea stars	☐ Basket stars	■ Sea urchins	■ Feather stars
	■ Ascidians	■ Sea snakes	■ Dolphins	■ Turtles
	■ Sharks	■ Fish	☐ Numerous fish	■ Abundant fish
Experience level:	■ Pupil	■ Beginner	■ Intermediate	■ Advanced
Dive site rating:	■ Excellent	☐ Very good	☐ Fair	■ Photography
Management of resources:	■ Marine reserve	■ Protected species	■ Quotas	☐ Collecting

Watersport (32 divers)

Contact:
Watersport
252–256 Walker Street, Townsville Qld 4810
Phone (077) 72 3583

Remarks:

Due to local conditions there is little or no diving on the coast itself but Magnetic Island has some good spots for shallow water scuba diving and snorkelling during the winter months.

Off Townsville there are many excellent Great Barrier Reefs to dive, some of the most popular being Rib Reef, Helix Reef, Bramble Reef, Trunk Reef, Davis Reef, Wheeler Reef and Broadhurst. I can thoroughly recommend Broadhurst, Bramble, Kelso and the afore-mentioned John Brewer (on the outer face) having dived part of each of them.

On the inshore mainland islands there is also some good diving. The visibility isn't quite what it is on the outer reef, but areas around Orpheus Island, Pelorus Island and Great Palm Island (mostly shallow water) are extremely rich in underwater species with large healthy fringing coral reefs and some very *big* fish. Probably the most popular dive site is the *Yongala*, now a fully protected historic shipwreck zone 18 kilometres off Cape Bowling Green near Townsville. This is one of the most spectacular wreck dives in Australia: clear water, zillions of animals, huge fish and a 'bit' of current.

WHITSUNDAY ISLANDS

The Whitsundays, as they as known, are a scattered group of large and small mainland islands adjacent to the Conway Range National Park which borders Shute Harbour some 36 kilometres northeast of Proserpine. With the exceptions of Hayman Island, Dent Island and Hamilton Island, the entire group is proclaimed a National Park. In general, the islands have good beaches, fabulous scenery, dense sub-tropical rainforest, natural flora and fauna, sheltered aspects and, underwater, they are fringed with dense thickets of coral, teaming with tropical marine life.

Services:

H$_2$0 SPORTZ (HAMILTON ISLAND)
PADI instruction facility, modern classroom and teaching aids, equipment sales, workroom for servicing, large range of hire equipment, air 7 days a week, island dives, charter boat. Specialty courses include resort introductory courses, open water and/or advanced

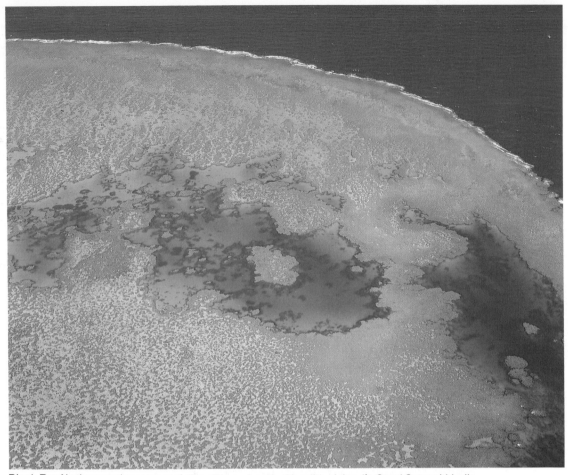

Black Reef is the popular outer reef dive site serviced by Hamilton Island's *Coral Cat* multi-hulls.

international certification, night diving, deep diving and equipment courses on request.

Contact:
Hamilton Island Resort
PMB Post Office, Mackay Qld 4740
Phone: (079) 46 9144

Sydney Office
Suite 609, Eastpoint,
180 Ocean Street, Edgecliff NSW 2027
Phone: (02) 327 1899

Melbourne Office
28 The Concourse, World Trade Centre,
Cnr Flinders & Spencer Streets, Melbourne Vic. 3005
Phone: (03) 611 3805

Gold Coast Office
PO Box 1985, Southport Qld 4215
Phone: (075) 32 8422

Whether you're a beginner or a serious diver, the Whitsundays have a lot to offer.

The new full colour brochure 'Dive H₂0 Sportz Hamilton Island' is one of the best presented information packages I've had the pleasure of reading.

By combining instruction in comfortable surroundings on Hamilton Island with helicopter rides and fast boat trips to the floating dive facility at Black Reef (on the outer Barrier Reef) and cruise diving on the luxurious *Coral Cat*, Hamilton Island has the facilities to take you where *you* want to go, at whatever level you wish. All you have to do is enjoy it!

Service:

BARRIER REEF DIVING SERVICES (Hayman Island)
PADI instruction, equipment sales, service, gear hire, air 7 days a week, resort and open water courses, dive charter to the outer Barrier Reef, local dives.

Contact:
Barrier Reef Diving Services
PO Box 180, Airlie Beach Qld 4802
Phone: (079) 46 6204

Service:

BARRIER REEF DIVING SERVICES (Airlie Beach)
As above.
Phone: (079) 46 6204

Service:

BARRIER REEF DIVING SERVICES (Day Dream Island)
As above.
Phone: (079) 46 9200

Service:

BARRIER REEF DIVING SERVICES (Lindeman Island)
Lindeman Island services can be arranged on request.
Phone: (079) 46 6204

Not as common as its relative, the feather duster worm, the giant tube worm may build a tube over 250 mm in length.

Service:

Airlie Beach Dive Centre
NAUI pro facility, instruction, equipment sales, service, gear hire, air, trips to the Great Barrier Reef.

Contact:
Whitsunday Centre
Shute Harbour Road, Airlie Beach Qld 4802
Phone: (079) 46 6508

Service:

BARNES REEFDIVING SERVICES
PADI instruction, equipment sales, service, gear hire, air, local dives, day charter boat to the outer islands and overnight trips to the Whitsundays (charter boat *Reefdiver*).

Contact:
Barnes Reefdiving Services
153 Victoria Street, Mackay Qld 4740
Phone: (079) 51 1472 (for diving or charter)

Service:

MACKAY DIVING
NAUI and PADI instruction, equipment sales, service, gear hire, air 7 days a week, local dive trips on dive boat *Charisma*. Dive holidays to Lady Elliott Island and Great Barrier Reef cruises.

Contact:
Mackay Diving
1 Mangrove Road, Mackay Qld 4740
Phone: (079) 51 1640 (for diving and charter)

Service:

WHITSUNDAY DIVE SERVICES
PADI instruction, equipment sales, service, gear hire, air, local dives, charter boat to the Great Barrier Reef. Services to South Mole Island, Whitsunday 100 Island and Hook Island.

Contact:
Whitsunday Dive Services
PO Box 546, Airlie Beach Qld 4802
Phone: (079) 46 6811

Charter Boats:

Charisma

Contact:
Mackay Island Tours
PO Box 941, Mackay Qld 4740
Phone: (079) 52 1870, (079) 59 8328

Spirit of Roylen

Contact:
Roylen Cruises
PO Box 169, Mackay Qld 4740
Phone: (079) 55 3066

Remarks:

There are about seventy-four islands in the Whitsunday group and although I haven't dived them all, I have spent just on three months in the area diving every day, photographing and recording the marine life.

Although the visibility around the mainland islands of the Whitsundays may not be the same as it is on the outer barrier, it is important to remember the reason why. The inner waters are richer in life; nutrients, plankton, suspended detritus, etc. (being closer to the coast). Quite simply, the clearer the water the less there is in it.

With an average visibility of 5 to 10 metres in the summer and 10 to 15 metres in the winter, the majority of what you see on the outer reefs is also present in the Whitsundays, you just have to look a little closer. Take my word for it, with the right weather and conditions, you can see more species in one dive off the Whitsundays than on the outer barrier. However, if you want clear water all year round, without fail, the outer barrier is the place to get it. The outer reefs off the Whitsundays are right in the heart of the Great Barrier Reef and you can't get any closer than that.

GENERAL INFORMATION

Best times of the year:	■ Summer	□ Winter	■ Spring	□ Autumn
Typical weather:	■ Excellent	□	■	□
	□ Very good	■	□	□
	□ Average	□	□	□
	□ Fair	□	□	■
Accommodation available:	■ Camping	□ Hostel	■ Hotel	□ Motel
Airport:	■ Light aircraft	■ Jet	□ International	■ Helicopter

DIVE SITE GUIDE

Access:	□ Boat ramp	■ Charter boat	■ Air	
Dive methods.	■ Scuba	■ Hookah	■ Snorkel	■ Snorkel diving
Types of diving:	■ Boat	■ Jetty	■ Shore	
Description of dive site:	■ Island	■ Submerged reef	■ Shore	
	□ Wreck	■ Shallow water	■ Deep water	
Conditions at site:	■ Current	■ Swell	■ Wind chop	
	■ Tide changes	□ Boat traffic	□ Good visibility (outer barrier)	
	■ Fair visibility	□ Poor visibility		
Dive time:	■ In-coming tide	■ Out-going tide		
	□ Spring tide	■ Neap tide	■ Slack tide	
Underwater terrain:	□ Drop offs	■ Gutters	■ Patch reefs	
	□ Sand & rubble	■ Rocky reef	■ Flat bottom	
	■ Low profile reef	■ Coral reef	■ Slope	
	□ Caves	□ Swim-throughs	■ Silty bottom	
Marine life:	□ Kelp	■ Sea grass	■ Sponges	■ Corals
	□ Sea whips	■ Sea fans	□ Black coral	■ Soft corals
	■ Anemones	■ Fan worms	■ Bryozoans	□ Brachiopods
	■ Crays	■ Crabs	■ Shells	■ Commensal shrimps
	■ Nudibranchs	□ Cuttles	■ Scallops	□ Abalone
	■ Sea stars	□ Basket stars	■ Sea urchins	■ Feather stars
	■ Ascidians	□ Sea lions	■ Dolphins	■ Turtles
	■ Sharks	■ Fish	□ Numerous fish	□ Abundant fish
Experience level:	■ Pupil	■ Beginner	■ Intermediate	■ Advanced
Dive site rating:	■ Excellent(outer barrier)	■ Very good	□ Fair	■ Photography
Management of resources:	■ Marine reserve	■ Protected species	□ Quotas	□ Collecting

The waters around the Keppel Islands are rich in soft corals and gorgonia sea fans similar to those this young tiera batfish is sheltering behind.

GREAT KEPPEL ISLAND

Just 12 kilometres off the coast of Yeppoon, Great Keppel was discovered in 1770 by Captain Cook, who named all the islands in the Keppel group.

The entire system of islands and reefs within the Keppel complex is staggering in the number of different habitats and micro-habitats it contains. There are more species of animals in this area than in places with 50 metre visibility, 400 kilometres out in the Coral Sea. The beginner scuba diver learning to dive in and around Great Keppel Island would gain experience on most types of underwater terrain and conditions.

Service:

HAVEN DIVING SERVICES (Great Keppel Island)
NAUI pro facility, instruction to all levels, equipment sales, services, gear hire, air 7 days a week, local dives and charter boat *Saracen*, 12 divers.

When diving Underwater Australia new discoveries like this red-margined casella nudibranch are made almost daily.

Contact:
Haven Diving Services (Great Keppel Island)
PO Box 108, Rockhampton Qld 4700
Phone: (079) 39 4217

Service:

HAVEN DIVING SERVICES (Rockhampton)
Same services as Haven Diving Services on Great Keppel.

Contact:
Haven Diving Services (Rockhampton)
158 Musgrave Street, North Rockhampton Qld 4701
Phone: (079) 39 4217

Charter Boats:

New Horizon (12 divers)

Contact:
New Horizon Tours
PO Box 360, Yeppoon Qld 4703
Phone: (079) 39 2307

Coralita (12 divers)

Contact:
Barrier Reef Cruises
PO Box 268, Yeppoon Qld 4703
Phone: (079) 39 1588

Victory or *Aquajet* (catamarans)
Daily departures from Roslyn Bay Harbour to Great Keppel Island

Contact:
Great Keppel Island Tourist Services
Phone: (079) 33 6744, A/H (079) 27 2948

Remarks: Diving around the Keppels has always been a great treat for me. On every dive I've always discovered one or two new species and some of the most interesting photographs used in my books were taken there.

I haven't dived all the dive sites that are available from Haven Diving but some of the best sites are Barron Island, Egg Rock, Man & Wife Rocks, Halfway Island, Half Tide Rocks and Middle Island. There are many more so I'll just have to keep going back.

GENERAL INFORMATION

Best times of the year: □ Summer ■ Winter ■ Spring □ Autumn

Typical weather:
- □ Excellent ■ ■ □
- ■ Very good □ □ □
- □ Average □ □ □
- □ Fair □ □ ■

Accommodation available: ■ Camping ■ Hostel ■ Hotel (Resort) ■ Motel

Airport: □ Light aircraft □ Jet □ International □ Helicopter

DIVE SITE GUIDE

Access: □ Boat ramp ■ Charter boat ■ Air

Dive methods: ■ Scuba ■ Hookah ■ Snorkel ■ Snorkel diving

Types of diving: ■ Boat □ Jetty ■ Shore

Description of dive site:
- ■ Island ■ Submerged reef □ Shore
- □ Wreck ■ Shallow water ■ Deep water

Conditions at site:
- ■ Current ■ Swell ■ Wind chop
- ■ Tide changes □ Boat traffic □ Good visibility
- ■ Fair visibility □ Poor visibility

Dive time:
- ■ In-coming tide ■ Out-going tide
- ■ Spring tide ■ Neap tide ■ Slack tide

Underwater terrain:
- ■ Drop offs ■ Gutters ■ Patch reefs
- ■ Sand & rubble ■ Rocky reef ■ Flat bottom
- ■ Low profile reef ■ Coral reef ■ Slope
- ■ Caves ■ Swim-throughs ■ Silty bottom

Marine life:
- □ Kelp ■ Sea grass ■ Sponges ■ Corals
- ■ Sea whips ■ Sea fans ■ Black coral ■ Soft corals
- ■ Anemones ■ Fan worms ■ Bryozoans □ Brachiopods
- ■ Crays ■ Crabs ■ Shells ■ Commensal shrimps

- ■ Nudibranchs ■ Cuttles ■ Scallops □ Abalone
- ■ Sea stars □ Basket stars ■ Sea urchins ■ Feather stars
- ■ Ascidians ■ Sea Snakes ■ Dolphins ■ Turtles
- ■ Sharks ■ Fish ■ Numerous fish □ Abundant fish

Experience level: ■ Pupil ■ Beginner ■ Intermediate ■ Advanced

Dive site rating: □ Excellent ■ Very good □ Fair ■ Photography

Management of resources: □ Marine reserve ■ Protected species ■ Quotas ■ Collecting

As the largest dive resort on the Great Barrier Reef, people from all over the world visit Heron Island to take part in its underwater activities.

HERON ISLAND

One of the twelve small coral cays in the Capricorn Bunker group, Heron Island lies some 80 kilometres offshore northeast of Gladstone. The whole island environment is carefully managed by the Queensland National Parks and Wildlife Service in conjunction with P & O Resorts, who operate the present lease and run all tourist functions on the Island. Lease operators of Heron Island have, for over twenty years, been a major force in popularizing scuba diving on the Great Barrier Reef and today the island boasts the largest professionally run operation on the Reef.

Due to it being a marine reserve for such a long time, the fish at Heron Island are extremely tame and will allow observers at close quarters.

Service:

HERON ISLAND DIVE SHOP
PADI instruction, complete scuba diving courses and resort courses, snorkelling instruction, equipment sales, service, gear hire, air, local dive trips and charter boat to other islands and reefs.

Contact:
Proprietors – P & O Resorts
482 Kingsford Smith Drive, Hamilton, Brisbane Qld 4000
Phone: (07) 268 8222

Service:

LAVER BROS SPORTS STORE
PADI instruction, equipment sales, service, gear hire, air, charter boat.

Contact:
Laver Bros Sports Store
55 Goondoon Street, Gladstone Qld 4680
Phone: (079) 72 1412

Some of the hundreds of tame fish ever present at the famous Heron Island Bommie.

Charter Boats:

Vacationer (12 divers)

Contact:
PO Box 500, Gladstone Qld 4680
Phone: (079) 72 4103, (043) 84 1219

Sea Reef (16 divers)

Contact:
PO Box 237, Gladstone Qld 4680
Phone: (079) 72 5842

Capricorn Star (12 divers)

Contact:
PO Box 340, Gladstone Qld 4680
Phone: (079) 72 2806

Odessa (day trips only)

Contact:
PO Box 406, Gladstone Qld 4680
Phone: (079) 72 3455

Tropic Rover (10 divers)

Contact:
12 Auckland Street, Gladstone Qld 4680
Phone: (079) 72 1680

Remarks:

This has been one of my all-time favourite dive spots for many years and I am certainly not alone. Heron Island has played host to more divers than any other resort in Australia.

The buoyed dive sites number sixteen and even though they see a lot of divers from time to time, each site is healthy and in good shape. Some of these sites include my good 'friend' the famous Heron Island Bommie, Wistari Reef, the Blue Pools, the Gorgonia Hole, the Hole in the Wall, Coral Gardens, Cascades and Pam's Point, and all within a 15 minute boat ride.

Each October/November P & O Resorts sponsor the Heron Island Underwater Festival, which is also supported by the diving industry. Top underwater educators assist by holding a wide variety of educational seminars complemented by films and audio-visuals. Free introductory underwater photography workshops are given by the Nikon School of Underwater Photography (see page 256).

All in all, Heron has some magnificent diving, excellent facilities, professional and knowledgeable dive staff and I can thoroughly recommend it.

GENERAL INFORMATION

Best times of the year:	■ Summer	□ Winter	■ Spring	□ Autumn
Typical weather:	■ Excellent	□	■	□
	□ Very good	■	□	■
	□ Average	□	□	□
	□ Fair	□	□	□
Accommodation available:	□ Camping	□ Hostel	■ Hotel (Resort)	□ Motel
Airport:	□ Light aircraft	□ Jet	□ International	■ Helicopter

DIVE SITE GUIDE

Access:	□ Boat ramp	■ Charter boat	■ Air	
Dive methods:	■ Scuba	□ Hookah	■ Snorkel	■ Snorkel diving
Types of diving:	■ Boat	□ Jetty	■ Shore	
Description of dive site:	■ Island	■ Submerged reef	■ Shore	
	■ Wreck	■ Shallow water	■ Deep water	
Conditions at site:	■ Current	■ Swell	■ Wind chop	
	■ Tide changes	□ Boat traffic	■ Good visibility	
	□ Fair visibility	□ Poor visibility		
Dive time:	■ In-coming tide	■ Out-going tide		
	■ Spring tide	■ Neap tide	■ Slack tide	
Underwater terrain:	■ Drop offs	■ Gutters	■ Patch reefs	
	■ Sand & rubble	□ Rocky reef	■ Flat bottom	
	■ Low profile reef	□ Coral reef	■ Slope	
	■ Caves	■ Swim-throughs	□ Silty bottom	
Marine life:	□ Kelp	■ Sea grass	■ Sponges	■ Corals
	■ Sea whips	■ Sea fans	□ Black coral	■ Soft corals
	■ Anemones	■ Fan worms	■ Bryozoans	■ Brachiopods
	■ Crays	■ Crabs	■ Shells	■ Commensal shrimps
	■ Nudibranchs	■ Cuttles	□ Scallops	□ Abalone
	■ Sea stars	□ Basket stars	■ Sea urchins	■ Feather stars
	■ Ascidians	■ Manta rays	■ Dolphins	■ Turtles
	■ Sharks	■ Fish	□ Numerous fish	■ Abundant fish
Experience level:	■ Pupil	■ Beginner	■ Intermediate	■ Advanced
Dive site rating:	■ Excellent	□ Very good	□ Fair	■ Photography
Management of resources:	■ Marine reserve	■ Protected species	□ Quotas	□ Collecting

Manta rays are common visitors around Lady Elliott Island and throughout the entire Capricorn Group of islands.

LADY ELLIOTT ISLAND

A part of the Capricornia section of the Great Barrier Reef Marine Park, this 42 hectares of true coral cay is situated 80 kilometres northeast of Bundaberg. It was discovered in 1816 by Captain Thomas Stewart and named after his ship, the *Lady Elliott*. It is the only coral cay on the Great Barrier Reef with an airstrip.

Service:

LADY ELLIOTT ISLAND DIVE
NAUI instruction facility, equipment sales, service, gear hire, air, local boat dives or shore dives, escorted or unescorted buddy pairs.

Contact:
Lady Elliott Island Dive
Locked Mail Bag No 6, PO Bundaberg Qld 4670
Phone (071) 72 2322

Book with:
Sea Life Holidays
27 Alfreda Street, Coogee NSW 2034
Phone: (02) 665 6333

At the southern end of the reef the beautiful Watanabei's angelfish lives in much shallower depths (15 metres) than those found at the northern end (40 metres).

Remarks:

For families on a budget this is the ideal holiday island: reef walking, wading, snorkelling, snorkel diving and scuba diving can all be done from shore, with snorkelling and diving instruction available from the Island's dive shop.

Below the water, Lady Elliott is a living treasure trove; there is no other Great Barrier Reef island or cay like it. It is unique: the underwater topography, the corals, the manta rays, the abundant fishlife and the mixture of species produce an amazing aggregation. The island has yet to be surveyed underwater, and when I first dived there in 1982 I discovered dozens of unrecorded species and some undescribed ones. It's really virgin diving country.

Rarely observed above 30 metres, the red-striped fairy basslet is one of the most beautiful fishes inhabiting southern reef waters.

GENERAL INFORMATION

Best times of the year:	■ Summer	■ Winter	■ Spring	□ Autumn
Typical weather:	■ Excellent	■	■	□
	□ Very good	□	□	■
	□ Average	□	□	□
	□ Fair	□	□	□
Accommodation available:	■ Camping	■ Hostel	■ Hotel (Resort)	□ Motel
Airport:	■ Light aircraft	□ Jet	□ International	□ Helicopter

DIVE SITE GUIDE

Access:	□ Boat ramp	■ Charter boat	■ Air	
Dive methods:	■ Scuba	□ Hookah	■ Snorkel	■ Snorkel diving
Types of diving:	■ Boat	□ Jetty	■ Shore	
Description of dive site:	■ Island	■ Submerged reef	■ Shore	
	□ Wreck	■ Shallow water	■ Deep water	
Conditions at site:	■ Current	■ Swell	■ Wind chop	
	■ Tide changes	□ Boat traffic	■ Good visibility	
	□ Fair visibility	□ Poor visibility		
Dive time:	■ In-coming tide	■ Out-going tide		
	■ Spring tide	■ Neap tide	■ Slack tide	
Underwater terrain:	■ Drop offs	■ Gutters	■ Patch reefs	
	■ Sand & rubble	□ Rocky reef	■ Flat bottom	
	■ Low profile reef	■ Coral reef	■ Slope	
	■ Caves	■ Swim-throughs	□ Silty bottom	
Marine life:	□ Kelp	□ Sea grass	■ Sponges	■ Corals
	■ Sea whips	■ Sea fans	□ Black coral	■ Soft corals
	■ Anemones	■ Fan worms	■ Bryozoans	□ Brachiopods
	■ Crays	■ Crabs	■ Shells	■ Commensal shrimps
	■ Nudibranchs	□ Cuttles	□ Scallops	□ Abalone
	■ Sea stars	□ Basket stars	■ Sea urchins	■ Feather stars
	■ Ascidians	■ Manta rays	■ Dolphins	■ Turtles
	■ Sharks	■ Fish	□ Numerous Fish	■ Abundant Fish
Experience level:	■ Pupil	■ Beginner	■ Intermediate	■ Advanced
Dive site rating:	■ Excellent	□ Very good	□ Fair	■ Photography
Management of resources:	■ Marine reserve	■ Protected species	□ Quotas	□ Collecting

With several hundred species of nudibranchs already recorded from the Great Barrier Reef, species such as the varicose nudibranch are now becoming well known to divers.

BUNDABERG – HERVEY BAY – MARYBOROUGH

Established in 1867, Bundaberg is 374 kilometres north of Brisbane and has a population of around 56,000. It is an important sugar cane district and home of the distillery for Bundaberg Rum.

Good shore diving can be had along the coast from Burnett Heads to Elliott Heads but only during winter when the offshore winds blow at irregular intervals. My first dives off places like Hoffman's Rocks and Bagara were unforgettable due to the richness of marine life: gorgonia gardens, butterfly fish, angel fish, sea snakes galore, nudibranchs and many, many more invertebrates. However, I saw no big fish due to the years of heavy spearfishing this area has suffered.

Mon Repos Environmental Park between Burnett Heads and Bagara is the site of the largest turtle rookery on the Australian mainland. Over 400 marine turtles of three species (logger head, flat back and green) come ashore to lay eggs from November onwards; the hatchlings appear in mid January to late March.

Built on the Burnett River, Bundaberg is the most southerly point of access to the Great Barrier Reef.

Lady Elliott Island, the Great Barrier Reef's southernmost coral cay, is only a half hour flight away; Lady Musgrave Island is just 49 kilometres offshore, a 40 minute flight or 2½ hours by a high speed catamaran like *Lady Musgrave*.

Hervey Bay is the location of the largest artificial reef in Australia, covering over fifty underwater sites of different compositions. However, diving in the Hervey Bay area (it has some good shallow-water coral covered reefs and lots of fish) is subject to slack water, due to the strong tidal movement. Visibility is restricted at times but the marine life here is extremely rich and varied. One of my first Queensland coastal dives was in Hervey Bay in 1966; luckily the tide was running in!

Centre of the Sugar Coast and peanut growing area, Maryborough, first settled in 1843, is one of Queensland's oldest cities. It has a population of 23,000. However, Hervey City, its coastal counterpart some 34 kilometres north of Maryborough, has steadily rivalled Maryborough in terms of tourism ever since the *Urangan* connection (ferry) to adjacent Fraser Island became popular.

Service:

ANGLO DIVING SERVICES
Instruction and specialty courses, equipment sales, service, gear hire, air, local diving, and Great Barrier Reef trips. Commercial diving and hull cleaning.

Contact:
Anglo Diving Services
Shop 3/47A Takalvan Street, Bundaberg Qld 4670
Phone: (071) 71 6422, A/H (071) 72 0903

Service:

BUNDABERG DIVE CENTRE
NAUI pro facility, instruction all levels, equipment sales, service, gear hire, air, local trips and dives to Lady Elliott Island.

Contact:
Bundaberg Dive Centre
46 Targo Street, Bundaberg Qld 4670
Phone: (071) 72 6707, A/H (071) 72 7000

Service:

HERVEY BAY DIVE SHOP
PADI instruction, equipment sales, service, gear hire, air, local trips together with trips to the Great Barrier Reef and overseas.

Contact:
Hervey Bay Dive Shop
429 Esplanade, Torquay Qld 4657
Phone: (071) 25 1311

Charter Boat:

Lady Musgrave
Day trips and holiday camp trips to Lady Musgrave Island.

Contact:
Barrier Reef Cruises
Phone: (071) 72 9011

GENERAL INFORMATION

Best times of the year:	□ Summer	■ Winter	■ Spring	□ Autumn
Typical weather:	□ Excellent	□	□	□
	□ Very good	■	■	□
	□ Average	□	□	□
	■ Fair	□	□	■
Accommodation available:	■ Camping	□ Hostel	■ Hotel	■ Motel
Airport:	■ Light aircraft	■ Jet	□ International	□ Helicopter

DIVE SITE GUIDE

Access:	■ Boat ramp	■ Charter boat	■ Air	
Dive methods:	■ Scuba	■ Hookah	■ Snorkel	■ Snorkel diving
Types of diving:	■ Boat	□ Jetty	■ Shore	
Description of dive site:	■ Island	■ Submerged reef	■ Shore	
	■ Wreck	■ Shallow water	□ Deep water	
Conditions at site:	■ Current	■ Swell	■ Wind chop	
	■ Tide changes	□ Boat traffic	□ Good visibility	
	■ Fair visibility	■ Poor visibility		
Dive time:	■ In-coming tide	□ Out-going tide		
	□ Spring tide	■ Neap tide	■ Slack tide	
Underwater terrain:	□ Drop offs	□ Gutters	■ Patch reefs	
	■ Sand & rubble	■ Rocky reef	■ Flat bottom	
	■ Low profile reef	■ Coral reef	■ Slope	
	□ Caves	■ Swim-throughs	■ Silty bottom	
Marine life:	□ Kelp	□ Sea grass	■ Sponges	■ Corals
	□ Sea whips	■ Sea fans	□ Black coral	■ Soft corals
	■ Anemones	■ Fan worms	■ Bryozoans	□ Brachiopods
	■ Crays	■ Crabs	■ Shells	■ Commensal shrimps
	■ Nudibranchs	□ Cuttles	□ Scallops	□ Abalone
	■ Sea stars	□ Basket stars	■ Sea urchins	■ Feather stars
	■ Ascidians	■ Sea snakes	■ Dolphins	■ Turtles
	■ Sharks	■ Fish	□ Numerous fish	□ Abundant fish
Experience level:	■ Pupil	■ Beginner	■ Intermediate	■ Advanced
Dive site rating:	□ Excellent	□ Very good	■ Fair	■ Photography
Management of resources:	■ Marine reserve	■ Protected species	■ Quotas	■ Collecting

Bottlenose dolphins are very common in Moreton Bay where there is a large resident population.

BRISBANE – MORETON BAY

As capital of the Sunshine State, Brisbane is the Queensland centre of finance, manufacturing and trade, and with a population of over 1 million it supports a healthy diving fraternity who have access to both tropical and subtropical dive sites. As the waters of inshore Moreton Bay are shallow and influenced by the huge output of silt from the Brisbane River and shoreline mangroves, all sites are boat dives.

Service:

A.N. ROBINSON'S SPORTS AND SCUBA SCHOOL
PADI instruction, equipment sales, service, gear hire, air, local dive trips, overseas holidays, club.

Contact:
A.N. Robinson's Sports and Scuba School
300 Queen Street, Brisbane Qld 4000
Phone: (07) 221 5011

Service:

ADVENTURE SPORTS
NAUI pro facility, instruction to all levels, speciality courses, equipment sales, service, gear hire, air, local dive trips, dive charter boat *Spirit of Adventure*.

Contact:
Adventure Sports
11 James Street, Toowoomba Qld 4350
Phone: (076) 32 7227

Prevalent around inshore mainland reefs, Cavanagh's ovulid inhabits the same soft corals upon which it feeds.

Service:

BRISBANE DIVE SYSTEMS
PADI instruction facility, speciality courses, equipment sales, service, gear hire, air, local dive trips, overseas dive holidays, charter boat *Diversion I*.

Contact:
Brisbane Dive Systems
536 Rode Road, Chermside Qld 4032
Phone: (07) 359 3925

Service:

BRISBANE SCUBA SCHOOL
NAUI pro facility instruction to all levels, specialty courses, equipment sales, service, gear hire, air, local dive trips, and trips to Byron Bay NSW.

Contact:
Brisbane Scuba School
Shop 8E, Shawna Downs Centre,
Old Beenleigh Road,
Sunny Bank Hills Qld 4109
Phone: (07) 344 1488

Service:

GET WET SPORTS
NAUI pro facility, instruction, equipment sales, service, gear hire, dive trips.

Contact:
Get Wet Sports
Tangalooma Resort, Moreton Island Qld 4004
Phone: (075) 48 2666

Service:

MICK SIMMONS BRISBANE
Air, equipment sales and service.

Contact:
Mick Simmons Brisbane
280 Adelaide Street, Brisbane Qld 4000
Phone: (07) 221 3866

Service:

MORETON ACADEMY OF DIVING
PADI instruction, equipment sales, service, hire gear, air, local dive trips, overseas dive holidays, club.

Contact:
Moreton Academy of Diving
Shop 9/65 Gawain Road, Bracken Ridge, Brisbane Qld 4017
Phone: (07) 211 4301, A/H (07) 261 2344

Service:

NORTHSIDE DIVING CENTRE
PADI instruction, equipment sales, service, gear hire, air 7 days a week, specialty courses, local dive trips, overseas dive holidays, boat charter.

Contact:
Northside Diving Centre
20 Samford Road, Alderley, Brisbane Qld 4051
Phone: (07) 352 6244

Service:

SPORTS FAIR
Equipment sales, service, gear hire, air 5 days a week.

Contact:
Sports Fair
Cnr Redland Bay & Mt. Cotton Roads, Capalaba Qld 4157
Phone: (07) 390 3322

Service:

THE DIVE SITE
NAUI pro facility, equipment sales, service, gear hire, air, specialty courses, dive trips.

Contact:
The Dive Site
652 Ipswich Road, Annerley, Brisbane Qld 4103
Phone: (07) 848 0696

Service:

SPORTSMAN'S WAREHOUSE
FAUI instruction, equipment sales, dive trips, charter boat.

Contact:
Sportsman's Warehouse
32 Strathaird Road, Bundall Qld 4217
Phone: (075) 38 9077 (sales); (075) 56 0030 (instruction)

Sunshine Coast

Service:

SUN DIVE SCUBA SCHOOL
NAUI/PADI instruction, equipment sales, service, gear hire, air 7 days, day trips, charter boat (12 divers).

Contact:
Sun Dive Scuba School
40 River Esplanade, Mooloolabah Qld 4557
Phone: (071) 44 5656, (071) 44 5545

Although feather stars occur in all the seas surrounding Australia the tropical forms are by far the most colourful.

Service:

SHARKS INCORPORATED
NAUI pro facility, equipment sales, service, gear hire, air 5½ days a week, local dive trips.

Contact:
Sharks Incorporated
Game Fishing Jetty, Gympie Terrace, Noosaville Qld 4566
Phone: (071) 49 8009

Gold Coast

Service:

GOLD COAST DIVE CENTRE
PADI instruction to all levels (Qld Course Director), speciality courses, equipment sales, service, gear hire, repairs, local dives, dive charters arranged.

Contact:
Gold Coast Dive Centre
20 Railway Street, Southport Qld 4215
Phone: (075) 32 8830, (075) 91 4575

Charter Boat:

Calypso Kristie
Camping holidays to the Capricorn Bunker Group.

Contact:
Aqua-Photo
PO Box 225, East Brisbane Qld 4169
Phone: (07) 391 6665, *or*

Contact:
Calypso Kristie
PO Box 886, Gladstone Qld 4680
Phone: (079) 72 3300

Remarks:

Once across Moreton Bay there are a number of good dive sites, ranging from shallow waters on the inside of Moreton Island to the deeper reefs off Cape Moreton and North Stradbroke. Within this area there is a fabulous range of different types of underwater terrain and an exciting array of different types of animals that inhabit them. As yet not everybody in Brisbane realizes the fantastic potential they have on their doorstep. The reefs here are as rich in species as anywhere I've been; it's just a different richness.

It is probable that Brisbane has been overshadowed due to the close proximity of the Great Barrier Reef. Brisbane has a totally different type of environment, and has, in my opinion, never been properly marketed.

GENERAL INFORMATION

Best times of the year:	□ Summer	■ Winter	■ Spring	□ Autumn
Typical weather:	□ Excellent	□	□	□
	□ Very good	■	■	□
	□ Average	□	□	□
	■ Fair	□	□	■
Accommodation available:	■ Camping	□ Hostel	■ Hotel	■ Motel
Airport:	■ Light aircraft	■ Jet	■ International	■ Helicopter

DIVE SITE GUIDE

Access:	■ Boat ramp	■ Charter boat	■ Air	
Dive methods:	■ Scuba	■ Hookah	■ Snorkel	■ Snorkel diving
Types of diving:	■ Boat	□ Jetty	□ Shore	
Description of dive site:	■ Island	■ Submerged reef	□ Shore	
	■ Wreck	■ Shallow water	■ Deep water	
Conditions at site:	■ Current	■ Swell	■ Wind chop	
	■ Tide changes	□ Boat traffic	■ Good visibility	
	■ Fair visibility	■ Poor visibility		
Dive time:	■ In-coming tide	□ Out-going tide		
	■ Spring tide	■ Neap tide	■ Slack tide	
Underwater terrain:	■ Drop offs	■ Gutters	■ Patch reefs	
	■ Sand & rubble	■ Rocky reef	■ Flat bottom	
	■ Low profile reef	■ Coral reef	■ Slope	
	□ Caves	□ Swim-throughs	■ Silty bottom	
Marine life:	■ Kelp	■ Sea grass	■ Sponges	■ Corals
	□ Sea whips	■ Sea fans	□ Black coral	■ Soft corals
	■ Anemones	■ Fan worms	■ Bryozoans	□ Brachiopods
	■ Crays	■ Crabs	■ Shells	■ Commensal shrimps
	■ Nudibranchs	■ Cuttles	■ Scallops	■ Abalone
	■ Sea stars	□ Basket stars	■ Sea urchins	■ Feather stars
	■ Ascidians	■ Whales	■ Dolphins	■ Turtles
	■ Sharks	■ Fish	□ Numerous fish	□ Abundant fish
Experience level:	■ Pupil	■ Beginner	■ Intermediate	■ Advanced
Dive site rating:	□ Excellent	■ Very good	□ Fair	■ Photography
Management of resources:	□ Marine reserve	□ Protected species	□ Quotas	■ Collecting

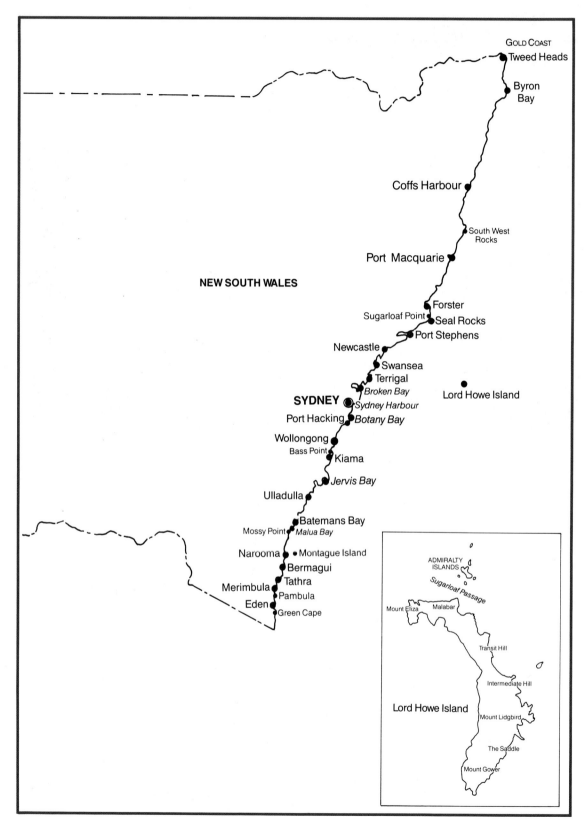

GOLD COAST
Tweed Heads

Byron
Bay

Coffs Harbour

South West
Rocks

Port Macquarie

NEW SOUTH WALES

Forster
Sugarloaf Point
Seal Rocks
Port Stephens

Newcastle

Swansea
Terrigal
Broken Bay

Lord Howe Island

SYDNEY
Sydney Harbour

Port Hacking
Botany Bay

Wollongong
Bass Point
Kiama

Jervis Bay

Ulladulla

Batemans Bay
Mossy Point *Malua Bay*

Narooma ● Montague Island
Bermagui
Tathra
Merimbula
Pambula
Eden
Green Cape

ADMIRALTY
ISLANDS

Sugarloaf Passage

Mount Eliza   Malabar

Transit Hill

Intermediate Hill

Lord Howe Island

Mount Lidgbird

The Saddle

Mount Gower

Diving
NEW SOUTH WALES

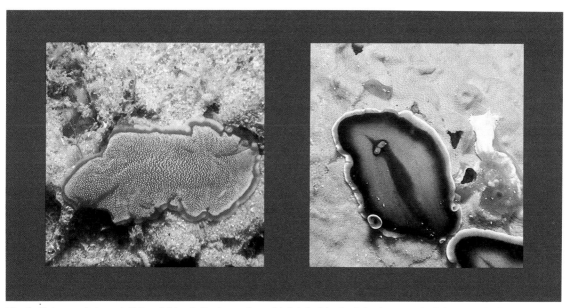

Kent's flatworm (*above left*) is a fairly distinct species which inhabits both inshore and offshore reefs. By comparison the margined flatworm (*above right*) is generally only found beneath rocks and, unlike Kent's flatworm, has two distinct head tentacles.

TWEED HEADS (includes Gold Coast)

Geographically linked with Coolangatta on Queensland's Gold Coast, Tweed Heads lies at the mouth of the Tweed River and is New South Wales' most northerly town. An important fishing port for the area, its biggest claim to fame is tourism. While a lot of the offshore bottom off the Tweed is sandy and flat without much high terrain, there are still some interesting dive sites.

Cook Island off Fingal Head is probably the most popular dive. It offers lots and lots of species but most of the bottom growth is not very interesting due to the tremendous bashing it gets from the swells. Five Mile and Nine Mile Reefs are good dives depending on the sea, and the *Kingscliffe* wreck is okay.

When the sea is up, there is always the Tweed River, which is a particularly good dive after a dry spell when the tide is in and the water is clear, but it must be dived on a slack tide.

Service: TWEED DIVE SHOP (ANGLER'S WAREHOUSE)
NAUI instruction, equipment sales, service, gear hire, air and local dive trips. Charter boat.

GENERAL INFORMATION

Best times of the year:	□ Summer	■ Winter	■ Spring	□ Autumn
Typical weather:	□ Excellent	□	□	□
	□ Very good	■	■	□
	□ Average	□	□	□
	■ Fair	□	□	■
Accommodation available:	■ Camping	□ Hostel	■ Hotel	■ Motel
Airport:	■ Light aircraft	■ Jet	□ International	□ Helicopter

DIVE SITE GUIDE

Access:	■ Boat ramp	■ Charter boat	■ Air	
Dive methods:	■ Scuba	□ Hookah	■ Snorkel	■ Snorkel diving
Types of diving:	■ Boat	□ Jetty	■ Shore	
Description of dive site:	■ Island	■ Submerged reef	■ Shore	
	■ Wreck	■ Shallow water	■ Deep water	
Conditions at site:	■ Current	■ Swell	■ Wind chop	
	■ Tide changes	□ Boat traffic	□ Good visibility	
	■ Fair visibility	■ Poor visibility		
Dive time:	■ In-coming tide	□ Out-going tide		
	■ Spring tide	■ Neap tide	■ Slack tide	
Underwater terrain:	□ Drop offs	■ Gutters	■ Patch reefs	
	■ Sand & rubble	■ Rocky reef	■ Flat bottom	
	■ Low profile reef	□ Coral reef	■ Slope	
	□ Caves	□ Swim-throughs	■ Silty bottom	
Marine life:	■ Kelp	■ Sea grass	■ Sponges	■ Corals
	□ Sea whips	□ Sea fans	□ Black coral	■ Soft corals
	■ Anemones	■ Fan worms	■ Bryozoans	□ Brachiopods
	■ Crays	■ Crabs	■ Shells	■ Commensal shrimps
	■ Nudibranchs	■ Cuttles	□ Scallops	□ Abalone
	■ Sea stars	□ Basket stars	■ Sea urchins	■ Feather stars
	■ Ascidians	■ Whales	■ Dolphins	■ Turtles
	■ Sharks	■ Fish	□ Numerous fish	■ Abundant fish
Experience Level:	■ Pupil	■ Beginner	■ Intermediate	■ Advanced
Dive site rating:	□ Excellent	□ Very good	■ Fair	■ Photography
Management of resources:	□ Marine reserve	■ Protected species	■ Quotas	■ Collecting

Contact:
Tweed Dive Shop
14 Wharf Street, Tweed Heads NSW 2485
Phone: (075) 36 3822, A/H (075) 36 8558

Remarks:

I think islands are special even when they are only a little way off-shore. They appeal to the imagination; they beckon, just like a home port beacon beckons to a sailor. Somehow they exert an attraction, it's as though their very isolation makes them mysterious. Islands are harder to get to, while the mainland is everybody's. When you dive an island it's just the island, the sea and you.

Wobbegong sharks, like this ornate wobbegong, often use large plate corals as hunting platforms and sleep ins.

BYRON BAY

Byron Bay is a prosperous fast-developing community of around 3000 people who live in what must be considered one of the most idyllic playgrounds of the South Pacific. All professional diving services are provided and the good year-round weather conditions enable continuous participation in all water sports. The view from the steep slopes atop Cape Byron, Australia's most easterly point,

Although Dana's brittle star is well known as a multi-host commensal, Byron Bay is one of the few locations it is known to inhabit sea urchins.

is a joy in itself: breathtaking white sandy beaches as far as the eye can see, with white-capped rolling swells washing in from the Pacific.

Service:

BYRON BAY DIVE CENTRE
The largest NAUI training facility on the north coast, this centre provides dive instruction to all levels, a full range of equipment, service, gear hire, air and regular boat dives 7 days a week, boat charter, and dive holidays.

Contact:
Byron Bay Dive Centre
9 Lawson Street, Byron Bay NSW 2481
Phone: (066) 85 7149

Remarks:

Julian Rocks out from Byron Bay offers the diver a host of different dive sites within the perimeter of its granite shores. From the Nursery to the Cod Hole, the scuba diver can see a vast array of micro habitats, hundreds of different species of animals and plants, and has the chance to discover species unknown to science. The area can be dived even during 'rough seas' as the rocks themselves give shelter from wind-driven swells. Around the rocks are dozens of other excitingly different dives such as the Mackeral Bowl, Cape Pinnacles, Kendricks Reef and many, many more. The divemasters at Byron Bay Dive Centre know them all and can cater for every diver safely and conveniently. Remember, Julian Rocks is a marine reserve. Respect it as such.

GENERAL INFORMATION

Best times of the year:	■ Summer	■ Winter	■ Spring	☐ Autumn
Typical weather:	☐ Excellent	☐	☐	☐
	■ Very good	■	■	☐
	☐ Average	☐	☐	■
	☐ Fair	☐	☐	☐
Accommodation available:	■ Camping	■ Hostel	■ Hotel	■ Motel
Airport:	☐ Light aircraft	☐ Jet	☐ International	☐ Helicopter

DIVE SITE GUIDE

Access:	■ Boat ramp	■ Charter boat	■ Air	
Dive methods:	■ Scuba	■ Hookah	■ Snorkel	■ Snorkel diving
Types of diving:	■ Boat	■ Jetty	☐ Shore	
Description of dive site:	■ Island	■ Submerged reef	☐ Shore	
	☐ Wreck	■ Shallow water	■ Deep water	
Conditions at site:	■ Current	■ Swell	■ Wind chop	
	■ Tide changes	☐ Boat traffic	■ Good visibility	
	■ Fair visibility	☐ Poor visibility		
Dive time:	■ In-coming tide	■ Out-going tide		
	■ Spring tide	■ Neap tide	■ Slack tide	
Underwater terrain:	■ Drop offs	■ Gutters	■ Patch reefs	
	■ Sand & rubble	■ Rocky reef	■ Flat bottom	
	■ Low profile reef	☐ Coral reef	■ Slope	
	■ Caves	☐ Swim-throughs	☐ Silty bottom	
Marine life:	■ Kelp	■ Sea grass	■ Sponges	■ Corals
	■ Sea whips	■ Sea fans	■ Black coral	■ Soft corals
	■ Anemones	■ Fan worms	■ Bryozoans	☐ Brachiopods
	■ Crays	■ Crabs	■ Shells	■ Commensal shrimps
	■ Nudibranchs	■ Cuttles	■ Scallops	■ Abalone
	■ Sea stars	☐ Basket stars	■ Sea urchins	■ Feather stars
	■ Ascidians	■ Whales	■ Dolphins	■ Turtles
	■ Sharks	☐ Fish	☐ Numerous Fish	■ Abundant Fish
Experience level:	■ Pupil	■ Beginner	■ Intermediate	■ Advanced
Dive site rating:	■ Excellent	☐ Very good	☐ Fair	■ Photography
Management of resources:	■ Marine reserve	■ Protected species	■ Quotas	■ Collecting

Slipper lobsters are nocturnal dwellers on the reefs. Related to rock lobsters, they make excellent eating.

COFF'S HARBOUR

Named after the founder John Korff in 1861, Coff's Harbour, with a population of 18,000, is the fastest growing district in New South Wales. With updated harbour facilities now completed, it is also one of the safest ports, and the largest banana producing region in Australia.

Diving around the Solitary Islands north of Coff's Harbour is a fantastic experience. I took part in the first underwater fauna survey of the Solitaries in 1976–78. The results of this survey enabled the New South Wales Fisheries and concerned divers and residents of Coff's Harbour to have the area designated as a marine park.

Service:

BLUE WATER DIVERS
NAUI/FAUI/PADI dive instruction, equipment sales, service, gear hire, air 5½ days a week, dive trips, boat charter, weekly and weekend trips to the Solitaries.

Feeding on their soft coral host are two Costellate egg cowries (ovulids). These molluscs prey on at least three different species of soft corals.

Contact:
Solitary Islands Diver Services
396 High Street, Coff's Harbour Jetty, Coff's Harbour NSW 2450
Phone: (066) 52 2422, A/H (066) 53 6087

Service:

DIVE QUEST, MULLAWAY
PADI instruction, equipment sales, service, gear hire, air, local dive trips to Solitaries 7 days a week subject to weather, boat charter.

Contact:
Dive Quest, Mullaway
30 Mullaway Drive, Mullaway NSW 2456
Phone: (066) 54 1930

Contact:
Dive Quest, Woolgoolga
53 Beach Street, Woolgoolga NSW 2456
Phone: (066) 54 1930

Remarks:

The diving off Coff's Harbour is all boat diving and there are enough exciting dive sites to keep even the most avid underwaterer satisfied. The waters off the Solitary Islands are a meeting place, where temperate-water animals and those of tropical origin live side by side. They also contain fauna peculiar to the Solitaries and not found off the mainland or any other coastal areas. The waters are alive with fish, both big and small – from tiny gobies 20 millimetres fully grown to large cods – and with hundreds of species of invertebrates.

Local knowledge can make or break your dive; go with the good people here who know what you will want and who can put you on to the best spots.

GENERAL INFORMATION

Best times of the year:	■ Summer	□ Winter	■ Spring	■ Autumn
Typical weather:	□ Excellent	□	□	□
	■ Very good	□	■	■
	□ Average	□	□	□
	□ Fair	■	□	□
Accommodation available:	■ Camping	■ Hostel	■ Hotel	■ Motel
Airport:	■ Light aircraft	□ Jet	□ International	□ Helicopter

DIVE SITE GUIDE

Access:	■ Boat ramp	■ Charter boat	■ Air	
Dive methods:	■ Scuba	■ Hookah	■ Snorkel	■ Snorkel diving
Types of diving:	■ Boat	□ Jetty	□ Shore	
Description of dive site:	■ Island	■ Submerged reef	□ Shore	
	□ Wreck	■ Shallow water	■ Deep water	
Conditions at site:	■ Current	■ Swell	■ Wind chop	
	■ Tide changes	□ Boat traffic	■ Good visibility	
	■ Fair visibility	□ Poor visibility		
Dive time:	■ In-coming tide	■ Out-going tide		
	■ Spring tide	■ Neap tide	■ Slack tide	
Underwater terrain:	■ Drop offs	■ Gutters	■ Patch reefs	
	■ Sand & rubble	■ Rocky reef	■ Flat bottom	
	■ Low profile reef	□ Coral reef	■ Slope	
	■ Caves	□ Swim-throughs	□ Silty bottom	
Marine life:	■ Kelp	■ Sea grass	■ Sponges	■ Corals
	■ Sea whips	■ Sea fans	■ Black coral	■ Soft corals
	■ Anemones	■ Fan worms	■ Bryozoans	□ Brachiopods
	■ Crays	■ Crabs	■ Shells	■ Commensal shrimps
	■ Nudibranchs	■ Cuttles	□ Scallops	■ Abalone
	■ Sea stars	■ Basket stars	■ Sea urchins	■ Feather stars
	■ Ascidians	■ Whales	■ Dolphins	■ Turtles
	■ Sharks	■ Fish	□ Numerous fish	■ Abundant fish
Experience level:	■ Pupil	■ Beginner	■ Intermediate	■ Advanced
Dive site rating:	■ Excellent	□ Very good	□ Fair	■ Photography
Management of resources:	■ Marine reserve	■ Protected species	■ Quotas	■ Collecting

Fish Rock Cave and its environs support rich growths of marine life.

SOUTH WEST ROCKS – PORT MACQUARIE

The small township of South West Rocks is snuggled in behind Smoky Cape, 35 kilometres north of Kempsey. On the tourist maps it is renowned for the old Trail Bay Gaol, but for divers there are far greater attractions. Fish Rock is one of the best yet least-known dives on the north coast. With a diveable tunnel right through it, fringed with gorgonians, sponges and sunshine corals, the rock itself is surrounded by spectacular sponge gardens, shark gutters, sea whip forests and canyons of black coral. The huge population of fish makes taking good photographs a difficult task due to the milling schools.

Established in 1821 as a penal colony, Port Macquarie today has a population of some 26,000 and is a very popular tourist resort. The best diving is all offshore: see Lighthouse Reef, The Pinnacles, Coral Reef, The Cod Hole, Kelp Reef and many more.

A resident commensal, the black coral shrimp is not always easy to see amongst the branches of its host.

Service:

BLUE WATER DIVERS
SOUTH WEST ROCKS MARINE CENTRE
PADI instruction, equipment sales, service, air 7 days a week, charter boat dives to Fish Rock and local sites.

Contact:
South West Rocks Marine Centre
100/104 Gregory Street, South West Rocks NSW 2431
Phone: (065) 66 6474

Service:

ACTION DIVERS DIVE INN
PADI instruction, equipment sales, gear hire, air 7 days a week, live-in courses, boat trips and charters to Fish Rock and other sites.

Contact:
Action Divers Dive Inn
Costa Rica Motel, Gregory Street,
South West Rocks NSW 2431
Phone: (065) 66 6614

Service:

MID COAST DIVERS
PADI instruction, equipment sales, service, gear hire, dive trips, charter, air 7 days a week.

Contact:
Mid Coast Divers
Port Marina, Park Street, Port Macquarie NSW 2444
Phone: (065) 83 8483, A/H (065) 83 3892

Remarks:

With scuba facilities relatively new to these areas, much of the coast offshore is still unexplored; many of the smaller animals will be new to science and as yet undescribed. Yet in time the explorers from the local dive facilities will secure more knowledge, discover more exciting dive sites and uncover their secrets. Book in at your local facility and explore the unknown.

GENERAL INFORMATION

Best times of the year:	■ Summer	□ Winter	■ Spring	■ Autumn
Typical weather:	□ Excellent	□	□	□
	■ Very good	□	■	■
	□ Average	□	□	□
	□ Fair	■	□	□
Accommodation available:	■ Camping	□ Hostel	■ Hotel	■ Motel
Airport:	■ Light aircraft	■ Jet	□ International	□ Helicopter

DIVE SITE GUIDE

Access:	■ Boat ramp	■ Charter boat	■ Air	
Dive methods:	■ Scuba	■ Hookah	■ Snorkel	■ Snorkel diving
Types of diving:	■ Boat	□ Jetty	□ Shore	
Description of dive site:	■ Island	■ Submerged reef	□ Shore	
	■ Wreck	■ Shallow water	■ Deep water	
Conditions at site:	■ Current	■ Swell	■ Wind chop	
	■ Tide changes	□ Boat traffic	■ Good visibility	
	□ Fair visibility	□ Poor visibility		
Dive time:	■ In-coming tide	■ Out-going tide		
	□ Spring tide	■ Neap tide	■ Slack tide	
Underwater terrain:	■ Drop offs	■ Gutters	□ Patch reefs	
	■ Sand & rubble	■ Rocky reef	□ Flat bottom	
	■ Low profile reef	□ Coral reef	■ Slope	
	■ Caves	■ Swim-throughs	□ Silty bottom	
Marine life:	■ Kelp	■ Sea grass	■ Sponges	■ Corals
	■ Sea whips	■ Sea fans	■ Black coral	■ Soft corals
	■ Anemones	■ Fan worms	■ Bryozoans	□ Brachiopods
	■ Crays	■ Crabs	■ Shells	■ Commensal shrimps
	■ Nudibranchs	■ Cuttles	■ Scallops	■ Abalone
	■ Sea stars	□ Basket stars	■ Sea urchins	■ Feather stars
	■ Ascidians	■ Whales	□ Dolphins	■ Turtles
	■ Sharks	■ Fish	□ Numerous fish	■ Abundant fish
Experience level:	■ Pupil	■ Beginner	■ Intermediate	■ Advanced
Dive site rating:	■ Excellent	□ Very good	□ Fair	■ Photography
Management of resources:	■ Marine reserve	■ Protected species	■ Quotas	■ Collecting

Lord Howe Island has the southernmost coral reefs in the world.

LORD HOWE ISLAND

The rim and remains of a submerged volcano, Lord Howe Island is of ancient origins. It lies some 708 kilometres northeast of Sydney on the same latitude as Port Macquarie and as such enjoys a sub-tropical climate.

Being so far off the coast it has excellent visibility and during the diver tourist season (August to May) the water at most dive sites is crystal clear.

Over 440 species of fish have so far been recorded at Lord Howe Island (65 new records from my observations and photographs), along with 60 species of corals. Over 600 species of underwater animals have been photographed during Sea Australia Resource Centre fauna surveys, and lots of new species discovered. Lord Howe Island has it all: the best scuba diving, the best climate, the best snorkelling, the tamest hand fed fish and the best snorkel diving in the best and safest lagoon in New South Wales.

Service:

SEA LIFE INTERNATIONAL
Total package dive tours for one week, two weeks, or as long as required. Complete information kits including brochure, available

Feeding the fish at Ned's Beach is a favourite pastime for divers waiting out surface intervals between dives.

on inquiry. Island services include air, gear hire, tee shirt sales, excellent divemaster, reliable charter boat, 2 dives a day, cheerful courteous assistance.

Contact:
Sea Life International
27 Alfreda Street, Coogee NSW 2034
Phone: (02) 665 6333

Service:

Polynesian Apartments
Accommodation, local diving services, gear hire, island tours.

Contact:
Rupert Giles
Polynesian Apartments
Lord Howe Island NSW 2034
Phone: (065) 632 093

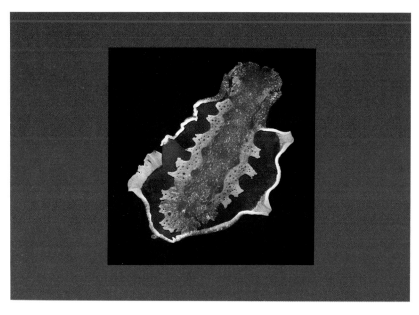

Common at Lord Howe Island, the Spanish dancer is the largest nudibranch in Australia.

Endemic to Australia, the short dragonfish has only been seen by a handful of divers.

Remarks:

(Extracted from 'Lord Howe, Island of Make Believe' by Neville Coleman, *Underwater, The Diver's Journal*, No. I, November 1981, p. 9.)

What do I feel about Lord Howe Island?

I feel a lot of things about Lord Howe Island. To me it is a magnificent place of make-believe, straight out of a fairy tale. It has everything anybody could ever wish for in a holiday resort. It is the perfect place for everybody to be introduced to the underwater world. Clear, safe, shallow waters, schools of tame fish, a sheltered lagoon, an unhurried lifestyle and a magnetism which really has to be experienced to be believed.

I could expound on the virtues of Lord Howe Island for a lifetime, using these and a hundred other superlatives. I could talk about freedom, about spirit, about adventure, about beauty, about individuality, about discovery. I could talk about dreams, experiences, escapism, rejuvenation; of living, breathing, smelling, tasting, touching and loving, all these and more would be true.

This special place, this perfect paradise, this idyllic island is for me the rendezvous of a million magic memories.

Lord Howe Island means so much to me because it was here that one of my most memorable experiences on land occurred. Something I would never try to explain fully, but if I were to start the story would begin: 'The night was black and clear, broken only by the twinkling crystals of a billion far-off worlds. The wind sighed, gently caressing the needle-leafed pines and rippling the surface waters into soft, velvety shimmers...' An uncanny experience, it had quite a lot of bearing on my work in the waters surrounding Lord Howe Island.

So, come along on one of our Underwater Task Force Lord Howe Island Underwater Adventures and discover a new species, or a new you. Everybody is welcome, from grandmothers to gridiron players...Bring your camera and have your Ektachrome or Fuji film processed on the spot. Dive such world-renowned sites as Flat Rock,

North Rock, Roach Island, Tenth of June, Sugarloaf Island, Noddy Island, Deacon's Reef, Gary's Reef, Wolf Rock, Phillip Rock, the Landslide, Malabar, the Gulch and lots more. For shallow-water scuba dives and snorkelling, Ned's Beach, Comet's Hole, Erscotts Hole, Sylphs Hole, Rabbit Island, and Blunt's Hole, make for fantastic 1 metre to 5 metre diving, or are good when your *no-decompression* bottom time has run out. If you decide to come to Lord Howe Island, be warned, the infatuation is catching, but what a way to go!

GENERAL INFORMATION

Best times of the year:	■ Summer	□ Winter	■ Spring	■ Autumn
Typical weather:	■ Excellent	□	□	□
	□ Very good	□	■	■
	□ Average	□	□	□
	□ Fair	■	□	□
Accommodation available:	□ Camping	□ Hostel	□ Hotel	■ Motel
Airport:	■ Light aircraft	□ Jet	□ International	□ Helicopter

DIVE SITE GUIDE

Access:	■ Boat ramp	■ Charter boat	■ Air	
Dive methods:	■ Scuba	□ Hookah	■ Snorkel	■ Snorkel diving
Types of diving:	■ Boat	□ Jetty	■ Shore	
Description of dive site:	■ Island	■ Submerged reef	■ Shore	
	□ Wreck	■ Shallow water	■ Deep water	
Conditions at site:	■ Current	■ Swell	■ Wind chop	
	□ Tide changes	□ Boat traffic	■ Good visibility	
	□ Fair visibility	□ Poor visibility		
Dive time:	■ In-coming tide	■ Out-going tide		
	■ Spring tide	■ Neap tide	■ Slack tide	
Underwater terrain:	■ Drop offs	■ Gutters	■ Patch reefs	
	■ Sand & rubble	■ Rocky reef	■ Flat bottom	
	■ Low profile reef	■ Coral reef	■ Slope	
	■ Caves	■ Swim-throughs	□ Silty bottom	
Marine life:	□ Kelp	■ Sea grass	■ Sponges	■ Corals
	■ Sea whips	■ Sea fans	■ Black coral	■ Soft corals
	■ Anemones	■ Fan worms	■ Bryozoans	□ Brachiopods
	■ Crays	■ Crabs	■ Shells	■ Commensal shrimps
	■ Nudibranchs	□ Cuttles	□ Scallops	□ Abalone
	■ Sea stars	■ Basket stars	■ Sea urchins	■ Feather stars
	■ Ascidians	■ Manta rays	■ Dolphins	■ Turtles
	■ Sharks	■ Fish	□ Numerous fish	■ Abundant fish
Experience level:	■ Pupil	■ Beginner	■ Intermediate	■ Advanced
Dive site rating:	■ Excellent	□ Very good	□ Fair	■ Photography
Management of resources:	■ Marine reserve	■ Protected species	□ Quotas	□ Collecting

Sub-tidal reefs are crowned with luxuriant growths of *Ecklonia* kelp at most New South Wales dive sites.

FORSTER – SEAL ROCKS

As well as offering fantastic scenery along white sandy beaches, the lakes country, and fabulous waterways and fishing, Forster is fast making a name for itself on the underwater scene. It has an excellent selection of offshore dive sites and more being discovered all the time.

Seal Rocks made its name as a popular fishing and spearfishing site but it loses nothing when judged by today's diving standards. The Sugarloaf Bay headland, with its little islands, has excellent shore dives. The place is literally alive with fish and makes for exciting photography.

Service: BLUE WATER DIVERS (Forster Dive School)
PADI instruction facility, equipment sales, service, gear hire, air 7 days a week, live-in courses available, local dives, charter boat.

Contact:
Forster Dive School
Fisherman's Wharf, Wharf Street, Forster NSW 2428
Phone: (065) 54 7478, A/H (065) 54 7945

Service: EAST COAST UNDERWATER SAFARIS
Equipment sales, air 5½ days a week, local dives, dive boat for charter.

GENERAL INFORMATION

Best times of the year: ■ Summer □ Winter ■ Spring □ Autumn
Typical weather:
■ Excellent □ □ □
■ Very good □ ■ □
□ Average □ □ □
□ Fair ■ □ ■
Accommodation available: ■ Camping □ Hostel ■ Hotel ■ Motel
Airport: □ Light aircraft □ Jet □ International □ Helicopter

DIVE SITE GUIDE

Access: ■ Boat ramp ■ Charter boat ■ Air
Dive methods: ■ Scuba ■ Hookah ■ Snorkel ■ Snorkel diving
Types of diving: ■ Boat ■ Jetty ■ Shore
Description of dive site: ■ Island ■ Submerged reef ■ Shore
■ Wreck ■ Shallow water ■ Deep water
Conditions at site: ■ Current ■ Swell ■ Wind chop
■ Tide changes □ Boat traffic ■ Good visibility
■ Fair visibility □ Poor visibility
Dive time: ■ In-coming tide ■ Out-going tide
■ Spring tide ■ Neap tide ■ Slack tide
Underwater terrain: ■ Drop offs ■ Gutters □ Patch reefs
■ Sand & rubble ■ Rocky reef ■ Flat bottom
■ Low profile reef □ Coral reef ■ Slope
■ Caves □ Swim-throughs □ Silty bottom
Marine life: ■ Kelp ■ Sea grass ■ Sponges ■ Corals
□ Sea whips ■ Sea fans ■ Black coral ■ Soft corals
■ Anemones ■ Fan worms ■ Bryozoans □ Brachiopods
■ Crays ■ Crabs ■ Shells ■ Commensal shrimps
■ Nudibranchs ■ Cuttles ■ Scallops ■ Abalone
■ Sea stars □ Basket stars ■ Sea urchins ■ Feather stars
■ Ascidians ■ Whales ■ Dolphins ■ Turtles
■ Sharks ■ Fish □ Numerous fish ■ Abundant fish
Experience level: ■ Pupil ■ Beginner ■ Intermediate ■ Advanced
Dive site rating: □ Excellent ■ Very good □ Fair ■ Photography
Management of resources: □ Marine reserve ■ Protected species ■ Quotas ■ Collecting

Contact:
East Coast Underwater Safaris
Shop 2B/115 The Parade, North Haven NSW 2445
Phone: (065) 59 9782

Remarks:

For most offshore boat diving in this area local knowledge is important, so book in at your choice of professional diving facility for
dives to Crowdy Head, Snapper Rock, Latitude Rock, the Pinnacles,
Skeleton Rock, the Shark Hole, Seal Rocks, the wreck of the *Catherine* and of the *Satara* and many, many more.

Broughton Island off Port
Stephens has picturesque
bays, clear water and good
diving.

PORT STEPHENS
– NEWCASTLE

Referred to as the Blue Water Wonderland, Port Stephens has every
possible attraction for the holiday maker, and for the diver, it's a
mecca. Nelson Bay, the commercial centre and home of a large fishing fleet, also has two of the most wonderful shoreline dive sites
imaginable. Fly Point and Halifax Park can be dived in almost any
weather conditions but only on slack tide due to the currents. Both
these areas are now designated marine reserves and rightly so. The
marine life is incredibly rich; the fish, tame and prolific. The offshore boat diving is spectacular, Boondelbah Island and Broughton
Island sport clear water and every possible type of underwater
terrain, while a wealth of wreck sites offshore prove that it is not

If these two half-banded sea perch were in the air they would be defying gravity, but as their medium is 800 times denser then air, they can 'perch' at almost any angle.

always smooth sailing. Check with local and/or Newcastle pro facilities for detailed information and dive trips.

Newcastle has a population of some 300,000 and is the second largest city in New South Wales, with a huge industrial area taking in the giant BHP Steelworks. The diving around Newcastle itself has limitations and generally is restricted to places like Merewether Reef and a number of offshore wrecks. Most divers prefer the short drive north to Nelson Bay or south to Swansea.

Port Stephens

Service:

PRO-DIVE
PADI instruction facility, equipment sales, service, gear hire, air 7 days a week, local dives, charters and courteous advice.

Contact:
Pro-Dive
59 Donald Street, Nelson Bay NSW 2315
Phone: (049) 81 4331

Service:

BAY AQUATICS AND ALL SPORTS
FAUI/PADI instruction, open 7 days a week for air, equipment sales, service, gear hire and local dives.

Contact:
Bay Aquatics and All Sports
1–2 Cinema Mall, Stockton Road, Nelson Bay NSW 2315
Phone: (049) 81 1888

Newcastle

Service:
ACTION DIVERS (Newcastle – Port Stephens – Erina – Tuncurry)
PADI instruction facility, equipment sales, service, gear hire, air, local dives, charter boat, club and specialty courses.

Contact:
Action Divers
410 Maitland Road, Mayfield West NSW 2304
Phone: (049) 67 6122 for locations in each area.

Service:
OCEAN DIVERS
PADI instruction facility, equipment sales, service, gear hire, air, local dives.

Contact:
Ocean Divers
87 Beaumont Street, Hamilton NSW 2303
Phone: (049) 69 6196

Service:
THE DIVE SHOP (NEWCASTLE AQUA DIVERS)
NAUI/FAUI/PADI instruction facility at all levels, equipment sales, service, gear hire, air, local dives, club, interstate and overseas holidays.

Contact:
The Dive Shop
645–658 Hunter Street, Newcastle West NSW 2303
Phone: (049) 24 234

Service:
NEWCASTLE DIVING ACADEMY
PADI instruction, equipment sales, service, gear hire, air, local dives.

Contact:
Newcastle Diving Academy
432 Pacific Highway, Belmont NSW 2280
Phone: (049) 45 3676

Maitland

Service:
SCUBAROO DIVING
PADI instruction, equipment sales, service, gear hire, air.

Contact:
Scubaroo Diving
36 Melbourne Street, East Maitland NSW 2323
Phone: (049) 33 4042

Remarks: It's funny, through the years you just tend to fall in love with some dive sites and others leave you cold. I suppose every person has his or her own favourites, both close to home and away. That's why diving is such an exciting and challenging pastime. You can never dive it all, and you can never see it all, and you can never know it all, but, what the heck, Fly Point, here I come!

GENERAL INFORMATION

Best times of the year: ■ Summer　■ Winter　■ Spring　□ Autumn

Typical weather:
□ Excellent　□　□　□
■ Very good　■　■　□
□ Average　□　□　■
□ Fair　□　□　□

Accommodation available: ■ Camping　□ Hostel　■ Hotel　■ Motel

Airport: □ Light aircraft　□ Jet　□ International　□ Helicopter

DIVE SITE GUIDE

Access: ■ Boat ramp　■ Charter boat　■ Air

Dive methods: ■ Scuba　■ Hookah　■ Snorkel　■ Snorkel diving

Types of diving: ■ Boat　■ Jetty　■ Shore

Description of dive site:
■ Island　■ Submerged reef　■ Shore
■ Wreck　■ Shallow water　■ Deep water

Conditions at site:
■ Current　■ Swell　■ Wind chop
■ Tide changes　■ Boat traffic　■ Good visibility
■ Fair visibility　□ Poor visibility

Dive time:
■ In-coming tide　■ Out-going tide
□ Spring tide　■ Neap tide　■ Slack tide

Underwater terrain:
■ Drop offs　■ Gutters　□ Patch reefs
■ Sand & rubble　■ Rocky reef　■ Flat bottom
■ Low profile reef　□ Coral reef　■ Slope
■ Caves　□ Swim-throughs　■ Silty bottom

Marine life:
■ Kelp　■ Sea grass　■ Sponges　■ Corals
□ Sea whips　■ Sea fans　■ Black coral　■ Soft corals
■ Anemones　■ Fan worms　■ Bryozoans　□ Brachiopods
■ Crays　■ Crabs　■ Shells　■ Commensal shrimps

■ Nudibranchs　■ Cuttles　■ Scallops　■ Abalone
■ Sea stars　■ Basket stars　■ Sea urchins　■ Feather stars
■ Ascidians　■ Whales　■ Dolphins　■ Turtles
■ Sharks　■ Fish　■ Numerous fish　□ Abundant fish

Experience level: ■ Pupil　■ Beginner　■ Intermediate　■ Advanced

Dive site rating: ■ Excellent　□ Very good　□ Fair　■ Photography

Management of resources: ■ Marine reserve　■ Protected species　■ Quotas　■ Collecting

The annual Terrigal Dive School treasure hunt has been a feature of the boat harbour for many years.

SWANSEA – TERRIGAL

A popular seaside holiday resort, Swansea is at the entrance of Lake Macquarie, the largest saltwater lake in Australia. Well known for its excellent fishing, this area is also becoming a popular diving venue both inshore and offshore. By contrast, Terrigal, some kilometres to the south, is famous for its surfing beaches. It was the first area on this part of the coast to have a professional facility; e.g., Terrigal Dive School at the Haven, which opened in 1968.

Service:

GOSFORD DIVING SERVICES
PADI instruction, equipment sales, service, gear hire, local dive trips, etc. Operates a commercial salvage, demolition and construction division.

Contact:
Gosford Diving Services
310 Trafalgar Avenue, Umina NSW 2257
Phone: (043) 42 1855, A/H (043) 42 1695

Service:

TERRIGAL DIVE SCHOOL
A FAUI instruction facility, equipment sales, service, gear hire, air 7 days a week, local dive trips and charter. Plus *Vacationer*, a charter boat on the Great Barrier Reef.

GENERAL INFORMATION

Best times of the year:	■ Summer	☐ Winter	■ Spring	☐ Autumn
Typical weather:	☐ Excellent	☐	☐	☐
	■ Very good	☐	■	☐
	☐ Average	☐	☐	☐
	☐ Fair	■	☐	■
Accommodation available:	■ Camping	☐ Hostel	■ Hotel	■ Motel
Airport:	☐ Light aircraft	☐ Jet	☐ International	☐ Helicopter

DIVE SITE GUIDE

Access:	■ Boat ramp	■ Charter boat	■ Air	
Dive methods:	■ Scuba	☐ Hookah	■ Snorkel	■ Snorkel diving
Types of diving:	■ Boat	■ Jetty	■ Shore	
Description of dive site:	■ Island	■ Submerged reef	■ Shore	
	■ Wreck	■ Shallow water	■ Deep water	
Conditions at site:	■ Current	■ Swell	■ Wind chop	
	■ Tide changes	☐ Boat traffic	☐ Good visibility	
	■ Fair visibility	☐ Poor visibility		
Dive time:	■ In-coming tide	■ Out-going tide		
	☐ Spring tide	■ Neap tide	■ Slack tide	
Underwater terrain:	■ Drop offs	■ Gutters	■ Patch reefs	
	■ Sand & rubble	■ Rocky reef	☐ Flat bottom	
	■ Low profile reef	☐ Coral reef	■ Slope	
	■ Caves	☐ Swim-throughs	■ Silty bottom	
Marine life:	■ Kelp	■ Sea grass	■ Sponges	☐ Corals
	☐ Sea whips	■ Sea fans	☐ Black coral	■ Soft corals
	■ Anemones	■ Fan worms	■ Bryozoans	☐ Brachiopods
	■ Crays	■ Crabs	■ Shells	☐ Commensal shrimps
	■ Nudibranchs	■ Cuttles	■ Scallops	■ Abalone
	■ Sea stars	☐ Basket stars	■ Sea urchins	■ Feather stars
	■ Ascidians	☐ Sea lions	■ Dolphins	☐ Whales
	■ Sharks	■ Fish	■ Numerous fish	☐ Abundant fish
Experience level:	■ Pupil	■ Beginner	■ Intermediate	■ Advanced
Dive site rating:	☐ Excellent	■ Very good	☐ Fair	■ Photography
Management of resources:	■ Marine reserve	■ Protected species	■ Quotas	■ Collecting

Contact:
Terrigal Dive School
The Haven, Terrigal NSW 2260
Phone: (043) 84 1219

Remarks:

Catherine Hill bay offers some good cave diving but with such an open coastline, diving from shore is only possible during reasonable conditions. From Swansea the deep dive wrecks of the *Advance* and *Bonnie Dundee* are possible, along with sites such as Blue Groper

Found in both shallow and deep waters, variable dorids often form into mating groups with over 20 individuals participating.

Reef, Moon Island and Redhead. In 'wipe out' weather, the bridge at Swansea is a great little dive for close ups and for observing fish behaviour, but it can only be dived on the slack tide. Check details at the Dive Store. Out of Terrigal are places such as the Skillion, the *Lord Ashley* wreck, the Shark Gutters, Forester's Reef and Foggy Reef. The annual Treasure Hunt, which attracts hundreds of divers, takes place on the first weekend in November.

A very common spring and summer resident in Sydney Harbour, the red-lined aeolid nudibranch is generally associated with hydroids, its food source.

BROKEN BAY – SYDNEY HARBOUR – PORT HACKING

The capital of New South Wales, Sydney, with a population of nearly 4 million people, is built on the shores of Sydney Harbour, one of the most picturesque natural deep-water harbours in the world. Whilst Sydney, together with its environs, is the diving capital of

Once thought to be very rare, the vermilion biscuit star is now known to be common on inshore and offshore reefs around Sydney.

Australia in terms of the number of dive shops which operate within its boundaries, divers will find the diving is only as good as their attitude...they must be flexible and prepared to take weather conditions as they find them.

North Shore

Service:

ATLANTIS DIVERS
FAUI dive school, equipment sales, air, service and hire, dive trips and charter boat.

Contact:
Atlantis Divers
Barrenjoey Boatshed, Governor Phillip Park,
Palm Beach NSW 2108
Phone: (02) 919 4261

Service:

DIVE 2000
PADI instruction facility, equipment sales, service, gear hire, air, dive trips and charter boat.

Contact:
Dive 2000
2 Military Road, Neutral Bay NSW 2089
Phone: (02) 953 7783

Service:

MID-COAST DIVERS – ST IVES
PADI 5 star training facility, instruction to all levels, equipment sales, service, gear hire, local boat dives on charter boat *New World V*; club, regular and overseas tours.

Contact:
Mid-Coast Divers
4/194 Mona Vale Road, St Ives NSW 2075

Service:

FROG DIVE SERVICES
NAUI instruction facility, equipment sales, service, gear hire, air, dive trips and charters.

Contact:
Frog Dive Services
35a Albany Street, Crows Nest NSW 2065
Phone: (02) 439 5323

Service:

SUNDIVE CENTRE
PADI instruction facility, equipment sales, service, gear hire, air, dive trips and charters.

Contact:
Sundive Centre
West Esplanade, Manly NSW 2095
Phone: (02) 948 0240

Service:

DEEP 6 DIVING
PADI instruction training facility, equipment sales, service, gear hire, air, dive trips, charters and club.

Contact:
Deep 6 Diving
Chatswood Village, Chatswood NSW 2067
Phone: (02) 411 1833

Service:

FATHOM DIVING
NAUI instruction facility, equipment sales, service, gear hire, air, dive trips and charters.

Contact:
Fathom Diving
178 Sydney Road, Fairlight NSW 2094
Phone: (02) 94 7221

Western Side

Service:

AQUASPORT DIVE SHOP
NAUI/FAUI/PADI instruction facility, equipment sales, service, gear hire, air, dive trips and charter boat.

Contact:
Aquasport Dive Shop
430 Hume Highway, Yagoona NSW 2199
Phone: (02) 708 2826

Service:
CAMPBELLTOWN DIVE
PADI dive school, equipment sales, service, gear hire, air, dive trips, club.

Contact:
Campbelltown Dive
Dumaresq Street, Campbelltown NSW 2560
Phone: (046) 27 2351

Service:
DEEP 6 DIVING
PADI instruction facility, equipment sales, service, gear hire, air, dive trips, club and charter boat.

Contact:
Deep 6 Diving
461A Church Street, Parramatta NSW 2150
Phone: (02) 630 7422, *or*

Contact:
Deep 6 Diving
1091 Victoria Road, West Ryde NSW 2114
Phone: (02) 858 4592

Service:
SCUBA WAREHOUSE
PADI 5 star training facility, equipment sales, service, gear hire, air, dive trips and club, charters arranged.

Contact:
Scuba Warehouse
Shop I, Para Mall, Parramatta NSW 2150
Phone: (02) 689 1389

Service:
PRO-DIVE
PADI instruction facility, equipment sales, service, gear hire, air, dive trips, charter, 7 days a week.

Contact:
Pro-Dive
227 Victoria Road, Drummoyne NSW 2047
Phone: (02) 819 7639

Service:
FROG DIVE SERVICES
NAUI instruction facility, equipment sales, service, gear hire, air, dive trips, charter and club.

Contact:
Frog Dive Services
Shop 1/20 Castelreagh Street, Penrith NSW 2750
Phone: (047) 32 3511, *or*

Contact:
Frog Dive Services
7A Miller Street, Merrylands NSW 2160
Phone: (02) 637 2144

Service: WILDERNESS SEA 'n' SKI
PADI instruction, equipment sales, service, gear hire, air, dive trips.

Contact:
Wilderness Sea 'n' Ski
137 George Street, Liverpool NSW 2170
Phone: (02) 601 3130

South Side

Service: CRONULLA DIVE SHOP
NAUI instruction, equipment sales, service, gear hire, air, dive trips, charter boat.

Contact:
Cronulla Dive Shop
130 Cronulla Street, Cronulla NSW 2230
Phone: (02) 523 0596

Service: PRO-DIVE
PADI instruction facility, equipment sales, service, gear hire, air, dive trips, charter boat, dive tours.

Contact:
Pro-Dive
22 Alfreda Street, Coogee NSW 2034
Phone: (02) 665 6333

Service: MIRANDA DIVE
PADI training, equipment sales, service, gear hire, air, dive trips, charter boat.

Contact:
Miranda Dive
7 Beach Park Arcade, Cronulla NSW 2230
Phone: (02) 527 1518

Service: SHIPROCK DIVE
PADI instruction, equipment sales, service, gear hire, air, local dive trips, open 7 days.

Contact:
Shiprock Dive
709 Port Hacking Road, Dolans Bay NSW 2229
Phone: (02) 526 2664

Service:

SNORKEL IN
PADI instruction, equipment sales, service, gear hire, air, specialty courses, dive trips, Great Barrier Reef budget holidays.

Contact:
Snorkel In
Shop 4 President Avenue, Kogarah NSW 2217
Phone: (02) 588 1152

Service:

SUB-AQUATIC TRAINING
NAUI/FAUI/PADI instruction, specialty courses, equipment sales, service, gear hire, air, dive trips, charter boat.

Contact:
Sub-Aquatic Training
2C Edgbaston Road, Beverly Hills NSW 2209
Phone: (02) 57 2851

Remarks:

Each one of the facilities listed is a professional operation and can be depended upon to provide good service, good advice, good equipment, and highly skilled diver operators. One thing which must be remembered is that they will do their best for you, their customers, but they are not magicians. *In diving you must learn to take the weather as it comes, you can't order it at the dive shop.*

Diving around the Sydney area is like a smorgasbord, there are lots of good shore dives in and around the harbour where depths range from 2 metres to 20 metres. Some of these dive sites are listed below but care must be taken to observe sea conditions at the site.

North Side: Shore Dives   Hole in the Wall (Avalon Beach), Bungan Head (Bungan Beach), Shelly Beach (Manly), Clifton Gardens (Chowder Bay), Fairlight Reef (Manly).

South Side: Shore Dives   Camp Cove (Green Point), Clovelly Pool (Clovelly), Thompson's Beach (Clovelly), Bare Island (La Perouse Botany Bay), Cape Solander (Cronulla), Oak Park (Cronulla), Shiprock (Dolan's Bay, Caringbah, Pt. Hacking), Bass and Flinders Point (Cronulla), Boat Harbour (Cronulla).

There are more, lots more, and your friendly pro facility can direct or take you to the best locations depending on the weather of the day. Each dive shop has its own special dive sites; fraternize, get to know what cost the operators years of diving, money and time to learn. Let them share with you their knowledge — after all, they *are* the professionals.

Offshore dive sites are many and varied, ranging in depth from 5 to 50 metres. Visibility also varies from 3 to 30 metres; visibility is best when the currents bring the clear blue water inshore at times during winter. But for the most, visibility is around 5 to 20 metres depending on the sea, the sewerage outfalls and the general dive site conditions. Some of the more well-known boat dive sites are listed below.

North Side: Boat Dives   The *Valiant* wreck, Barrenjoey Bombora, Barrenjoey Sponge Gardens, South Palm Beach Reef, Trawley's Reef,

GENERAL INFORMATION

Best times of the year:	□ Summer	■ Winter	■ Spring	□ Autumn
Typical weather:	□ Excellent	□	□	□
	□ Very good	■	■	□
	■ Average	□	□	□
	□ Fair	□	□	■
Accommodation available:	■ Camping	■ Hostel	■ Hotel	■ Motel
Airport:	■ Light aircraft	■ Jet	■ International	■ Helicopter

DIVE SITE GUIDE

Access:	■ Boat ramp	■ Charter boat	■ Air	
Dive methods:	■ Scuba	■ Hookah	■ Snorkel	■ Snorkel diving
Types of diving:	■ Boat	■ Jetty	■ Shore	
Description of dive site:	■ Island	■ Submerged reef	■ Shore	
	■ Wreck	■ Shallow water	■ Deep water	
Conditions at site:	■ Current	■ Swell	■ Wind chop	
	■ Tide changes	■ Boat traffic	□ Good visibility	
	■ Fair visibility	■ Poor visibility		
Dive time:	■ In-coming tide	■ Out-going tide		
	■ Spring tide	■ Neap tide	■ Slack tide	
Underwater terrain:	■ Drop offs	■ Gutters	■ Patch reefs	
	■ Sand & rubble	■ Rocky reef	■ Flat bottom	
	■ Low profile reef	□ Coral reef	■ Slope	
	■ Caves	■ Swim-throughs	■ Silty bottom	
Marine life:	■ Kelp	■ Sea grass	■ Sponges	■ Corals
	□ Sea whips	■ Sea fans	□ Black coral	■ Soft corals
	■ Anemones	■ Fan worms	■ Bryozoans	■ Brachiopods
	■ Crays	■ Crabs	■ Shells	■ Commensal shrimps
	■ Nudibranchs	■ Cuttles	■ Scallops	■ Abalone
	■ Sea stars	■ Basket stars	■ Sea urchins	■ Feather stars
	■ Ascidians	□ Sea lions	■ Dolphins	■ Whales
	■ Sharks	■ Fish	□ Numerous fish	□ Abundant fish
Experience level:	■ Pupil	■ Beginner	■ Intermediate	■ Advanced
Dive site rating:	□ Excellent	■ Very good	■ Fair	■ Photography
Management of resources:	■ Marine reserve	■ Protected species	■ Quotas	■ Collecting

The Ovens, The Pinnacles, *Birchgrove Park* wreck (only for experienced divers, and even these get bent), Ship Reef (artificial), Long Reef Wall.

Sydney Harbour: Boat Dives North Head, Old Man's Hat, Dobroyd Point, Middle Head.

South Side: Boat Dives Black Streak, Boat Harbour Reef, Osborne Shoals, Voodoo Reef, Jibbon Reef, Barren's Hut, Rockfall, Marley Reef, Rock Perch, Hanging Rock, Wattamolla Headland.

The southside boat dives from Jibbon Reef to Wattamolla Headland have some fond memories for me as they were my first boat dives. I used to go out with the local spearos – but I'd chase nudibranchs. They thought I was nuts! They couldn't see any value in what I was trying to do (and at that stage, back in 1964 to 1968, I wasn't too sure either). I just knew that one day identifying nudibranchs would be as important as putting holes in fish.

WOLLONGONG – BASS POINT – KIAMA

With a population of over 220,000, including its industrial centre at Pork Kembla, Wollongong is the third largest city in New South Wales and is positioned 82 kilometres south of Sydney. Although Wollongong is the centre of dive operators in the area, it has only a minor percentage of the diving spots; the majority of spots are concentrated in the Bass Point – Kiama districts.

Service:

UNITED DIVERS
PADI/FAUI instruction, all dive services and air, hydro test station, local dives and dive charters.

Contact:
United Divers
6 Victoria Street, Wollongong NSW 2500
Phone: (042) 28 5962

Typical sponge garden scene at the 20 metre depth in the Kiama/Bass Point reefs.

Service:

SHELLHARBOUR FISHING & SCUBA SUPPLIES
Equipment sales, service, gear hire, air 6 days a week and good dive site advice.

Contact:
ShellHarbour Fishing & Scuba Supplies
Shop No 2/19 Addison Street, Shellharbour NSW 2529
Phone: (042) 96 6931

Remarks:

If I had to choose between Wollongong, Kiama and Bass Point as dive sites I'd choose Bass Point. Sure, the others are nice, but a lot of those sites are open to the sea, while Bass Point always has shelter, either on one side or the other, with really first-class dives on both sides. Bass Point also has fantastic shore diving in relatively sheltered waters. Dive sites along this stretch of coast include Wollongong Reef, Ballambi Reef, the Fire Islands, The Gravel Loader, The Church Grounds, The Lumps, the *Boston* wreck, Bushranger's Bay, the Archway, Hole in the Wall, Minamurra Reef, Gerroa Bommie and many more.

GENERAL INFORMATION

Best times of the year:	□ Summer	■ Winter	■ Spring	□ Autumn
Typical weather:	□ Excellent	□	□	□
	□ Very good	■	■	□
	■ Average	□	□	■
	□ Fair	□	□	□
Accommodation available:	■ Camping	□ Hostel	■ Hotel	■ Motel
Airport:	■ Light aircraft	□ Jet	□ International	■ Helicopter

DIVE SITE GUIDE

Access:	■ Boat ramp	■ Charter boat	■ Air	
Dive methods:	■ Scuba	■ Hookah	■ Snorkel	■ Snorkel diving
Types of diving:	■ Boat	■ Jetty	■ Shore	
Description of dive site:	■ Island	■ Submerged reef	■ Shore	
	■ Wreck	■ Shallow water	■ Deep water	
Conditions at site:	■ Current	■ Swell	■ Wind chop	
	■ Tide changes	□ Boat traffic	■ Good visibility	
	■ Fair visibility	□ Poor visibility		
Dive time:	■ In-coming tide	■ Out-going tide		
	■ Spring tide	■ Neap tide	■ Slack tide	
Underwater terrain:	■ Drop offs	■ Gutters	□ Patch reefs	
	■ Sand & rubble	■ Rocky reef	■ Flat bottom	
	■ Low profile reef	□ Coral reef	■ Slope	
	■ Caves	□ Swim-throughs	□ Silty bottom	
Marine life:	■ Kelp	■ Sea grass	■ Sponges	■ Corals
	■ Sea whips	■ Sea fans	■ Black coral	■ Soft corals
	■ Anemones	■ Fan worms	■ Bryozoans	□ Brachiopods
	■ Crays	■ Crabs	■ Shells	□ Commensal shrimps
	■ Nudibranchs	■ Cuttles	■ Scallops	■ Abalone
	■ Sea stars	■ Basket stars	■ Sea urchins	■ Feather stars
	■ Ascidians	□ Sea lions	■ Dolphins	■ Whales
	■ Sharks	■ Fish	■ Numerous fish	□ Abundant fish
Experience level:	■ Pupil	■ Beginner	■ Intermediate	■ Advanced
Dive site rating:	□ Excellent	■ Very good	□ Fair	■ Photography
Management of resources:	■ Marine reserve	■ Protected species	■ Quotas	■ Collecting

Known for many years under the common name of red rock cod, the cardinal scorpionfish is very good to eat, but, like all scorpionfish, it has venomous dorsal spines.

JERVIS BAY

Only a two and a half hour drive south from Sydney, Jervis Bay is served by the township of Huskisson. Originally opened up by the Naval College Training Operation Centre, it is somewhat of a coincidence that the dive site area should have been pioneered by a then navy diver (Steve Parish, 1968). Jervis Bay diving is so good and so extensive it could fill a book, let alone be part of one.

The largest mollusc on the south east coast, the magnificent volute comes inshore to lay its eggs during the spring and summer months.

Service:

JERVIS BAY SEA SPORTS
A complete in-house PADI/FAUI training service facility with air 7 days a week, equipment sales, service, gear hire, local dives and dive charter on *Sea Life III* and *Sea Sports II*. Large guesthouse catering to dive groups; live-in dive courses.

Contact:
Jervis Bay Sea Sports
47 Owen Street, Huskisson NSW 2540
Phone: (044) 41 5012, A/H (044) 41 5598

Service:

PRO-DIVING SERVICES
PADI pro instruction facility, open 7 days a week for air, equipment sales, service, gear hire, local dives and charter on *Bay Explorer*.

Contact:
Pro-Diving Services
Shop 6/74 Owen Street, Huskisson NSW 2540
Phone: (044) 41 5255

Service:

JOHN GRAY DIVE COMPANY
Air 7 days a week.

Contact:
John Gray Dive Company
25 Excellent Street, Vincentia NSW 2540
Phone: (044) 41 532

Service:

AQUA MEDIUM DIVE CENTRE (CANBERRA)
FAUI dive training facility, equipment service, sales, gear hire, air, boat dives and club, charter boat *Aqua Medium* available to Jervis Bay dive sites.

Contact:
Aqua Medium Dive Centre
3/43 Colbee Court, Phillip, Canberra ACT 2606
Phone: (062) 82 3919 Canberra; (044) 41 5044 Huskisson

Remarks:
I did my first photography and deep diving (below 33 metres) at
Jervis Bay and its environs on my Australian Coastal Marine Expe-
dition (1969–1973) and since then I've logged up quite a few dives.
Some of my favourite sites are listed on page 101. Contact your choice

GENERAL INFORMATION

Best times of the year:	■ Summer	□ Winter	□ Spring	■ Autumn
Typical weather:	□ Excellent	□	□	□
	□ Very good	■	■	□
	□ Average	□	□	□
	□ Fair	□	□	□
Accommodation available:	■ Camping	■ Hostel	□ Hotel	■ Motel
Airport:	□ Light aircraft	□ Jet	□ International	□ Helicopter

DIVE SITE GUIDE

Access:	■ Boat ramp	■ Charter boat	■ Air	
Dive methods:	■ Scuba	■ Hookah	■ Snorkel	■ Snorkel diving
Types of diving:	■ Boat	□ Jetty	■ Shore	
Description of dive site:	■ Island	■ Submerged reef	■ Shore	
	■ Wreck	■ Shallow water	■ Deep water	
Conditions at site:	■ Current	■ Swell	■ Wind chop	
	□ Tide changes	■ Boat traffic	■ Good visibility	
	■ Fair visibility	□ Poor visibility		
Dive time:	■ In-coming tide	■ Out-going tide		
	■ Spring tide	■ Neap tide	■ Slack tide	
Underwater terrain:	■ Drop offs	■ Gutters	■ Patch reefs	
	■ Sand & rubble	■ Rocky reef	■ Flat bottom	
	■ Low profile reef	□ Coral reef	■ Slope	
	■ Caves	■ Swim-throughs	■ Silty bottom	
Marine life:	■ Kelp	■ Sea grass	■ Sponges	■ Corals
	■ Sea whips	■ Sea fans	■ Black coral	■ Soft corals
	■ Anemones	■ Fan worms	■ Bryozoans	□ Brachiopods
	■ Crays	■ Crabs	■ Shells	■ Commensal shrimps
	■ Nudibranchs	■ Cuttles	■ Scallops	■ Abalone
	■ Sea stars	■ Basket stars	■ Sea urchins	■ Feather stars
	■ Ascidians	□ Sea lions	■ Dolphins	■ Whales
	■ Sharks	■ Fish	■ Numerous fish	□ Abundant fish
Experience level:	■ Pupil	■ Beginner	■ Intermediate	■ Advanced
Dive site rating:	■ Excellent	□ Very good	□ Fair	■ Photography
Management of resources:	■ Marine reserve	■ Protected species	■ Quotas	■ Collecting

of professional facility and let them introduce you to places like Currarong, Whale Point, Drum and Drumsticks, Crocodile Head, Smuggler's Cave, The Arch, Point Perpendicular, Middle Ground, The Streets, Bowen Island, The Docks, Stoney Creek, Hole in the Wall, The Nursery, Scallop Beds and Fifteen Fathom Bank, The Tubes, or The Plane; they *all* make for really good diving.

Giants sea squirts growing from the side of a huge underwater boulder are covered in encrusting sponges.

ULLADULLA – BATEMAN'S BAY – MALUA BAY – MOSSY POINT

Located at the foot of the Clyde Mountain in the Clyde River estuary, Bateman's Bay is one of the largest amateur fishing holiday areas on the south coast. Ten kilometres further south is Malua Bay, the hub of an active dive site area that extends to the *Dureenbee* wreck on the north of Broulee Island in the south. Mossy Point is on the southern side of the Tamago River outlet headland, overlooking the site of the *John Penn*, wrecked on Burrewarra Point in 1879.

Although most flatheads inhabit sand or mud, the tassel-snouted flathead is a rock and rubble dweller.

Service:

CHARLIE BIRD'S SCUBA SHOP
FAUI instruction, equipment sales, service, gear hire, air, an accommodation block for divers, regular boat dives and a charter service.

Contact:
Charlie Bird's Scuba Shop
4 Kuppa Avenue, Malua Bay NSW 2536
Phone: (044) 71 1659

Service:

BAY DIVE
FAUI instruction, equipment sales, service, gear hire, air and dive charters.

Contact:
Bay Dive
Old Punt Road, Bateman's Bay NSW 2536
Phone: (044) 72 6735, A/H (044) 71 7796

Service:

ULLADULLA DIVERS SUPPLIES
PADI training facility 7 days a week, all brands of diving equipment, service, gear hire, air. Local dive trips and charters arranged on *M.V. Warrigal*.

Contact:
Ulladulla Divers Supplies
Shop 10, Wason Street Arcade, Ulladulla NSW 2539
Phone: (044) 55 2695 (044) 55 3766

Charter Boats:

M.V. Warrigal (21 divers)

Contact:
Ulladulla Divers Supplies
PO Box 361, Ulladulla NSW 2539
Phone: (044) 55 3589, (044) 55 2810

Dive Co (9 divers)

Contact:
Same as above.

Remarks: Although there are a number of good dive sites around the Ulladulla area, my favourite is always Lighthouse Reef and I must admit that whenever I go to Ulladulla that's the only place I want to dive.
The reef has a magnificent wall and the bottom is covered in

GENERAL INFORMATION

Best times of the year:	■ Summer	☐ Winter	☐ Spring	■ Autumn
Typical weather:	☐ Excellent	☐	☐	☐
	■ Very good	☐	☐	■
	☐ Average	■	■	☐
	☐ Fair	☐	☐	☐
Accommodation available:	■ Camping	☐ Hostel	■ Hotel	■ Motel
Airport:	☐ Light aircraft	☐ Jet	☐ International	☐ Helicopter

DIVE SITE GUIDE

Access:	■ Boat ramp (Mossy Pt)	■ Charter boat	■ Air	
Dive methods:	■ Scuba	■ Hookah	■ Snorkel	■ Snorkel diving
Types of diving:	■ Boat	☐ Jetty	■ Shore	
Description of dive site:	■ Island	■ Submerged reef	■ Shore	
	■ Wreck	■ Shallow water	■ Deep water	
Conditions at site:	■ Current	■ Swell	■ Wind chop	
	■ Tide changes	☐ Boat traffic	☐ Good visibility	
	■ Fair visibility	☐ Poor visibility		
Dive time:	■ In-coming tide	■ Out-going tide		
	■ Spring tide	■ Neap tide	■ Slack tide	
Underwater terrain:	■ Drop offs	■ Gutters	☐ Patch reefs	
	■ Sand & rubble	■ Rocky reef	■ Flat bottom	
	■ Low profile reef	☐ Coral reef	■ Slope	
	■ Caves	■ Swim-throughs	☐ Silty bottom	
Marine life:	■ Kelp	■ Sea grass	■ Sponges	■ Corals
	■ Sea whips	■ Sea fans	☐ Black coral	■ Soft corals
	■ Anemones	■ Fan worms	■ Bryozoans	☐ Brachiopods
	■ Crays	■ Crabs	■ Shells	☐ Commensal shrimps
	■ Nudibranchs	■ Cuttles	■ Scallops	■ Abalone
	■ Sea stars	■ Basket stars	■ Sea urchins	☐ Feather stars
	■ Ascidians	☐ Sea lions	■ Dolphins	■ Whales
	■ Sharks	■ Fish	■ Numerous fish	☐ Abundant fish
Experience level:	■ Pupil	■ Beginner	■ Intermediate	■ Advanced
Dive site rating:	☐ Excellent	■ Very good	☐ Fair	■ Photography
Management of resources:	☐ Marine reserve	■ Protected species	☐ Quotas	■ Collecting

sponge gardens, sea whips, gorgonian fans, hydroids and bunches of sea tulips (purple, yellow and brown in their cloaks of encrusting sponges), and tame fish by the zillion.

Other dive sites include Brush Island, Bannister Point, Sullivan Reef drop off, Burrill Rocks Reef, the Golf Course Bommie and, for close ups on a bad day, the Burrill Lake Bridge pylons.

Some of the interesting dive sites around Bateman's Bay include Black Rock with its Bubble Cave, the Arch and the Crevice; Tollgate Reef, with its tunnel and chimney; Jemmy Island surrounded by huge boulders; Guerilla Bay, Broulee Island with its cave and the *John Penn* in Broulee Bay. When in an unknown area don't just take 'pot luck', take the time to visit the local pro facility dive shop and let them tell you where the action is and save you time and money.

Found from New South Wales to Tasmania, the sweet dorid is one of the most commonly noticed local nudibranchs.

NAROOMA – MONTAGUE ISLAND – BERMAGUI – TATHRA

Built at the mouth of the Wagonga Inlet, Narooma and its northern and southern counterparts could all be described in terms of its Aboriginal meaning (clear blue water). Initially a timber milling and ship building port, today it is more dependent on fishing and tourism.

Bermagui is legendary for its clear waters and big pelagics (an open-ocean fish, generally migratory, i.e. tuna, marlin). As the birth-place of game fishing in Australia (1930s), today Bermagui is home port to a large commercial fishing fleet.

Tathra is famous for its old steamer jetty which makes for good shore diving and snorkelling, and provides excellent macro photography.

Service:

DARRYL'S FISHING TACKLE AND DIVE SHOP
Complete dive shop services: FAUI instruction, equipment sales, service, gear hire, air 7 days a week, charters and dive trips to Montague Island.

Contact:
Darryl's Fishing Tackle and Dive Shop
Princes Highway, Narooma NSW 2546
Phone: (044) 76 2111, A/H (044) 76 2240

Service:

MONTAGUE DIVE AND MARINE
FAUI instruction, equipment sales, service, gear hire, charter boat and local daily dive trips to Montague Island.

Contact:
Montague Dive and Marine
8 Bunga Street, Bermagui West NSW 2547
Phone: (064) 93 4184

Service:

TATHRA MARINE AQUARIUM & DIVE CENTRE
PADI training, good range of dive equipment, service, gear hire, air 7 days a week, organised dives.

Contact:
Tathra Marine Aquarium & Dive Centre
15 Bega Street, Tathra NSW 2550
Phone: (064) 94 1697, A/H (064) 94 1161

Remarks:

Without doubt the major diving spot hereabouts is Montague Island, and it deserves to be. Certainly Narooma is the closest mainland town to the island, and so the shortest trip to Montague is between the two, but the sand bar at the entrance of the inlet can be a real problem and has claimed many a boat and broken many a bone. Big shark catamarans don't seem to have too much trouble, but in moderate seas it's best to try from Bermagui.

This area offers southern New South Wales diving at its best: clear water, lots of good locations, big fish, drop offs, sharks, sea lions, brilliant sea fans and a myriad of species. Regular dive sites include the famous Montague Island, Aughinish Rock, the Three Brothers Rocks, Gorgonia Reef and Blue Pool Bombora.

Montague Island is a must – brilliant. I've found new species of nudibranchs and soft corals, and numerous unrecorded species. In these waters sea turtles, manta rays and tropical lionfish swim amongst temperate water species. One of my favourite southern New South Wales dive sites.

GENERAL INFORMATION

Best times of the year:	■ Summer	□ Winter	□ Spring	■ Autumn
Typical weather:	□ Excellent	□	□	□
	■ Very good	■	■	■
	□ Average	□	□	□
	□ Fair	□	□	□
Accommodation available:	■ Camping	■ Hostel	■ Hotel	■ Motel
Airport:	□ Light aircraft	□ Jet	□ International	□ Helicopter

DIVE SITE GUIDE

Access:	■ Boat ramp	■ Charter boat	■ Air	
Dive methods:	■ Scuba	■ Hookah	■ Snorkel	■ Snorkel diving
Types of diving:	■ Boat	■ Jetty	■ Shore	
Description of dive site:	■ Island	■ Submerged reef	■ Shore	
	□ Wreck	■ Shallow water	■ Deep water	
Conditions at site:	■ Current	■ Swell	■ Wind chop	
	■ Tide changes	□ Boat traffic	■ Good visibility	
	□ Fair visibility	□ Poor visibility		
Dive time:	■ In-coming tide	■ Out-going tide		
	■ Spring tide	■ Neap tide	■ Slack tide	
Underwater terrain:	■ Drop offs	■ Gutters	□ Patch reefs	
	■ Sand & rubble	■ Rocky reef	□ Flat bottom	
	■ Low profile reef	□ Coral reef	■ Slope	
	■ Caves	□ Swim-throughs	□ Silty bottom	
Marine life:	■ Kelp	■ Sea grass	■ Sponges	■ Corals
	■ Sea whips	■ Sea fans	□ Black coral	■ Soft corals
	■ Anemones	■ Fan worms	■ Bryozoans	□ Brachiopods
	■ Crays	■ Crabs	■ Shells	□ Commensal shrimps
	■ Nudibranchs	■ Cuttles	■ Scallops	■ Abalone
	■ Sea stars	■ Basket stars	■ Sea urchins	□ Feather stars
	■ Ascidians	■ Sea lions	■ Dolphins	■ Whales
	■ Sharks	■ Fish	□ Numerous fish	■ Abundant fish
Experience level:	■ Pupil	■ Beginner	■ Intermediate	■ Advanced
Dive site rating:	■ Excellent	□ Very good	□ Fair	■ Photography
Management of resources:	■ Marine reserve	■ Protected species	■ Quotas	■ Collecting

Yet to be scientifically described, these bryozoan anemones belong to no known family or genus, and are unique to Australia.

MERIMBULA – PAMBULA – EDEN – GREEN CAPE

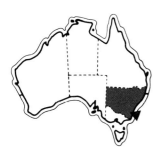

Approximately 26 kilometres north of Eden, Merimbula is one of the most popular seaside resorts along the Sapphire Coast (so named because of its brilliant clear blue waters). Midway between Sydney and Melbourne, Merimbula has a population of around 4000 and some excellent surfing beaches.

Six kilometres further south is Pambula, a smaller resort built on the Pambula River.

A former whaling station, Eden is the most southern port in New South Wales and the third deepest natural harbour in the world. Now an important deep-water fishing village, it supplies markets in both Sydney and Melbourne. Eden is surrounded by the Ben Boyd National Park; the park is named after the man who first established whaling in Twofold Bay.

Service:

MERIMBULA DIVE CENTRE
FAUI instruction, equipment sales, service, air 5½ days a week, charter boat.

Contact:
Merimbula Dive Centre
63 Lakeview Avenue, Merimbula NSW 2548
Phone: (064) 95 1447

107

Service:

HYDRA DIVE CENTRE
PADI instruction, equipment sales, service, gear hire, air, local dives, dive charters, accommodation.

Contact:
Hydra Dive Centre
Shop 7 Alice Street, Merimbula NSW 2548
Phone: (064) 95 1928, A/H (064) 95 2310

Service:

DAVIS MITCHELL MARINE
Air 5½ days a week.

Contact:
Davis Mitchell Marine
Storey Avenue, Eden NSW 2551
Phone: (064) 96 1339

Charter Boat:

Neptune Explorer (air on board)

Contact:
3 Ida Rodd Drive, Eden NSW 2551
Phone: (064) 96 1927

Remarks:

Good diving and snorkelling may be had all along this stretch of coast: from the old jetty shallows near the entrance to Merimbula Lake, to the wreck of the *Empire Gladstone* parked for all eternity in 15 metres at Gladstone Rock, and out to the deeper offshore reefs.

No spearfishing is allowed in any area of enclosed waters in New South Wales and it is against the law to spear on scuba or hookah.

Further south at Green Cape the topography is a boon for divers, for no matter which way the wind blows there is a sheltered spot. An excellent shore dive and snorkelling area, with either aspect having good entry sites depending on the seas. Named sites include the Gutter and Cathedral Rocks. There are a number of wreck sites but these require a boat and local knowledge (see charter boat *Neptune Explorer*). The wrecks are *Empire Gladstone*, *S.S. City of Sydney*, the *New Guinea*, and the *Ly-ee-Moon*.

The Pambula – Green Cape area is excellent for underwater photography.

GENERAL INFORMATION

Best times of the year:	■ Summer	□ Winter	□ Spring	■ Autumn
Typical weather:	■ Excellent	□	□	■
	□ Very good	□	■	□
	□ Average	■	□	□
	□ Fair	□	□	□
Accommodation available:	■ Camping	□ Hostel	■ Hotel	■ Motel
Airport:	■ Light aircraft	■ Jet	□ International	□ Helicopter

DIVE SITE GUIDE

Access:	■ Boat ramp	■ Charter boat	■ Air	
Dive methods:	■ Scuba	■ Hookah	■ Snorkel	■ Snorkel diving
Types of diving:	■ Boat	■ Jetty	■ Shore	
Description of dive site:	□ Island	■ Submerged reef	■ Shore	
	■ Wreck	■ Shallow water	■ Deep water	
Conditions at site:	■ Current	■ Swell	■ Wind chop	
	■ Tide changes	■ Boat traffic	■ Good visibility	
	□ Fair visibility	□ Poor visibility		
Dive time:	■ In-coming tide	■ Out-going tide		
	■ Spring tide	■ Neap tide	■ Slack tide	
Underwater terrain:	■ Drop offs	■ Gutters	■ Patch reefs	
	■ Sand & rubble	■ Rocky reef	■ Flat bottom	
	■ Low profile reef	□ Coral reef	■ Slope	
	■ Caves	□ Swim-throughs	□ Silty bottom	
Marine life:	■ Kelp	■ Sea grass	■ Sponges	□ Corals
	■ Sea whips	■ Sea fans	■ Black coral	■ Soft corals
	■ Anemones	■ Fan worms	■ Bryozoans	□ Brachiopods
	■ Crays	■ Crabs	■ Shells	□ Commensal shrimps
	■ Nudibranchs	■ Cuttles	■ Scallops	■ Abalone
	■ Sea stars	■ Basket stars	■ Sea urchins	■ Feather stars
	■ Ascidians	□ Sea lions	■ Dolphins	■ Whales
	■ Sharks	■ Fish	■ Numerous fish	□ Abundant fish
Experience level:	■ Pupil	■ Beginner	■ Intermediate	■ Advanced
Dive site rating:	■ Excellent	■ Very good	□ Fair	■ Photography
Management of resources:	□ Marine reserve	■ Protected species	□ Quotas	■ Collecting

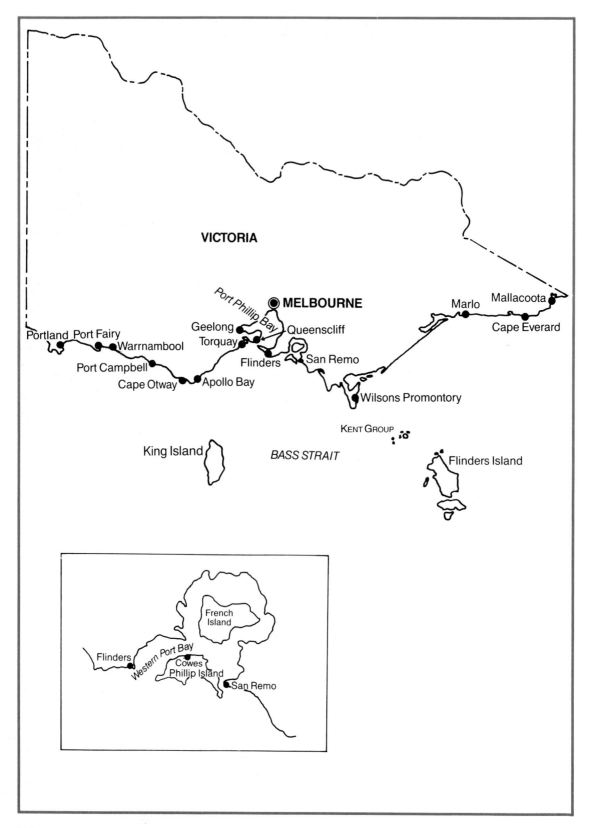

Diving
VICTORIA

Common on sub-tidal reefs, the mosaic sea star is known to cause numbness to the skin when handled.

MALLACOOTA – MARLO – CAPE EVERARD

Mallacoota is on the southern side of the Mallacoota inlet, 95 kilometres of which is protected inside Croajingalong National Park. The offshore islands of Gabo and Tullaberga have deep-water surrounds, fantastic sponge gardens over a metre in height, drop offs, gorgonian fans, clouds of butterfly perch and a trillion sea urchins.

A small fishing village situated on the Brodrib River inlet, Marlo is between the big fishing port of Lakes Entrance and Mallacoota. It has access to the sea and offers some good diving locations along the coast in good weather, notably at Cape Canron and Cape Everard. Seeking local knowledge is advisable as I can vouch for the giant ground swells that roll in from the Tasman Sea. Cape Everard has a sea lion colony and giant kelp beds, though the kelp does not grow as high as in Tasmania.

This country was originally pioneered by abalone divers working out of Mallacoota, the largest abalone-producing town in Victoria.

Service:

MARLO DIVE AND HIRE
FAUI, NAUI instruction, air and services.

Contact:
Marlo Dive and Hire
59 Jorgensen Street, Marlo Vic. 3888
Phone: (051) 54 8392

GENERAL INFORMATION

Best times of the year:	■ Summer	□ Winter	□ Spring	■ Autumn
Typical weather:	□ Excellent	□	□	□
	□ Very good	□	□	■
	□ Average	■	■	□
	■ Fair	□	□	□
Accommodation available:	■ Camping	■ Hostel	□ Hotel	■ Motel
Airport:	□ Light aircraft	□ Jet	□ International	□ Helicopter

DIVE SITE GUIDE

Access:	■ Boat ramp	□ Charter boat	■ Air (At Marlo only)	
Dive methods:	■ Scuba	■ Hookah	□ Snorkel	□ Snorkel diving
Types of diving:	■ Boat	□ Jetty	□ Shore	
Description of dive site:	■ Island	■ Submerged reef	□ Shore	
	■ Wreck	□ Shallow water	■ Deep water	
Conditions at site:	■ Current	■ Swell	■ Wind chop	
	■ Tide changes	□ Boat traffic	□ Good visibility	
	■ Fair visibility	□ Poor visibility		
Dive time:	■ In-coming tide	■ Out-going tide		
	■ Spring tide	■ Neap tide	■ Slack tide	
Underwater terrain:	■ Drop offs	■ Gutters	□ Patch reefs	
	□ Sand & rubble	■ Rocky reef	□ Flat bottom	
	□ Low profile reef	□ Coral reef	■ Slope	
	■ Caves	■ Swim-throughs	□ Silty bottom	
Marine life:	■ Kelp	■ Sea grass	■ Sponges	□ Corals
	■ Sea whips	■ Sea fans	□ Black coral	■ Soft corals
	■ Anemones	■ Fan worms	■ Bryozoans	□ Brachiopods
	■ Crays	■ Crabs	■ Shells	□ Commensal shrimps
	■ Nudibranchs	■ Cuttles	□ Scallops	■ Abalone
	■ Sea stars	■ Basket stars	■ Sea urchins	■ Feather stars
	■ Ascidians	■ Sea lions	■ Dolphins	■ Whales
	■ Sharks	■ Fish	■ Numerous fish	□ Abundant fish
Experience level:	□ Pupil	■ Beginner	■ Intermediate	■ Advanced
Dive site rating:	□ Excellent	□ Very good	■ Fair	■ Photography
Management of resources:	■ Marine reserve	■ Protected species	■ Quotas	■ Collecting

Descendants of the few survivors left by the Bass Strait's sealers, the Australian fur seals are slowly making a comeback.

WILSONS PROMONTORY NATIONAL PARK

First visited by explorer George Bass in 1799, Wilsons Promontory is a great natural wonderland both above and below the tideline.

The water surrounding the 'Prom' is deep, clear and lonely: a place without people. The offshore islands are giant granite castles, sparsley wooded and rounded by screaming gales which sweep in from the southwest and without warning turn the straits into a boiling cauldron of giant swells and blinding rain.

Diving in the straits around the 'Prom' is not for the faint hearted; it takes a good boat, good organising, good seamanship, good safety procedures, a good divemaster and a bit of good luck to make it work. This is heart-stopping country – incredible fish life, strong currents, blue, blue water, and reefs that are alive with such a profusion of creatures that it's hard to take it in all at once. Everything is big, or bigger, than you've ever seen before (but it's deep, so be extra careful!); giant sea fans, sea whips and hydroids sway in the swells or lean away in the current.

With water so clear you can almost breathe it, underwater photography is the perfect way to capture this beauty and share it with the world.

Large numbers of red gurnard scorpionfish are rarely seen in depths above 30 metres. The species is more common in Bass Strait and Tasmanian waters than in Victorian.

Charter Boats:

Only charter boats services are available.
Polperro II (group charters: 14 metre, 9 berth boat)

Contact:
Phone: (056) 86 2395 (out of Port Franklin)

Osprey (17 metre, 8 berth)

Contact:
Bob Cumberland's Dive Shop
Phone: (03) 589 2084 for bookings or (059) 88 9739 for departures out of Port Franklin.

GENERAL INFORMATION

Best times of the year:	■ Summer	□ Winter	□ Spring	■ Autumn
Typical weather:	□ Excellent	□	□	□
	□ Very good	□	□	□
	□ Average	■	■	□
	■ Fair	□	□	■
Accommodation available:	■ Camping	□ Hostel	□ Hotel	□ Motel
Airport:	□ Light aircraft	□ Jet	□ International	□ Helicopter

DIVE SITE GUIDE

Access:	■ Boat ramp	■ Charter boat	□ Air	
Dive methods:	■ Scuba	■ Hookah	■ Snorkel	■ Snorkel diving
Types of diving:	■ Boat	□ Jetty	□ Shore	
Description of dive site:	■ Island	■ Submerged reef	□ Shore	
	■ Wreck	□ Shallow water	■ Deep water	
Conditions at site:	■ Current	■ Swell	■ Wind chop	
	■ Tide changes	□ Boat traffic	■ Good visibility	
	□ Fair visibility	□ Poor visibility		
Dive time:	■ In-coming tide	■ Out-going tide		
	□ Spring tide	■ Neap tide	■ Slack tide	
Underwater terrain:	■ Drop offs	■ Gutters	□ Patch reefs	
	■ Sand & rubble	■ Rocky reef	□ Flat bottom	
	□ Low profile reef	□ Coral reef	■ Slope	
	■ Caves	■ Swim-throughs	□ Silty bottom	
Marine life:	■ Kelp	■ Sea grass	■ Sponges	■ Corals
	■ Sea whips	■ Sea fans	■ Black coral	■ Soft corals
	■ Anemones	■ Fan worms	■ Bryozoans	□ Brachiopods
	■ Crays	■ Crabs	■ Shells	□ Commensal shrimps
	■ Nudibranchs	■ Cuttles	■ Scallops	■ Abalone
	■ Sea stars	■ Basket stars	■ Sea urchins	■ Feather stars
	■ Ascidians	■ Sea lions	■ Dolphins	■ Whales
	■ Sharks	■ Fish	□ Numerous fish	■ Abundant fish
Experience level:	□ Pupil	□ Beginner	■ Intermediate	■ Advanced
Dive site rating:	■ Excellent	□ Very good	□ Fair	■ Photography
Management of resources:	■ Marine reserve	■ Protected species	■ Quotas	■ Collecting

Mostly seen on night dives, the very appealing undulate volute shell is inhabited by an even more attractive animal.

SAN REMO – PHILLIP ISLAND – WESTERN PORT BAY – FLINDERS

A mainland commercial fishing village, San Remo is also the centre of a large dairying district. It is connected to Phillip Island by a 640 metre bridge. Phillip Island is famous for its resident protected Fairy Penguin colony at Summerland Beach and is also a popular holiday resort.

Western Port Bay is smaller than Port Phillip Bay and is an important shallow-water estuary complex with hectares of mangrove forests, mudflats and sea grass meadows rich in viable primary resource for coastal protein conversion food webs. Due to the low visibility, few divers stray to its upper reaches, but Crawfish Rock is a marine biologist's dream (or nightmare – depending on how you see work).

At the entrance to Western Port Bay there are some more conventional dive sites and of these the most popular for beginners, underwater photographers and night divers is the Flinder's Jetty. Flinder's Jetty can be a shore dive if you like walking and swimming, but makes a more comfortable boat dive. Only 5 metres deep, it is a marvellous dive to build up bottom time with no chance of a bend. Beautiful weedy sea dragons abound around the sea grass meadows; sea horses, pipefish, boxfish, scorpion fish, angler fish, octopus and sea stars are everywhere. Good dives are also found around Seal Rock, The Nobbies, Pyramid Rock and, on good days, Cape Woolamai.

Service:

No diving facilities exist as such but air is available from the Shell Service Station at San Remo. For other services see Melbourne.

Verco's nudibranch feeds exclusively on the blue polyzoan *Bugula dentata*. Periodically common in Victorian waters, it has only recently been discovered inhabiting waters off central New South Wales.

Contact:
Bone's San Remo Motors
133 Marine Parade, San Remo Vic. 3925
Phone: (056) 78 5315, air 7 days a week; *or*
Phone: (056) 78 5403, air on booking.

Contact:
Boat Charter for The Pinnacles, etc.
Phone: (056) 78 5245

Remarks:

For me the best dive around San Remo (apart from the bridge pylons at slack tide) are The Pinnacles – volcanic 'needles' which sit in 45 metres of water, coming straight up to within 10 metres of the surface. The tops of The Pinnacles are crowned with a headdress of *Ecklonia* kelp, but over the edge the kelp gives way to walls of thickly encrusted invertebrates. In some places the growth is half a metre thick with sea fans, bryozoans, huge bunches of bright yellow zoanthids, sea whips and mobile invertebrates of every phyla, all surrounded by fish. The visibility isn't all that brilliant (10 metres) but the sea life makes up for it. The photographic subjects here are exceptional.

Other dive sites in the area include Red Rock, Cape Woolamai, Smiths Beach, Pyramid Rock, the *George Kermode* wreck, Current run (a drift dive in the San Remo channel on the incoming tide), Seal Rocks and The Nobbies.

All diving from jetties in Victoria requires a permit, but shore entry from the beach or rocks is within the law as long as care is taken not to swim in areas that have boat traffic or to cause obstruction to boats embarking or disembarking. Beware when diving in areas with sea lion colonies as sharks 'love' the sea lions that swim the slowest, even though they spit out the ones in wet suits!

GENERAL INFORMATION

Best times of the year:	■ Summer	□ Winter	■ Spring	□ Autumn
Typical weather:	□ Excellent	□	□	□
	■ Very good	□	■	□
	□ Average	■	□	■
	□ Fair	□	□	□
Accommodation available:	■ Camping	■ Hostel	■ Hotel	■ Motel
Airport:	■ Light aircraft	□ Jet	□ International	□ Helicopter

DIVE SITE GUIDE

Access:	■ Boat ramp	■ Charter boat	■ Air	
Dive methods:	■ Scuba	■ Hookah	■ Snorkel	■ Snorkel diving
Types of diving:	■ Boat	■ Jetty	■ Shore	
Description of dive site:	■ Island	■ Submerged reef	■ Shore	
	■ Wreck	■ Shallow water	■ Deep water	
Conditions at site:	■ Current	■ Swell	■ Wind chop	
	■ Tide changes	■ Boat traffic	□ Good visibility	
	■ Fair visibility	□ Poor visibility		
Dive time:	■ In-coming tide	□ Out-going tide		
	■ Spring tide	■ Neap tide	■ Slack tide	
Underwater terrain:	■ Drop offs	■ Gutters	■ Patch reefs	
	■ Sand & rubble	■ Rocky reef	■ Flat bottom	
	■ Low profile reef	□ Coral reef	■ Slope	
	■ Caves	□ Swim-throughs	■ Silty bottom	
Marine life:	■ Kelp	■ Sea grass	■ Sponges	□ Corals
	■ Sea whips	■ Sea fans	□ Black coral	■ Soft corals
	■ Anemones	■ Fan worms	■ Bryozoans	□ Brachiopods
	■ Crays	■ Crabs	■ Shells	□ Commensal shrimps
	■ Nudibranchs	■ Cuttles	■ Scallops	■ Abalone
	■ Sea stars	□ Basket stars	■ Sea urchins	■ Feather stars
	■ Ascidians	■ Sea lions	■ Dolphins	■ Whales
	■ Sharks	■ Fish	■ Numerous fish	□ Abundant fish
Experience level:	■ Pupil	■ Beginner	■ Intermediate	■ Advanced
Dive site rating:	□ Excellent	■ Very good	□ Fair	■ Photography
Management of resources:	■ Marine reserve	■ Protected species	■ Quotas	■ Collecting

Underwater photographer working amongst the dense algae beds at Pope's Eye, Port Phillip Bay.

MELBOURNE – PORT PHILLIP BAY

Melbourne, the garden city of Victoria, lies at the head of Port Phillip Bay. It is second only to Sydney in population (3 million) but second to none in the enthusiasm of its diving community.

Port Phillip is undoubtedly the centre of diving in Victoria. Its large area and circular topography ensure there will be adequate shelter for diving somewhere in the Bay, regardless of which way the wind is blowing.

Although dives can be made as far up the Bay as Williamstown (where there is a huge population of sea urchins) most of the diving is confined to the lower reaches which offer better visibility and an interesting variety of dive sites.

Service:

WESTERN DIVING SERVICES
Two shops run 7 days a week. Complete NAUI instruction facilities, equipment sales, service, gear hire, air and hydro tests. Regular dives each week from the *Sea Venture* charter boat.

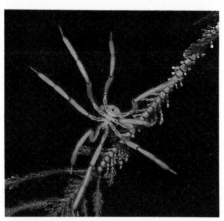

Although only 20 mm in size, the ambiguous sea spider's bright yellow colouring makes it easy to see amongst bottom growths.

The magnificent sea star can be separated from its nearest relative, the southern biscuit star, by its greater number of marginal plates.

Contact:
Western Diving Services
559 Mt. Alexander Road, Moonee Ponds Vic. 3039
Phone: (03) 370 9258, *or*

Contact:
Western Diving Services
227 Nelson Place, Williamstown Vic. 3016
Phone: (03) 397 6045

Service:

IN DEPTH SCUBA EDUCATION
FAUI instruction to all levels, 5½ days trading with full dive shop capacity, equipment sales, service, gear hire and air. Charters by *M.V. Medusa*.

Contact:
In Depth Scuba Education
589 Victoria Street, North Melbourne Vic. 3051
Phone: (03) 328 3217, (03) 328 3218

Service:

SOUTHERN CROSS DIVERS
Part of the largest chain of diving shops in Victoria, this shop and the others in the chain have top facilities catering to all a diver's needs. FAUI instruction to all levels, air, equipment sales, service, gear hire, open 5½ days a week, large dive club and three charter vessels: *M.V. Julie-Anne*, *M.V. Southern Star*, *M.V. Southern Cross 2*.

Contact:
Southern Cross Divers
1368 Toorak Road, Burwood Vic. 3125
Phone: (03) 299 1111, A/H (03) 233 9841, *or*

Contact:
Southern Cross Divers
99 Maroondah Highway, Ringwood Vic. 3134
Phone: (03) 870 8888 (services as above)

Service:

BOB CUMBERLAND'S DIVE SHOP
Complete dive shop with FAUI instruction to all levels (arranged through Diver Instruction Services), equipment sales, service, gear hire, air, hydro testing, club, local dive trips and overseas travel.

Contact:
Bob Cumberland's Dive Shop
34 East Concourse, Beaumaris Vic. 3193
Phone: (03) 99 2084

Service:

A.B. OCEAN DIVERS
Active dive club, with workshop to repair suits and service dive equipment on site. PADI training facility, equipment sales, gear hire and air.

Contact:
A.B. Ocean Divers
237 East Boundary Road, East Bentleigh Vic. 3165
Phone: (03) 578 2851

Service:

WARRICK'S DIVE CENTRES
Two complete dive shops. PADI facilities, equipment sales, service, gear hire, air, regular club dives, charters, open 5½ days, local and overseas trips.

Contact:
Warrick's Dive Centres
34 Station Street, Moorabbin Vic. 3189
Phone: (03) 555 9128, *or*

Contact:
Warrick's Dive Centres
167 Lonsdale Street, Dandenong Vic. 3175
Phone: (03) 794 8136

Remarks:

Port Phillip Bay sports a host of good dive sites, ones I have spent many, many hours enjoying, photographing and recording. My favourites are Pope's Eye (3 kilometres southeast of Queenscliff), now part of the Harold Holt Marine Reserves. Since this area has had a measure of protection the fish life has increased dramatically, to the point where it would now be one of the few places along the entire Victorian coast where fish are prolific and tame. Pope's Eye is an excellent place for photography, but care must be taken to dive on a slack tide due to the strong currents that run on the turn of the tides. The inside of the eye is a perfect training ground for beginners and snorkellers.

Rickett's Point, out of Beaumaris, is a shore dive but an extraordinary one in my book. The water may be shallow, but the marine life is superb and perfect for close up photography, with different sorts of animals from those divers generally see: gobies, shore eels,

GENERAL INFORMATION

Best times of the year:	■ Summer	□ Winter	■ Spring	□ Autumn
Typical weather:	□ Excellent	□	□	□
	■ Very good	□	■	□
	□ Average	■	□	■
	□ Fair	□	□	□
Accommodation available:	■ Camping	■ Hostel	■ Hotel	■ Motel
Airport:	■ Light aircraft	■ Jet	■ International	■ Helicopter

DIVE SITE GUIDE

Access:	■ Boat ramp	■ Charter boat	■ Air	
Dive methods:	■ Scuba	■ Hookah	■ Snorkel	■ Snorkel diving
Types of diving:	■ Boat	■ Jetty	■ Shore	
Description of dive site:	■ Island	■ Submerged reef	■ Shore	
	■ Wreck	■ Shallow water	■ Deep water	
Conditions at site:	■ Current	■ Swell	■ Wind chop	
	■ Tide changes	■ Boat traffic	□ Good visibility	
	■ Fair visibility	■ Poor visibility		
Dive time:	■ In-coming tide	■ Out-going tide		
	■ Spring tide	■ Neap tide	■ Slack tide	
Underwater terrain:	■ Drop offs	■ Gutters	■ Patch reefs	
	■ Sand & rubble	■ Rocky reef	■ Flat bottom	
	■ Low profile reef	□ Coral reef	■ Slope	
	■ Caves	■ Swim-throughs	■ Silty bottom	
Marine life:	■ Kelp	■ Sea grass	■ Sponges	□ Corals
	■ Sea whips	■ Sea fans	□ Black coral	■ Soft corals
	■ Anemones	■ Fan worms	■ Bryozoans	□ Brachiopods
	■ Crays	■ Crabs	■ Shells	□ Commensal shrimps
	■ Nudibranchs	■ Cuttles	■ Scallops	■ Abalone
	■ Sea stars	□ Basket stars	■ Sea urchins	■ Feather stars
	■ Ascidians	■ Sea lions	■ Dolphins	■ Whales
	□ Sharks	■ Fish	■ Numerous fish	□ Abundant fish
Experience level:	■ Pupil	■ Beginner	■ Intermediate	■ Advanced
Dive site rating:	□ Excellent	■ Very good	□ Fair	■ Photography
Management of resources:	■ Marine reserve	■ Protected species	■ Quotas	■ Collecting

bright red snapping shrimps, juvenile flounder and red-cake bryozoans.

Other places of interest are Portsea Jetty, Portsea Hole, the *Coogee* wreck, Sorrento Jetty, the *Eliza Ramsden* wreck, the kelp beds, South Channel Fort, the *City of Launceston* wreck, the *S.S. Hurricane* wreck, Quarantine Bay, the *William Salthouse* wreck and scores more.

The pro facility dive shops know all the good places, so if you are in Melbourne looking for a dive go and see the guys and girls I've listed; they'll look after you.

Growing to over 1 metre across, the cabbage bryozoan is the largest species of upright bryozoan found in Victoria.

GEELONG – QUEENSCLIFF

The closest major city (the second largest in Victoria) to the entrance of Port Phillip Bay is Geelong, with a population of 127,000 people.

Adjacent to Geelong, across the Bellarine Peninsula, is Queenscliff, one of the most popular diving locations in Victoria. The Point Lonsdale Reef Marine Reserve is part of the Harold Holt Marine Reserve complex, which also takes in Point Nepean, Swan Bay, Pope's Eye and Mud Islands. This reserve, covering 110 hectares, is an important 'type locality' for more than thirty species of opisthobranchs, with over 150 kinds of these nudibranch-like molluscs having already been recorded from the area.

Service:

GEELONG DIVING CENTRE
Open 5½ days a week for air, equipment sales, service and gear hire, this shop is a fully integrated NAUI pro facility with instruction and dive charters every weekend.

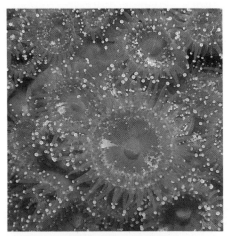

Found in a host of different colour variations, southern jewel anemones are commonly observed inside wrecks.

Zimmer's sea fan grows in areas of active water movement, along drop offs and in channels.

Contact:
Geelong Diving Centre
146 Ormond Road, East Geelong Vic. 3219
Phone: (052) 21 3342, A/H (052) 43 5894

Service:

QUEENSCLIFF DIVE CENTRE
Complete dive shop facility, FAUI instruction, open 7 days a week for air, equipment sales, service and gear hire. Charters on arrangement.

Contact:
Queenscliff Dive Centre
Shop 1, 62 Hesse Street, Queenscliff Vic. 3225
Phone: (052) 52 1188

Charter Boats:

M.V. Medusa

Contact:
In Depth Diving Centre
Phone: (03) 328 3217 (or as above)

M.V. Sea Venture

Contact:
Phone: (03) 397 6045

Service:

SOUTHERN CROSS DIVERS
Complete dive shop services and friendly advice. FAUI tuition, equipment sales, service, gear hire, tank testing, air station 4 days a week, 3 charter boats, club boat dives weekends and during weekdays.

Contact:
Southern Cross Divers
92 Parkington Street, Geelong West Vic. 3218
Phone: (052) 22 4899

Remarks:

Diving anywhere in the vicinity of Port Phillip Bay Heads requires guidance from local dive professionals in good boats. They can show you the best they have and take away the worry, indecision and risks. Places like the Lonsdale Wall have the most exciting visual

GENERAL INFORMATION

Best times of the year:	■ Summer	□ Winter	■ Spring	□ Autumn
Typical weather:	□ Excellent	□	□	□
	■ Very good	□	■	□
	□ Average	■	□	■
	□ Fair	□	□	□
Accommodation available:	■ Camping	■ Hostel	■ Hotel	■ Motel
Airport:	■ Light aircraft	■ Jet	□ International	□ Helicopter

DIVE SITE GUIDE

Access:	■ Boat ramp	■ Charter boat	■ Air	
Dive methods:	■ Scuba	■ Hookah	■ Snorkel	■ Snorkel diving
Types of diving:	■ Boat	□ Jetty	■ Shore	
Description of dive site:	■ Island	■ Submerged reef	■ Shore	
	■ Wreck	■ Shallow water	■ Deep water	
Conditions at site:	■ Current	■ Swell	■ Wind chop	
	■ Tide changes	■ Boat traffic	□ Good visibility	
	■ Fair visibility	□ Poor visibility		
Dive time:	■ In-coming tide	□ Out-going tide		
	■ Spring tide	■ Neap tide	■ Slack tide	
Underwater terrain:	■ Drop offs	■ Gutters	■ Patch reefs	
	■ Sand & rubble	■ Rocky reef	□ Flat bottom	
	■ Low profile reef	□ Coral reef	■ Slope	
	■ Caves	■ Swim-throughs	■ Silty bottom	
Marine life:	■ Kelp	■ Sea grass	■ Sponges	■ Corals
	■ Sea whips	■ Sea fans	□ Black coral	■ Soft corals
	■ Anemones	■ Fan worms	■ Bryozoans	□ Brachiopods
	■ Crays	■ Crabs	■ Shells	□ Commensal shrimps
	■ Nudibranchs	■ Cuttles	■ Scallops	■ Abalone
	■ Sea stars	□ Basket stars	■ Sea urchins	■ Feather stars
	■ Ascidians	■ Sea lions	□ Dolphins	□ Whales
	□ Sharks	■ Fish	■ Numerous fish	□ Abundant fish
Experience level:	■ Pupil	■ Beginner	■ Intermediate	■ Advanced
Dive site rating:	□ Excellent	■ Very good	□ Fair	■ Photography
Management of resources:	■ Marine reserve	□ Protected species	■ Quotas	■ Collecting

extravaganzas you will ever see: giant bryozoan colonies, bright yellow zoanthids that cover the sides of caverns, sponges, soft corals and fragile gorgonians, jewel anemones and sea whips are everywhere. But the 'Rip', as it is known, is one of the most dangerous pieces of water in the Southern Hemisphere and can only be dived on slack water.

The famous Twelve Apostles rock formations at Port Campbell are a stark reminder of the violence of the sea along this stretch of coastline.

TORQUAY – APOLLO BAY – CAPE OTWAY – PORT CAMPBELL

Torquay holds a lot more promise for diving than some previously mentioned places, and although most safe diving is done from boats, there are a number of local dive sites which can be reached in season. The wreck of the *Victoria Towers* is a popular, reasonably sheltered dive site when conditions are relatively calm, as are the

Southern rock lobsters will find a haven even in the roughest of conditions.

offshore reefs which feature big rocks, crevices, and undercuts rich in sessile marine life.

The only boat refuge between Point Lonsdale and Port Fairy is inside the huge artificial breakwaters at Apollo Bay (which also has some interesting sea life for macro photography). While much of the area may be good for spearfishing, wreck dive enthusiasts and professional abalone divers, for the average scuba diver or underwater photographer bad weather conditions and big seas make it a writeoff for most of the year.

Cape Otway is only open to boat diving and, as is the case with most dive locations in out-of-the-way places, local knowledge is required. All along the coastline here is good crayfish country (they love it rough) but, due to the heavy pounding, sedentary sea life (with the exception of algae), is fairly well restricted to protective ledges, gutters and deep fissures in the rocky sea floor.

Nestling between spectacular cliffs and reef is the small fishing village of Port Campbell, nucleus of the Port Campbell National Park that incorporates the famous Twelve Apostles and 40 kilometres of intertidal coastline.

To stand on the cliff tops and gaze down at the foaming maelstrom 130 metres below and as far as the eye can see in every direction makes you wonder how this stretch of coast could ever be dived. I've never seen it calm once. Yet I'm told on authority that on good days it's reasonable (for Victorians that is). Lots of wreck dives including the famous *Loch Ard*.

Service: MOBIL SERVICE STATION
Sells air.

GENERAL INFORMATION

Best times of the year:	■ Summer	□ Winter	□ Spring	□ Autumn
Typical weather:	□ Excellent	□	□	□
	□ Very good	□	□	□
	■ Average	■	■	□
	□ Fair	□	□	■
Accommodation available:	■ Camping	□ Hostel	■ Hotel	■ Motel
Airport:	□ Light aircraft	□ Jet	□ International	□ Helicopter

DIVE SITE GUIDE

Access:	■ Boat ramp	□ Charter boat	■ Air	
Dive methods:	■ Scuba	■ Hookah	■ Snorkel	■ Snorkel diving
Types of diving:	■ Boat	□ Jetty	□ Shore	
Description of dive site:	□ Island	■ Submerged reef	□ Shore	
	■ Wreck	■ Shallow water	■ Deep water	
Conditions at site:	■ Current	■ Swell	■ Wind chop	
	■ Tide changes	□ Boat traffic	□ Good visibility	
	■ Fair visibility	■ Poor visibility		
Dive time:	■ In-coming tide	■ Out-going tide		
	■ Spring tide	■ Neap tide	■ Slack tide	
Underwater terrain:	■ Drop offs	■ Gutters	□ Patch reefs	
	■ Sand & rubble	■ Rocky reef	■ Flat bottom	
	■ Low profile reef	□ Coral reef	■ Slope	
	■ Caves	□ Swim-throughs	□ Silty bottom	
Marine life:	■ Kelp	■ Sea grass	■ Sponges	□ Corals
	□ Sea whips	■ Sea fans	□ Black coral	□ Soft corals
	■ Anemones	■ Fan worms	■ Bryozoans	□ Brachiopods
	■ Crays	■ Crabs	■ Shells	□ Commensal shrimps
	■ Nudibranchs	□ Cuttles	■ Scallops	■ Abalone
	■ Sea stars	□ Basket stars	■ Sea urchins	□ Feather stars
	■ Ascidians	□ Sea lions	■ Dolphins	■ Whales
	□ Sharks	■ Fish	□ Numerous fish	□ Abundant fish
Experience level:	□ Pupil	□ Beginner	■ Intermediate	■ Advanced
Dive site rating:	□ Excellent	□ Very good	■ Fair	■ Photography
Management of resources:	□ Marine reserve	□ Protected species	■ Quotas	■ Collecting

Contact:
Mobil Service Station
Port Campbell Vic. 3269
Phone: (055) 89 6258

Remarks: Virtually the entire coastline east of Port Campbell along to Point Lonsdale (the entrance to Port Phillip Bay) is an area of fierce seas, many wrecks, unfavourable weather conditions and treacherous currents. Boat landing ramps are scarce and dive facilities non-existent, so that without local guidance and good weather, you would be ill-advised to dive.

The local Victorian diver, used to these ocean conditions, would find the diving quite normal. But it is imperative that overseas visitors or tourist divers used to calmer seas find experienced divers to accompany them on dive trips or to buddy with: if this describes you then check with the nearest pro facility before diving in the area.

Making full use of its distinctive colour pattern, Gunn's leatherjacket takes up a defensive position against a wharf pylon.

WARRNAMBOOL – PORT FAIRY – PORTLAND

Warrnambool is the largest city in Victoria's Western District with a population of over 22,000. The coastline east and west of the city has some reasonable diving locations but care must be exercised as it is open to the weather and there is no shelter. Some of the more well-known spots can be dived from shore but a boat makes for less risk and better diving. Locations like Roger's Rocks, Killarney,

Griffith Island and Lady Bay have a mixture of kelp-covered rocks, overhangs and gutters, with a rich display of invertebrates waiting to be discovered. Crays and abalone can also be found. Photography is mostly confined to close-ups.

Port Fairy is an historic pioneer port. First settled in 1810, it later became Australia's second largest port. It is still the base for one of the largest fishing fleets in Victoria. Within a 400 metre area of the habour lies the remains of some thirty wrecks: a stark reminder of the conditions that can occur there. Lady Julia Percy Island has a sea lion colony but, due to the efforts of game fishermen seeking to flush out a shark or two, care is required when diving. In the not-so-early days the sea lions were shot for shark and cray bait.

Originally the first permanent farming settlement in Victoria, Portland was established by Edward Henty in 1834. As the only deep-water port between Port Phillip Bay and Adelaide in South Australia, Portland has grown from a popular seaside resort to a multi-million dollar modern port operation with a huge new dock development.

Service:

SEA WORLD SERVICES
Most dive shop services available, dives arranged.

Contact:
Sea World Services
96 Kariot Street, Warrnambool Vic. 3280
Phone: (055) 62 2141

Service:

PORTLAND AQUANAUTS SCUBA FILLING STATION
Prior arrangements must be made to book air fills.

Contact:
Portland Aquanauts Scuba Filling Station
100 Palmer Street, Portland Vic. 3305
Phone: (055) 23 1445 (dive club)

Remarks:

Some of the known dive locations from shore include areas around Cape Bridgewater, inside Portland Bay (Breakwater), Blackrose Point and Point Danger, seas and weather permitting. Boat dive locations take in the town jetty, Minerva Reef, Lawrence Rocks, Cape Nelson and Seal Caves. Though the waters in the harbour have limited visibility diver's have discovered some rare species of molluscs beneath the old town jetty. The town breakwater itself is interesting, with lots of local marine life, silty on the inside and kelp covered on the outside. Quite a good spot for close-up photography.

GENERAL INFORMATION

Best times of the year:	■ Summer	□ Winter	□ Spring	□ Autumn
Typical weather:	□ Excellent	□	□	□
	□ Very good	□	□	□
	□ Average	■	■	□
	■ Fair	□	□	■
Accommodation available:	■ Camping	■ Hostel	■ Hotel	■ Motel
Airport:	■ Light aircraft	■ Jet	□ International	□ Helicopter

DIVE SITE GUIDE

Access:	■ Boat ramp	□ Charter boat	■ Air	
Dive methods:	■ Scuba	■ Hookah	■ Snorkel	■ Snorkel diving
Types of diving:	■ Boat	■ Jetty	■ Shore	
Description of dive site:	■ Island	■ Submerged reef	■ Shore	
	■ Wreck	■ Shallow water	■ Deep water	
Conditions at site:	■ Current	■ Swell	■ Wind chop	
	□ Tide changes	□ Boat traffic	□ Good visibility	
	■ Fair visibility	■ Poor visibility		
Dive time:	■ In-coming tide	■ Out-going tide		
	□ Spring tide	■ Neap tide	■ Slack tide	
Underwater terrain:	■ Drop offs	■ Gutters	□ Patch reefs	
	■ Sand & rubble	■ Rocky reef	■ Flat bottom	
	■ Low profile reef	□ Coral reef	■ Slope	
	□ Caves	□ Swim-throughs	□ Silty bottom	
Marine life:	■ Kelp	■ Sea grass	■ Sponges	□ Corals
	□ Sea whips	■ Sea fans	□ Black coral	□ Soft corals
	■ Anemones	■ Fan worms	■ Bryozoans	□ Brachiopods
	■ Crays	■ Crabs	■ Shells	□ Commensal shrimps
	■ Nudibranchs	□ Cuttles	■ Scallops	■ Abalone
	■ Sea stars	□ Basket stars	■ Sea urchins	□ Feather stars
	■ Ascidians	■ Sea lions	■ Dolphins	□ Whales
	■ Sharks	■ Fish	□ Numerous fish	□ Abundant fish
Experience level:	■ Pupil	■ Beginner	■ Intermediate	■ Advanced
Dive site rating:	□ Excellent	□ Very good	■ Fair	■ Photography
Management of resources:	□ Marine reserve	□ Protected species	□ Quotas	■ Collecting

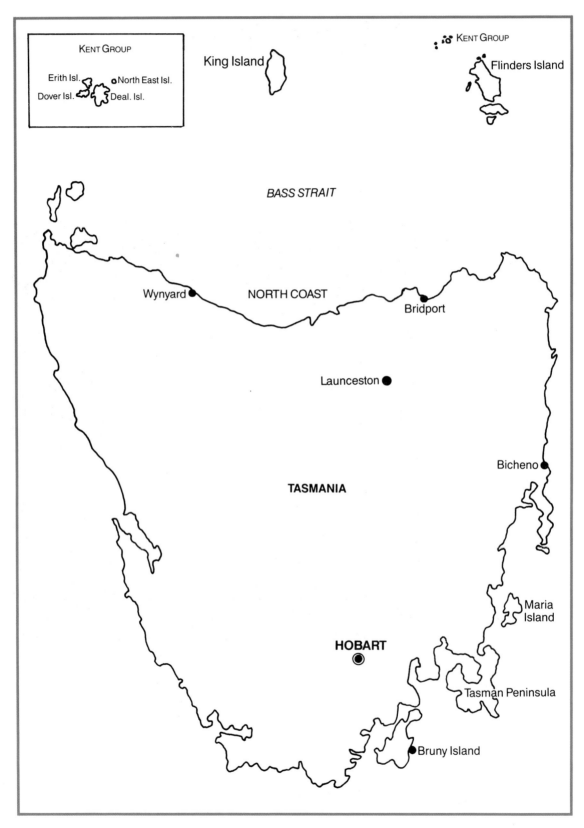

KENT GROUP

Erith Isl.   o North East Isl.
Dover Isl.   Deal. Isl.

KENT GROUP

King Island

Flinders Island

BASS STRAIT

Wynyard   NORTH COAST
                        Bridport

Launceston

Bicheno

TASMANIA

Maria
Island

HOBART

Tasman Peninsula

Bruny Island

Diving
TASMANIA

Curled into a protective ball during the daylight hours, at night-time the southern basket star unravels its many arms and catches plankton for food.

FLINDERS ISLAND & KENT GROUP, BASS STRAIT

As the largest island in the Furneaux group of islands, Flinders offers divers the thrill of untouched seascapes and an opportunity to explore some of the many wrecks in the area. Accessibility is restricted to light aircraft and dive charter boats from Victoria or Launceston, and day trips can be arranged from the island itself.

The female paper nautilus builds a shelly egg case in which she lays several layers of eggs. Just before they hatch she dies and the young argonauts begin their planktonic existence.

Service:

FLINDERS ISLAND SCUBA HIRE
The only air on the island, this moderate service offers full FAUI instruction and scuba hire plus information on the best dive sites and/or organised dives.

Contact:
Flinders Island Scuba Hire
PO Box 60, Whitemark, Flinders Island, Brass Strait Tas. 7255
Phone: (033) 59 2124, (003) 59 2077

Charter Boat:

Polperro

Contact:
Polperro
Port Franklin Vic.
Phone: (056) 86 2395 for information regarding the Kent Group, as no facilities are available on the island whatsoever. The only residents are the birds.

Remarks:

Understandably, visibility in the area changes, as does the weather. Sea conditions in Bass Strait storms can be devastating and it is advisable to plan excursions with professionals who are knowledgeable about Bass Strait. The Kent Group is accessible only by charter boat, but as anybody who's experienced the fantastic diving, 30 metre visibility, giant kelp beds, zillions of crays, fish and abalone, paper nautilus, sponge gardens and wrecks can tell you, it's worth the slog out from the mainland just to get there. Uninhabited island adventures!

GENERAL INFORMATION

Best times of the year: ■ Summer ☐ Winter ☐ Spring ■ Autumn

Typical weather:
☐ Excellent	☐	☐	☐
■ Very good	☐	☐	■
☐ Average	■	■	☐
☐ Fair	☐	☐	☐

Accommodation available: ■ Camping ☐ Hostel ■ Hotel ■ Motel

Airport: ■ Light aircraft ☐ Jet ☐ International ☐ Helicopter

DIVE SITE GUIDE

Access: ☐ Boat ramp ■ Charter boat ■ Air

Dive methods: ■ Scuba ■ Hookah ■ Snorkel ■ Snorkel diving

Types of diving: ■ Boat ☐ Jetty ■ Shore

Description of dive site: ■ Island ■ Submerged reef ■ Shore / ■ Wreck ■ Shallow water ■ Deep water

Conditions at site: ☐ Current ■ Swell ■ Wind chop / ☐ Tide changes ☐ Boat traffic ■ Good visibility / ■ Fair visibility ☐ Poor visibility

Dive time: ■ In-coming tide ■ Out-going tide / ■ Spring tide ■ Neap tide ■ Slack tide

Underwater terrain: ■ Drop offs ■ Gutters ☐ Patch reefs / ■ Sand & rubble ■ Rocky reef ☐ Flat bottom / ■ Low profile reef ☐ Coral reef ■ Slope / ■ Caves ☐ Swim-throughs ☐ Silty bottom

Marine life:
■ Kelp ■ Sea grass ■ Sponges ■ Corals
■ Sea whips ■ Sea fans ■ Black coral ■ Soft corals
■ Anemones ■ Fan worms ■ Bryozoans ☐ Brachiopods
■ Crays ■ Crabs ■ Shells ☐ Commensal shrimps

■ Nudibranchs ■ Cuttles ■ Scallops ■ Abalone
■ Sea stars ■ Basket stars ■ Sea urchins ■ Feather stars
■ Ascidians ■ Sea lions ■ Dolphins ■ Whales
■ Sharks ■ Fish ☐ Numerous fish ■ Abundant fish

Experience level: ☐ Pupil ☐ Beginner ■ Intermediate ☐ Advanced

Dive site rating: ■ Excellent ☐ Very good ☐ Fair ■ Photography

Management of resources: ☐ Marine reserve ☐ Protected species ■ Quotas ■ Collecting

Most hermit crabs are nocturnal, hiding away amongst rocks, under ledges or beneath the sand during the day.

NORTH COAST –
LAUNCESTON, WYNYARD

Both of these centres, situated respectively on the Tamar and Inglis rivers, are popular diving towns on the north coast. Launceston, the largest, has a population of around 65,000 and offers all modern conveniences. The North Coast attracts divers from the mainland during the season to dive on the many wreck sites in Bass Strait. Weather is the main consideration here as the entire coastline is open to prevailing westerlies and Bass Strait can be a pretty scary place in rough seas. Boat trips out to the Bass Strait Islands can be arranged from either location through the facilities listed below.

Service:

KINGS MEADOWS SPORTS CONNECTION
A fully integrated sports store, Kings Meadows nevertheless has a complete dive section with all services, a full range of equipment and air 5½ days a week, catering to both local and touring divers. The facility has both NAUI and PADI instruction and can arrange dive trips to all areas depending on conditions.

Being in the water with the fur seals at Barrenjoey Island (east of Launceston) is an experience no diver should miss.

Contact:
Kings Meadows Sports Connection
120 Hobart Road, Kings Meadows, Launceston Tas. 7249
Phone: (003) 44 9411

Service:

TERRY CHARLTON SPORTS STORE
Run in conjunction with other sporting services, the dive section has an in-house departmental manager backed up by staff and offers a full range of equipment catering for all scuba diving and snorkelling requirements. Air is available 5½ days a week as is PADI instruction and dive trips to the Bass Strait Islands; wreck site dives can be arranged depending on the weather.

Contact:
Terry Charlton Sports Store
155 Brisbane Street, Launceston Tas. 7250
Phone: (003) 31 6913

Service:

WYNYARD SCUBA CENTRE
The only totally complete single entity dive facility on the North or West Coast of Tasmania, Wynyards Scuba Centre, with its own fully heated indoor training pool, offers the largest pro facility services. PADI instruction, air 5½ days a week, regular boat dives, equipment sales, gear hire and servicing. Charter boat available for Bass Strait area including the notorious West Coast.

Contact:
Wynyard Scuba Centre
62 Bass Highway, Wynyard Tas. 7325
Phone: (004) 422 247

Remarks:

Bass Strait Islands are wild and woolly and hardly a place for 'whimps', yet their very nature has kept their secrets hidden from the prying eyes of most humans. The diving is adventurous and exciting and nothing surpasses the sea lion colony at Barrenjoey Island. To dive, surrounded by scores of sea lions, screaming up and down and around and through the giant kelp forests, is the most adrenaline-pumping high you could ever imagine. Dive-bombed by bubble-seekers that 'talk' with their eyes and swim with grace, divers can only stare in amazement and wonder as their clumsy attempts at swimming fail to emulate such perfection.

GENERAL INFORMATION

Best times of the year:	■ Summer	☐ Winter	☐ Spring	■ Autumn
Typical weather:	☐ Excellent	☐	☐	☐
	■ Very good	☐	☐	■
	☐ Average	■	■	☐
	☐ Fair	☐	☐	☐
Accommodation available:	■ Camping	☐ Hostel	■ Hotel	■ Motel
Airport:	■ Light aircraft	■ Jet	☐ International	☐ Helicopter

DIVE SITE GUIDE

Access:	■ Boat ramp	■ Charter boat	■ Air	
Dive methods:	■ Scuba	■ Hookah	■ Snorkel	■ Snorkel diving
Types of diving:	■ Boat	☐ Jetty	■ Shore	
Description of dive site:	■ Island	■ Submerged reef	■ Shore	
	■ Wreck	■ Shallow water	■ Deep water	
Conditions at site:	■ Current	■ Swell	■ Wind chop	
	■ Tide changes	☐ Boat traffic	☐ Good visibility	
	■ Fair visibility	☐ Poor visibility		
Dive time:	■ In-coming tide	■ Out-going tide		
	■ Spring tide	■ Neap tide	■ Slack tide	
Underwater terrain:	■ Drop offs	■ Gutters	■ Patch reefs	
	■ Sand & rubble	■ Rocky reef	■ Flat bottom	
	■ Low profile reef	☐ Coral reef	■ Slope	
	☐ Caves	☐ Swim-throughs	☐ Silty bottom	
Marine life:	■ Kelp	■ Sea grass	■ Sponges	☐ Corals
	☐ Sea whips	■ Sea fans	☐ Black coral	☐ Soft corals
	■ Anemones	■ Fan worms	■ Bryozoans	☐ Brachiopods
	■ Crays	■ Crabs	■ Shells	☐ Commensal shrimps
	■ Nudibranchs	■ Cuttles	☐ Scallops	■ Abalone
	■ Sea stars	☐ Basket stars	■ Sea urchins	■ Feather stars
	■ Ascidians	■ Sea lions	■ Dolphins	■ Whales
	☐ Sharks	■ Fish	■ Numerous fish	☐ Abundant fish
Experience level:	☐ Pupil	■ Beginner	■ Intermediate	■ Advanced
Dive site rating:	☐ Excellent	■ Very good	☐ Fair	■ Photography
Management of resources:	☐ Marine reserve	☐ Protected species	■ Quotas	■ Collecting

The underwater scenery at Bicheno is both spectacular and relatively unexplored.

BICHENO

Situated on the east coast 152 kilometres northeast of Hobart, Bicheno is rated as one of the best diving areas in Tasmania. Certainly the fantastic scenery at and picturesque setting of the Gulch, Governor Island and Waub's Bay add to the attraction, as does the hospitable, easygoing ways of the locals. A popular holiday resort and fishing port, Bicheno has a seabird sanctuary on Governor Island, penguins on nearby Diamond Island and, for those of you who don't wish to get their feet wet, the Bicheno Sea Life Centre, which has the world's biggest crabs on show.

Service:

BICHENO DIVE CENTRE
Originally set up by Dave Warth, an ex-abalone diver, the Bicheno Dive Centre is an excellent, thoroughly professional PADI facility offering instruction to all levels. Hostel accommodation; a 24 hour, 7-days-a-week air service; a complete range of equipment and gear hire. Dive trips from their 7 metre sharkcat scheduled every day depending on weather conditions.

Unlike any other fish in the world, the old wife is the only fish in its scientific family.

One of the many undescribed species of commensal zoanthids, this species (commonly called the yellow zoanthid) grows only on sponges.

Contact:
Bicheno Dive Centre
4 Tasman Highway, Bicheno Tas. 7215
Phone: (003) 75 1138

Remarks:

Diving Bicheno means deep-water sponge beds alive with colour and giant kelp forests – eerie underwater jungles where light rays beam down, flashing like shimmering quicksilver on a thousand rippling fronds as they sway back and forth in the surging swells. Some of the better known dive sites are the Giant Kelp Forests, Trap Reef, Bird Rock, the Castle, Muirs Rock and the Hairy Wall. The Rock and the Point out of Waub's Bay are interesting shallow-water dives with lots of life beneath the *Ecklonia* kelp canopy. Excellent sites for underwater photography.

GENERAL INFORMATION

Best times of the year:	□ Summer	■ Winter	■ Spring	□ Autumn
Typical weather:	□ Excellent	□	□	□
	■ Very good	■	■	□
	□ Average	□	□	■
	□ Fair	□	□	□
Accommodation available:	■ Camping	□ Hostel	■ Hotel	■ Motel
Airport:	□ Light aircraft	□ Jet	□ International	□ Helicopter

DIVE SITE GUIDE

Access:	■ Boat ramp	■ Charter boat	■ Air	
Dive methods:	■ Scuba	■ Hookah	■ Snorkel	■ Snorkel diving
Types of diving:	■ Boat	□ Jetty	■ Shore	
Description of dive site:	■ Island	■ Submerged reef	■ Shore	
	□ Wreck	■ Shallow water	■ Deep water	
Conditions at site:	■ Current	■ Swell	■ Wind chop	
	□ Tide changes	□ Boat traffic	■ Good visibility	
	□ Fair visibility	□ Poor visibility		
Dive time:	■ In-coming tide	■ Out-going tide		
	■ Spring tide	■ Neap tide	■ Slack tide	
Underwater terrain:	■ Drop offs	■ Gutters	□ Patch reefs	
	■ Sand & rubble	■ Rocky reef	□ Flat bottom	
	■ Low profile reef	□ Coral reef	■ Slope	
	■ Caves	■ Swim-throughs	□ Silty bottom	
Marine life:	■ Kelp	■ Sea grass	■ Sponges	□ Corals
	■ Sea whips	■ Sea fans	■ Black coral	■ Soft corals
	■ Anemones	■ Fan worms	■ Bryozoans	□ Brachiopods
	■ Crays	■ Crabs	■ Shells	□ Commensal shrimps
	■ Nudibranchs	■ Cuttles	■ Scallops	■ Abalone
	■ Sea stars	■ Basket stars	■ Sea urchins	■ Feather stars
	■ Ascidians	□ Sea lions	■ Dolphins	■ Whales
	■ Sharks	■ Fish	■ Numerous fish	■ Abundant fish
Experience level:	■ Pupil	■ Beginner	■ Intermediate	□ Advanced
Dive site rating:	■ Excellent	□ Very good	□ Fair	■ Photography
Management of resources:	■ Marine reserve	□ Protected species	■ Quotas	■ Collecting

Looking down on the giant kelp beds of Penguin Island from Fluted Cape, Bruny Island.

HOBART – BRUNY ISLAND – TASMAN PENINSULA – MARIA ISLAND

With a population of over 128,000, Hobart is the capital of Tasmania and the second oldest Australian city. A melting pot of old and new, it can be a place of extremes in terms of prevailing weather conditions. Diving in the Hobart Estuary has been somewhat hampered by the high level of pollution. Up until a few years ago the Derwent River had one of the highest heavy metal concentrations in the world. Most of the diving activity is centered south of Hobart along the 56 kilometre stretch of D'Entrecasteaux Channel, which is protected in the sheltering lee of Bruny Island.

Service:

THE DIVE SHOP
Complete dive shop facilities, air 6 days a week, diving instruction PADI facility, local boat tours to most dive sites, diving tours arranged.

Contact:
The Dive Shop
233 Liverpool Street, Hobart Tas. 7000
Phone: (002) 34 3428, A/H (002) 25 1539 for all local information.

Remarks:

Some of my favourite dive sites around the Bruny Island locality are Tinderbox, Simpson's Point, Adventure Bay, Fluted Cape, Penguin Island and Great Taylor Bay.

One of the weirdest of underwater creatures is the weedy sea dragon, another endemic Australian.

North of Hobart and only accessible by charter boat is the National Park of Maria Island. This area is also a marine reserve and has been the subject of an extensive fauna survey in which it was recorded as one of the richest sea life sites in Tassie. Wetsuits are a must – jacket, full long johns; 5 mm minimum, locals wear 8 mm. Photography is excellent at most sites.

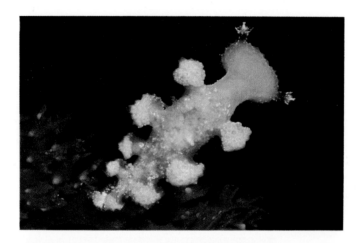

Only 25 mm in size, the southern melibe is a shell-less mollusc that captures food by sucking up prey in its huge, over-sized mouth.

Growing to over 1 metre in length, giant cuttles occur in all southern Australian waters and show little fear of divers.

GENERAL INFORMATION

Best times of the year: ■ Summer   □ Winter   □ Spring   ■ Autumn

Typical weather:

	Summer	Winter	Spring	Autumn
Excellent	□	□	□	□
Very good	■	□	□	■
Average	□	■	■	□
Fair	□	□	□	□

Accommodation available: ■ Camping   ■ Hostel   ■ Hotel   ■ Motel

Airport: ■ Light aircraft   ■ Jet   □ International   □ Helicopter

DIVE SITE GUIDE

Access: ■ Boat ramp   ■ Charter boat   ■ Air

Dive methods: ■ Scuba   ■ Hookah   ■ Snorkel   ■ Snorkel diving

Types of diving: ■ Boat   □ Jetty   ■ Shore

Description of dive site: ■ Island   ■ Submerged reef   ■ Shore
  ■ Wreck   ■ Shallow water   ■ Deep water

Conditions at site: □ Current   ■ Swell   ■ Wind chop
  □ Tide changes   □ Boat traffic   ■ Good visibility
  ■ Fair visibility   □ Poor visibility

Dive time: ■ In-coming tide   ■ Out-going tide
  ■ Spring tide   ■ Neap tide   ■ Slack tide

Underwater terrain: ■ Drop offs   ■ Gutters   □ Patch reefs
  ■ Sand & rubble   ■ Rocky reef   ■ Flat bottom
  ■ Low profile reef   □ Coral reef   ■ Slope
  ■ Caves   □ Swim-throughs   ■ Silty bottom

Marine life:

■ Kelp	■ Sea grass	■ Sponges	□ Corals
■ Sea whips	■ Sea fans	■ Black coral	□ Soft corals
■ Anemones	□ Fan worms	■ Bryozoans	□ Brachiopods
■ Crays	■ Crabs	■ Shells	□ Commensal shrimps
■ Nudibranchs	■ Cuttles	■ Scallops	■ Abalone
■ Sea stars	■ Basket stars	■ Sea urchins	■ Feather stars
■ Ascidians	□ Sea lions	■ Dolphins	■ Whales
□ Sharks	■ Fish	□ Numerous fish	□ Abundant fish

Experience level: ■ Pupil   ■ Beginner   ■ Intermediate   ■ Advanced

Dive site rating: □ Excellent   ■ Very good   ■ Fair   ■ Photography

Management of resources: ■ Marine reserve   ■ Protected species   ■ Quotas   ■ Collecting

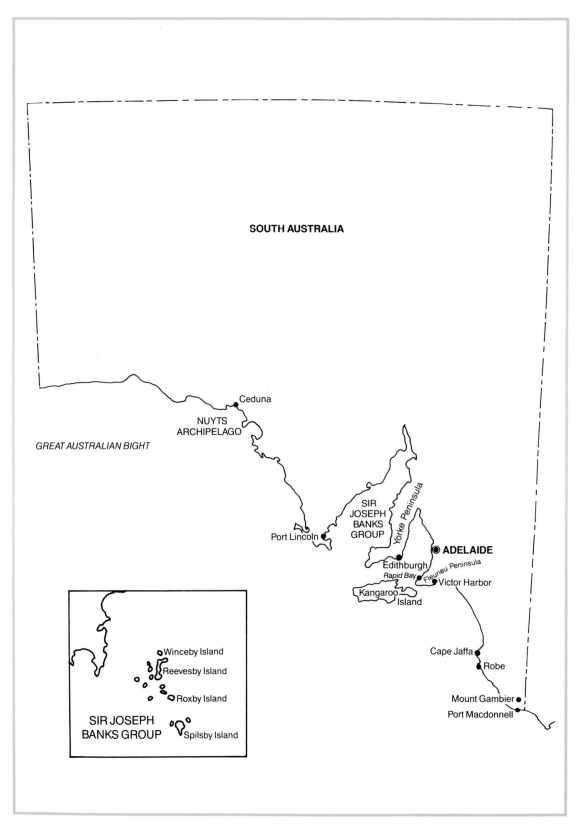

SOUTH AUSTRALIA

Ceduna

NUYTS
ARCHIPELAGO

GREAT AUSTRALIAN BIGHT

SIR
JOSEPH
BANKS
GROUP

Yorke Peninsula

Port Lincoln

◉ **ADELAIDE**

Edithburgh

Rapid Bay

Fleurieu Peninsula

Kangaroo
Island

Victor Harbor

Cape Jaffa

Robe

Mount Gambier

Port Macdonnell

Winceby Island

Reevesby Island

Roxby Island

SIR JOSEPH
BANKS GROUP

Spilsby Island

Diving
SOUTH AUSTRALIA

Although rarely seen by divers, the giant crab (which grows to over 400 mm) is regularly brought up in craypots from deep water reefs.

PORT MACDONNELL –
ROBE – CAPE JAFFA

Built a little to the east of Cape Northumberland on the southern-most tip of South Australia, 495 kilometres from Adelaide, Port Macdonnell is home to the largest rock lobster fishing fleet in the state. A busy seaside township of less than 1000 people, Port Mac-donnell has a man-made harbour breakwater which gives some meas-ure of protection from the weather along this rugged stretch of coastline.

This area can be dived from shore. The shallow reefs are kelp

Extremely
inquisitive, this
juvenile dusky
morwong shows
no alarm at the
photographer's
approach.

covered, but quite rich in invertebrates (but not many fish) and, surprisingly, there are quite a few rock lobsters.

The offshore reefs promise spectacular diving, but most are in fairly deep water. From what I've seen coming up in the rock lobster pots, giant 30 lb (13.5 kg) crabs included, the reefs have a whole new fauna to investigate.

Carpenter's Rocks to Cape Banks is an interesting shore dive with extensive sea grass meadows, giant pipefish, beautiul sea anemones, tube worms and lots of dusky morwong that can be caught in fish traps without bait. I knew dusky morwong were very inquisitive but I didn't believe they'd 'catch themselves' by investigating empty traps till someone showed me.

Robe on Guichen Bay has a safe harbour and was once a big shipping port. Today it is supported by fishing and tourism. The waters are clear, the sand white, and it's a nice place for snorkelling. The Godfrey Islands no doubt would be good diving locations, but the only access is by boat.

Further to the north at Cape Jaffa is a line of reefs stretching out to sea towards Margaret Brock Reef eight kilometres west of

Cape Jaffa. While the shallow reefs here offer good diving if the conditions are good, I bet Margaret Brock Reef is really something special. Situated right on the overlap between two biogeographical provinces, the western warm temperate and the cool temperate zones, some exciting discoveries should be made there one day. Margaret Brock Reef is a sanctuary. All rock lobsters are protected.

Services: None. (See Mt. Gambier.)

GENERAL INFORMATION

Best times of the year:	■ Summer	☐ Winter	☐ Spring	■ Autumn
Typical weather:	■ Excellent	☐	☐	☐
	☐ Very good	☐	■	■
	☐ Average	■	☐	☐
	☐ Fair	☐	☐	☐
Accommodation available:	■ Camping	☐ Hostel	☐ Hotel	■ Motel
Airport:	☐ Light aircraft	☐ Jet	☐ International	☐ Helicopter

DIVE SITE GUIDE

Access:	■ Boat ramp	☐ Charter boat	☐ Air	
Dive methods:	■ Scuba	■ Hookah	■ Snorkel	■ Snorkel diving
Types of diving:	■ Boat	☐ Jetty	■ Shore	
Description of dive site:	☐ Island	■ Submerged reef	■ Shore	
	■ Wreck	■ Shallow water	■ Deep water	
Conditions at site:	■ Current	■ Swell	■ Wind chop	
	■ Tide changes	☐ Boat traffic	■ Good visibility	
	☐ Fair visibility	☐ Poor visibility		
Dive time:	■ In-coming tide	■ Out-going tide		
	■ Spring tide	■ Neap tide	■ Slack tide	
Underwater terrain:	☐ Drop offs	■ Gutters	■ Patch reefs	
	■ Sand & rubble	■ Rocky reef	■ Flat bottom	
	■ Low profile reef	☐ Coral reef	☐ Slope	
	☐ Caves	☐ Swim-throughs	☐ Silty bottom	
Marine life:	■ Kelp	■ Sea grass	■ Sponges	☐ Corals
	☐ Sea whips	■ Sea fans	☐ Black coral	☐ Soft corals
	■ Anemones	■ Fan worms	■ Bryozoans	☐ Brachiopods
	■ Crays	■ Crabs	■ Shells	☐ Commensal shrimps
	■ Nudibranchs	☐ Cuttles	☐ Scallops	■ Abalone
	■ Sea stars	☐ Basket stars	■ Sea urchins	☐ Feather stars
	■ Ascidians	☐ Sea lions	■ Dolphins	☐ Turtles
	☐ Sharks	■ Fish	☐ Numerous fish	☐ Abundant fish
Experience level:	■ Pupil	■ Beginner	■ Intermediate	■ Advanced
Dive site rating:	☐ Excellent	☐ Very good	■ Fair	☐ Photography
Management of resources:	■ Marine reserve	■ Protected species	■ Quotas	■ Collecting

Ewen's ponds, a beautiful, crystal clear spring-fed freshwater dive site.

MT. GAMBIER

Built on the slopes of an extinct volcano containing four lakes, Mt. Gambier is South Australia's second largest provincial city with a population of 20,000. It is situated in the centre of white coraline limestone country that is famous for its sinkholes. These underground caverns with their spring-fed crystal clear water are said to be amongst the best in the world.

Due to inexperience, ineptitude and inadequate safety procedures

A freshwater crayfish.

in the past, a number of divers have lost their lives in these sink-holes. Stricter control measures introduced to save lives mean it is now against the law to dive in the freshwater sinkholes, lakes or ponds without a special cave diver's certificate. All visitors planning to dive in the area must contact the National Parks and Wildlife Service section at Mt. Gambier, or the Cave Divers Association of South Australia, PO Box 290, North Adelaide, SA 5006, well in advance so arrangements can be made for certification to the appropriate category.

Some of the more accessible sites are Ewen's Ponds, one of the few freshwater dives in the area not requiring cave diving certification, although a permit from National Parks and Wildlife is necessary, and Piccaninny Ponds. A category 2 cave diver's certification is required to scuba dive at Piccaninny Ponds. Snorkelling requires only a snorkelling permit from National Parks and Wildlife.

To dive in Ewen's Ponds and Piccaninny Ponds was certainly a highlight in my diving career: both are freezing cold and crystal clear, with freshwater sponges, hydroids, fish, crabs, shrimps, spectacular reedbeds, frogs and tortoises. Underwater springs well up from the bottom and big freshwater crayfish (or yabbies as they are sometimes called in Australia) crawl around feeding on the vegetation.

Other dive sites include Pinetrees, One Tree, The Sisters and Baby Blue. See the local pro facility for directions and advice.

Service:

PLOENGES MARINE & DIVING CENTRE
FAUI/PADI instruction, equipment sales, service, gear hire, air 6 days a week, advice and locations for all Mt. Gambier dive sites.

Contact:
Ploenges Marine & Diving Centre
343 Commercial Street West, Mt. Gambier SA 5390
Phone: (087) 25 7604

Service:

ARENA SPORTS STORE
No instruction, air fills, some sales.

Contact:
Arena Sports Store
Cnr Commercial Street East & Compton Street
Mt. Gambier SA 5290
Phone: (087) 25 7977, A/H (087) 25 5230

GENERAL INFORMATION

Best times of the year:	■ Summer	■ Winter	■ Spring	■ Autumn
Typical weather:	■ Excellent	□	□	□
	□ Very good	□	■	■
	□ Average	□	□	□
	□ Fair	■	□	□
Accommodation available:	■ Camping	□ Hostel	■ Hotel	■ Motel
Airport:	■ Light aircraft	□ Jet	□ International	□ Helicopter

DIVE SITE GUIDE

Access:	□ Boat ramp	□ Charter boat	□ Air	
Dive methods:	■ Scuba	□ Hookah	■ Snorkel	■ Snorkel diving
Types of diving:	□ Boat	□ Jetty	■ Shore	
Description of dive site:	□ Island	□ Submerged reef	■ Shore	
	□ Wreck	■ Shallow water	■ Deep water	
Conditions at site:	■ Current	□ Swell	□ Wind chop	
	□ Tide changes	□ Boat traffic	■ Good visibility	
	□ Fair visibility	□ Poor visibility		
Dive time:	□ In-coming tide	■ Out-going tide		
	□ Spring tide	□ Neap tide	□ Slack tide	
Underwater terrain:	■ Drop offs	□ Gutters	□ Patch reefs	
	■ Sand & rubble	■ Rocky reef	■ Flat bottom	
	□ Low profile reef	□ Coral reef	■ Slope	
	■ Caves	■ Swim-throughs	■ Silty bottom	
Marine life:	□ Kelp	□ Sea grass	■ Sponges	□ Corals
	□ Sea whips	□ Sea fans	□ Black coral	□ Soft corals
	□ Anemones	□ Fan worms	□ Bryozoans	□ Brachiopods
	■ Crays	■ Crabs	■ Shells	■ Commensal shrimps
	□ Nudibranchs	□ Cuttles	□ Scallops	□ Abalone
	□ Sea stars	□ Basket stars	□ Sea urchins	□ Feather stars
	□ Ascidians	□ Sea lions	□ Dolphins	□ Turtles
	□ Sharks	■ Fish	□ Numerous fish	□ Abundant fish
Experience level:	□ Pupil	□ Beginner	■ Intermediate	■ Advanced
Dive site rating:	■ Excellent	□ Very good	□ Fair	□ Photography
Management of resources:	□ Marine reserve	■ Protected species	□ Quotas	□ Collecting

Remarks: Mt. Gambier was my first introduction to freshwater diving and photography. It sure was different. Buoyancy control were the keywords, so as not to disturb the soft bottom. It was strange seeing saltwater fish such as bream and mullet swimming around quite happily in pure fresh water. The freshwater sponges were green with symbiotic algae and the little commensal temnocephalids on the crays were fascinating. Piccaninny Ponds from the surface is a spectacle: underwater it's breathtaking.

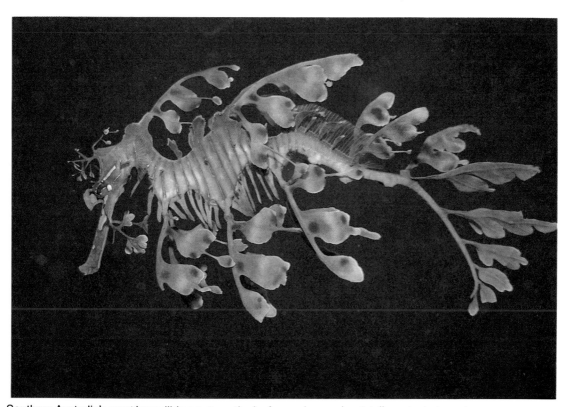

Southern Australia's most incredible creature, the leafy sea dragon, is a totally protected species.

VICTOR HARBOUR – RAPID BAY

Victor Harbour was founded on the slopes of Encounter Bay and with a population of 7000 it is the largest and most popular resort town on the south coast, being only 74 kilometres from Adelaide. Diving Victor Harbour and its offshore islands and reefs is by no means for the faint of heart. The visibility in the harbour isn't brilliant, and outside around Wright Island, West Island and the ensuing coastline, the huge ocean swells crash up the granite shore sending spray 20 metres in the air. Shore diving near the West Island Jetty is more feasible as is diving inside the harbour breakwater.

The offshore reefs are covered in kelp forests but many have ledges and caves stuffed with gorgonian sea fans, ascidians and all manner of invertebrates. Harlequin rock cod, schools of trevally and the ever-present sweep abound, and black cowries have been found.

A more pleasant dive in reasonable conditions (depending on the weather) is under the old jetty at Rapid Bay, some 70 kilometres away in St Vincent's Gulf.

Unique to Australia, the multi-spined sea star inhabits rocky reefs down to 60 metres.

Service:

VICTOR MARINE & WATERSPORT
Air 7 days a week, some equipment sales.

Contact:
Victor Marine & Watersport
160 Hindmarsh Road, Victor Harbour SA 5211
Phone: (085) 52 4757

Remarks:

For all the difficulties in getting to good diving sites and the all-too-often rough seas, Victor Harbour has one redeeming feature – leafy sea dragons. These fantastically shaped masters of mimicry inhabit the kelp beds and sometimes the close-by sea grass meadows.

Leafy sea dragons are found only in South Australia and southern Western Australia and are protected by law. They are so well camouflaged that only a few divers have ever seen them in the wild.

GENERAL INFORMATION

Best times of the year:	☐ Summer	■ Winter	■ Spring	■ Autumn
Typical weather:	☐ Excellent	☐	☐	☐
	☐ Very good	☐	☐	☐
	■ Average	☐	☐	■
	☐ Fair	■	■	☐
Accommodation available:	■ Camping	☐ Hostel	■ Hotel	■ Motel
Airport:	☐ Light aircraft	☐ Jet	☐ International	☐ Helicopter

DIVE SITE GUIDE

Access:	■ Boat ramp	☐ Charter boat	■ Air	
Dive methods:	■ Scuba	☐ Hookah	■ Snorkel	■ Snorkel diving
Types of diving:	■ Boat	■ Jetty	■ Shore	
Description of dive site:	■ Island	■ Submerged reef	■ Shore	
	☐ Wreck	■ Shallow water	■ Deep water	
Conditions at site:	■ Current	■ Swell	■ Wind chop	
	☐ Tide changes	☐ Boat traffic	☐ Good visibility	
	■ Fair visibility	■ Poor visibility		
Dive time:	■ In-coming tide	■ Out-going tide		
	■ Spring tide	■ Neap tide	■ Slack tide	
Underwater terrain:	■ Drop offs	■ Gutters	☐ Patch reefs	
	■ Sand & rubble	■ Rocky reef	■ Flat bottom	
	■ Low profile reef	☐ Coral reef	■ Slope	
	■ Caves	☐ Swim-throughs	■ Silty bottom	
Marine life:	■ Kelp	■ Sea grass	■ Sponges	☐ Corals
	☐ Sea whips	■ Sea fans	☐ Black coral	■ Soft corals
	■ Anemones	■ Fan worms	■ Bryozoans	☐ Brachiopods
	■ Crays	■ Crabs	■ Shells	☐ Commensal shrimps
	■ Nudibranchs	☐ Cuttles	☐ Scallops	■ Abalone
	■ Sea stars	■ Basket stars	■ Sea urchins	■ Feather stars
	■ Ascidians	☐ Sea lions	■ Dolphins	■ Whales
	☐ Sharks	■ Fish	☐ Numerous fish	☐ Abundant fish
Experience level:	☐ Pupil	■ Beginner	■ Intermediate	■ Advanced
Dive site rating:	☐ Excellent	☐ Very good	■ Fair	☐ Photography
Management of resources:	■ Marine reserve	■ Protected species	☐ Quotas	☐ Collecting

The Kingscote Jetty is excellent for macro photography.

KANGAROO ISLAND

Site of South Australia's first settlement, Kangaroo Island was discovered by Matthew Flinders. A large island of around 145 kilometres in length by 60 kilometres in width, it supports a population of nearly 4000 people. Most of the commercial facilities are located in the vicinity of three small coastal towns – Kingscote, American River and Penneshaw. The diving around the island is quite good and,

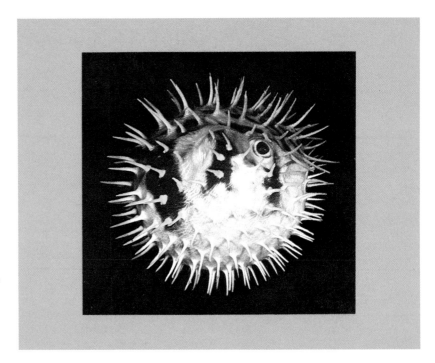

Although globefish are deadly poisonous if eaten by humans and have one of the best defence mechanisms in the underwater world, sharks often swallow them without ill effect.

due to the many bays, shore diving may be accomplished at most locations, though the main diving occurs on the northern side. Some of the better dive sites include Western River Cove, Stoke's Bay, Snug Cove, Kingscote Jetty and Penneshaw Jetty. Offshore reefs are all around but most require a boat, as to get to reasonably deep water otherwise calls for a long swim.

Service:

ADVENTURE DIVING SERVICE
FAUI instruction, gear hire, air, accommodation arranged.

Contact:
Adventure Diving Service
Lot 155, Beach Crescent, American Beach,
Penneshaw, Kangaroo Island SA 5222
Phone: (08) 483 1072

Service:

FERRETS HARDWARE STORE
Equipment sales, air.

Contact:
Ferrets Hardware Store
Telegraph Road, Kingscote, Kangaroo Island SA 5223
Phone: (08) 483 1072

Remarks:

Kangaroo Island offers dense kelp beds, lots of fish, clear shallow water, fantastic scenery, unique rock formations, a sea lion colony at seal beach and plenty of good diving and photography.

GENERAL INFORMATION

Best times of the year:	■ Summer	□ Winter	■ Spring	□ Autumn
Typical weather:	□ Excellent	□	■	□
	■ Very good	■	□	■
	□ Average	□	□	□
	□ Fair	■	□	□
Accommodation available:	■ Camping	□ Hostel	■ Hotel	■ Motel
Airport:	■ Light aircraft	□ Jet	□ International	□ Helicopter

DIVE SITE GUIDE

Access:	□ Boat ramp	□ Charter boat	■ Air	
Dive methods:	■ Scuba	□ Hookah	■ Snorkel	■ Snorkel diving
Types of diving:	■ Boat	■ Jetty	■ Shore	
Description of dive site:	□ Island	■ Submerged reef	■ Shore	
	■ Wreck	■ Shallow water	□ Deep water	
Conditions at site:	■ Current	■ Swell	■ Wind chop	
	■ Tide changes	□ Boat traffic	□ Good visibility	
	■ Fair visibility	□ Poor visibility		
Dive time:	■ In-coming tide	■ Out-going tide		
	■ Spring tide	■ Neap tide	■ Slack tide	
Underwater terrain:	□ Drop offs	■ Gutters	■ Patch reefs	
	■ Sand & rubble	■ Rocky reef	■ Flat bottom	
	■ Low profile reef	□ Coral reef	□ Slope	
	■ Caves	□ Swim-throughs	□ Silty bottom	
Marine life:	■ Kelp	■ Sea grass	■ Sponges	□ Corals
	□ Sea whips	■ Sea fans	□ Black coral	■ Soft corals
	■ Anemones	■ Fan worms	■ Bryozoans	□ Brachiopods
	■ Crays	■ Crabs	□ Shells	□ Commensal shrimps
	■ Nudibranchs	□ Cuttles	■ Scallops	■ Abalone
	■ Sea stars	■ Basket stars	■ Sea urchins	■ Feather stars
	■ Ascidians	■ Sea lions	■ Dolphins	■ Whales
	□ Sharks	■ Fish	□ Numerous fish	□ Abundant fish
Experience level:	■ Pupil	■ Beginner	■ Intermediate	■ Advanced
Dive site rating:	□ Excellent	■ Very good	□ Fair	□ Photography
Management of resources:	■ Marine reserve	■ Protected species	□ Quotas	□ Collecting

Aptly named, the Harlequin rock cod is the largest southern Australian serranid growing to over 1 metre in length.

ADELAIDE – FLEURIEU PENINSULA

To many people, Adelaide, with its wide, well-planned streets, church architecture and low property prices, appears to sit aloof amongst the Adelaide Hills and let the world go around beyond it. Well, Adelaide may appear to be a little behind the times, but for over twenty years or more it has implemented a more progressive, long-range marine conservation programme than all of the other states put together. While everybody else talked about marine reserves, the South Australian Department of Fisheries and Wildlife, which has its headquarters in Adelaide, did something about them.

The Fleurieu Peninsula runs from just south of Adelaide down

159

to Cape Jervis, and it is along this stretch of coastline that the main-stream of diving activities in South Australia take place. They start from Glenelg, with its hectares and hectares of beautiful shallow water 'broken-bottom' offshore reefs, and go on to the unsurpassed shore diving in Port Noarlunga Aquatic Reserve. And from the off-shore, they begin at Onkaparinga Headland patch reefs, and go down to the caves, undercuts and ledges of the Aldinga Drop Off, which bristles with gorgonian sea fans and where boarfish, gurnard perch, blue devils and nudibranchs abound. Then there is the selection of jetties on the way to Rapid Bay, where the shore diver can revel in examining the piles on the 487 metre long jetty. See your local pro facility for the right dives at the right times.

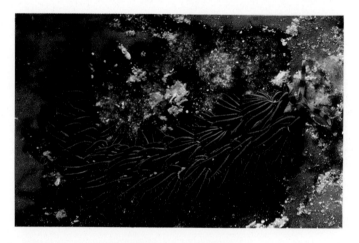

Shown here in its most common colour form, the opalescent nudibranch is found throughout all Australian seas.

Service:

ADELAIDE SKINDIVING CENTRE
FAUI instruction to all levels, specialty courses, air, equipment sales, service, gear hire, club, local dives, charter boat *Scuba*, escorted dive trips overseas.

Contact:
Adelaide Skindiving Centre
7 Compton Street, Adelaide SA 5000
Phone: (08) 51 6144, (08) 51 2140, (08) 51 6145

Service:

DIVERS INTERNATIONAL
PADI 5 star training facility, equipment sales, service, gear hire, air 6 days a week, test station, local dive trips, club, weekend trips.

Contact:
Divers International
510 Goodwood Road, Daw Park SA 5041
Phone: (08) 271 7065

Service:

RAPID MARINE
PADI instruction, equipment sales, service, gear hire, air 5½ days a week, local dive trips.

Only two colour variations of the round-armed sea star are known, yellow and wine red.

Contact:
Rapid Marine
254–256 Rundle Street, Adelaide SA 5000
Phone: (08) 223 2263, (08) 223 2725

Service:

DIVERS SERVICE
PADI/FAUI instruction, equipment sales, service, gear hire, air 5½ days a week, local dives, escorted overseas tours.

Contact:
Divers Service
80 Grange Road, Welland SA 5007
Phone: (08) 463 4222, A/H (08) 258 2834 (08) 372 7894

Service:

GLENELG MARINE
PADI instruction, equipment sales, service, gear hire, air, local diving.

Contact:
Glenelg Marine
Patawalonga Frontage, North Glenelg SA 5045
Phone: (08) 294 7744

Service:

SOUTHERN DIVING CENTRE
FAUI/PADI instruction, eqiupment sales, service, gear hire, air 5½ days a week.

Contact:
Southern Diving Centre
35 Beach Road, Christies Beach SA 5165
Phone: (08) 382 1322

Service:

UNDERWATER SPORTS DIVING CENTRE
FAUI instruction, cave diving, equipment sales, service, gear hire, air 5½ days a week, dive tours.

Contact:
Underwater Sports Diving Centre
1198 Grand Junction Road, Hope Valley SA 5090
Phone: (08) 263 3337

Remarks:

Although the Adelaide area has some very good dive sites and pro facilities, they are not well known outside of South Australia. It's a pity that the sinkholes at Mt. Gambier got their major publicity from diver deaths, rather than the pleasure and wonder they have given to many thousands. It's also a pity that due to profit-making

GENERAL INFORMATION

Best times of the year:	☐ Summer	■ Winter	■ Spring	■ Autumn
Typical weather:	☐ Excellent	■	■	☐
	■ Very good	☐	☐	■
	☐ Average	☐	☐	☐
	☐ Fair	☐	☐	☐
Accommodation available:	■ Camping	☐ Hostel	■ Hotel	■ Motel
Airport:	■ Light aircraft	■ Jet	☐ International	☐ Helicopter

DIVE SITE GUIDE

Access:	■ Boat ramp	■ Charter boat	■ Air	
Dive methods:	■ Scuba	■ Hookah	■ Snorkel	■ Snorkel diving
Types of diving:	■ Boat	■ Jetty	■ Shore	
Description of dive site:	☐ Island	■ Submerged reef	■ Shore	
	■ Wreck	■ Shallow water	■ Deep water	
Conditions at site:	■ Current	■ Swell	■ Wind chop	
	■ Tide changes	■ Boat traffic	■ Good visibility	
	■ Fair visibility	☐ Poor visibility		
Dive time:	■ In-coming tide	■ Out-going tide		
	■ Spring tide	■ Neap tide	■ Slack tide	
Underwater terrain:	■ Drop offs	■ Gutters	■ Patch reefs	
	■ Sand & rubble	■ Rocky reef	■ Flat bottom	
	■ Low profile reef	☐ Coral reef	■ Slope	
	■ Caves	☐ Swim-throughs	■ Silty bottom	
Marine life:	■ Kelp	■ Sea grass	■ Sponges	☐ Corals
	☐ Sea whips	■ Sea fans	☐ Black coral	■ Soft corals
	■ Anemones	■ Fan worms	■ Bryozoans	☐ Brachiopods
	■ Crays	■ Crabs	■ Shells	☐ Commensal shrimps
	■ Nudibranchs	■ Cuttles	■ Scallops	■ Abalone
	■ Sea stars	■ Basket stars	■ Sea urchins	■ Feather stars
	■ Ascidians	☐ Sea lions	■ Dolphins	☐ Turtles
	☐ Sharks	■ Fish	☐ Numerous fish	☐ Abundant fish
Experience level:	■ Pupil	■ Beginner	■ Intermediate	■ Advanced
Dive site rating:	☐ Excellent	■ Very good	☐ Fair	■ Photography
Management of resources:	■ Marine reserve	■ Protected species	☐ Quotas	☐ Collecting

sensationalism that really only benefits a few, South Australia has inherited such a fearsome image from white pointer shark promotions, shark fishing, shark cages, shark movies, shark videos, and shark baiting ventures.

South Australia really has a lot to offer the diver: blue water with lots of endemic Australian species and much to be explored. Take my word for it, put the negative publicity aside. South Australia is as safe as anywhere else in the world of water.

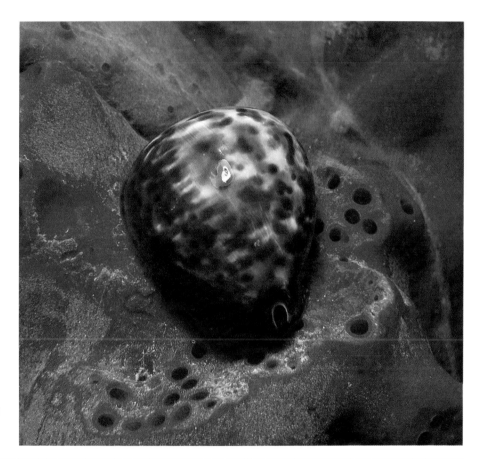

One of the first molluscs to receive protected status in Australia, the black cowry is a prohibited export.

YORKE PENINSULA

Comparing the evergreen coast of southeast Victoria to the dry barren wide-open treeless hectares of the Yorke Peninsula really brought home to me just what intensive farming does to the land. Wheat and sheep might have resulted in no small measure of prosperity in the early years, but a legacy of dry desolation seems a heck of a price to pay. Still, I forgot all this the moment I got in the water.

The jetties on the way down the inside leg of Yorke Peninsula

Gaimard's spider crab takes a defensive stance while retreating from the photographer.

are all worth a dive; they offer abundant invertebrate life, some fish, giant cuttles, lots of colour and are excellent for close up photography. Jetties occur at Ardrossan, Port Vincent, Stansbury, Port Giles, Edithburg and, to the west, Stenhouse Bay. Personally I liked Edithburg jetties best.

Troubridge Shoals off Edithburg makes a fantastic drift dive with the incoming tide – giant orange sponges, grey sponges and brown sponges cover the bottom, along with giant spider crabs, black cowries, huge sponge crabs and lots of invertebrates, but not many fish. Troubridge Island is also a good dive. Shore dives can be made anywhere there with adequate entry and sheltered water. There are some good diving spots on the south and west cape but these can best be located by checking with the local dive or air facility.

Coming up the western side of the Peninsula, Wardang Island off Port Victoria has interesting diving, but of the thirteen wreck sites eight exist in name only as the wrecks themselves are no longer recognisable. However, the new underwater wreck trails and accompanying information plaques placed by the National Heritage Commission are certainly a step in the right direction.

The islands off the northern tip of Wardang are all marine reserves. Tipara Reef out of Port Hughes has some interesting diving country but very few fish and the area is subject to tidal current and rough seas.

Service: NORTHERN UNDERWATER CENTRE
FAUI instruction, equipment sales, service, gear hire, air, club, local dive site information.

Contact:
Northern Underwater Centre
158 Balmoral Road, Port Pirie SA 5540
Phone: (086) 32 5110, A/H (086) 32 4929

GENERAL INFORMATION

Best times of the year:	□ Summer	■ Winter	■ Spring	□ Autumn
Typical weather:	□ Excellent	■	■	□
	■ Very good	□	□	■
	□ Average	□	□	□
	□ Fair	□	□	□
Accommodation available:	■ Camping	□ Hostel	■ Hotel	■ Motel
Airport:	□ Light aircraft	□ Jet	□ International	□ Helicopter

DIVE SITE GUIDE

Access:	■ Boat ramp	□ Charter boat	■ Air	
Dive methods:	■ Scuba	■ Hookah	■ Snorkel	■ Snorkel diving
Types of diving:	■ Boat	■ Jetty	■ Shore	
Description of dive site:	■ Island	■ Submerged reef	■ Shore	
	■ Wreck	■ Shallow water	■ Deep water	
Conditions at site:	■ Current	■ Swell	■ Wind chop	
	■ Tide changes	■ Boat traffic	■ Good visibility	
	■ Fair visibility	□ Poor visibility		
Dive time:	■ In-coming tide	■ Out-going tide		
	■ Spring tide	■ Neap tide	■ Slack tide	
Underwater terrain:	■ Drop offs	■ Gutters	■ Patch reefs	
	■ Sand & rubble	■ Rocky reef	■ Flat bottom	
	■ Low profile reef	□ Coral reef	■ Slope	
	□ Caves	□ Swim-throughs	■ Silty bottom	
Marine life:	■ Kelp	■ Sea grass	■ Sponges	□ Corals
	□ Sea whips	■ Sea fans	□ Black coral	■ Soft corals
	■ Anemones	■ Fan worms	■ Bryozoans	□ Brachiopods
	■ Crays	■ Crabs	■ Shells	□ Commensal shrimps
	■ Nudibranchs	■ Cuttles	■ Scallops	■ Abalone
	■ Sea stars	■ Basket stars	■ Sea urchins	■ Feather stars
	■ Ascidians	□ Sea lions	■ Dolphins	□ Turtles
	□ Sharks	■ Fish	□ Numerous fish	□ Abundant fish
Experience level:	■ Pupil	■ Beginner	■ Intermediate	■ Advanced
Dive site rating:	□ Excellent	■ Very good	□ Fair	■ Photography
Management of resources:	■ Marine reserve	■ Protected species	■ Quotas	■ Collecting

Service: KADINA MARINE & AUTO CENTRE
Air only, local dive site information.

Contact:
BP Service Station
29 Francis Terrace, Kadinay SA 5554
Phone: (088) 21 1225

Service: E.J. BRAUND & SONS
Air only.

Contact:
E.J. Braund & Sons
2 Stansbury Road, Yorketown SA 5576
Phone: (088) 52 1005

Service: BRAUNDS CARAVAN PARK
Air only.

Contact:
Braunds Caravan Park
Foreshore Davies Terrace, Port Victoria SA 5573
Phone: (088) 34 2012

Spending most of its daylight hours beneath the sand, the lightning volute hunts other molluscs under cover of darkness.

Cradled in a death grip by the predatory granular sea star, there is no hope for this bivalve and soon it will be eaten.

SIR JOSEPH BANKS GROUP

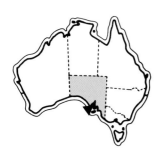

Situated off South Bay on the western side of Spencer Gulf some 628 kilometres from Adelaide, the Sir Joesph Banks Group is comprised of eighteen islands, seventeen of which have been proclaimed wildlife sanctuaries. The entire area abounds with sea life, much of which is only plentiful around these islands. The waters surrounding the islands are mostly shallow and clear, making for excellent diving conditions, beautiful sea grass meadows and broken bottom reefs rich in species.

Charter Boats:

Sea Jade (6 divers)
Alpaca (8 divers)

Contact:
Seajade Charters (Air Filling Station)
2 Pfitzner Street, Tumby Bay SA 5605
Phone: (086) 88 2098, A/H (086) 88 2424

Remarks: It is a pleasure diving around these islands; no depth to worry about, or currents to speak of, the sand on the bottom is shell grit and white (with a coating of brown or green algae in the summer months) and there are lots of things to find. Like many places in South Australia, the fish are fairly wary of divers.

GENERAL INFORMATION

Best times of the year:	■ Summer	■ Winter	□ Spring	☑ Autumn
Typical weather:	□ Excellent	□	□	□
	■ Very good	■	□	□
	□ Average	□	□	□
	□ Fair	□	■	■
Accommodation available:	■ Camping	□ Hostel	■ Hotel	■ Motel
Airport:	■ Light aircraft	□ Jet	□ International	□ Helicopter

DIVE SITE GUIDE

Access:	■ Boat ramp	■ Charter boat	□ Air	
Dive methods:	■ Scuba	■ Hookah	■ Snorkel	■ Snorkel diving
Types of diving:	■ Boat	□ Jetty	□ Shore	
Description of dive site:	■ Island	■ Submerged reef	□ Shore	
	□ Wreck	■ Shallow water	□ Deep water	
Conditions at site:	□ Current	■ Swell	■ Wind chop	
	□ Tide changes	□ Boat traffic	■ Good visibility	
	□ Fair visibility	□ Poor visibility		
Dive time:	■ In-coming tide	■ Out-going tide		
	■ Spring tide	■ Neap tide	■ Slack tide	
Underwater terrain:	□ Drop offs	■ Gutters	■ Patch reefs	
	■ Sand & rubble	■ Rocky reef	■ Flat bottom	
	■ Low profile reef	□ Coral reef	□ Slope	
	□ Caves	□ Swim-throughs	□ Silty bottom	
Marine life:	■ Kelp	■ Sea grass	■ Sponges	■ Corals
	□ Sea whips	■ Sea fans	□ Black coral	■ Soft corals
	■ Anemones	■ Fan worms	■ Bryozoans	□ Brachiopods
	■ Crays	■ Crabs	■ Shells	□ Commensal shrimps
	■ Nudibranchs	■ Cuttles	□ Scallops	■ Abalone
	■ Sea stars	□ Basket stars	■ Sea urchins	■ Feather stars
	■ Ascidians	■ Sea lions	■ Dolphins	□ Turtles
	■ Sharks	■ Fish	□ Numerous fish	□ Abundant fish
Experience level:	■ Pupil	■ Beginner	■ Intermediate	■ Advanced
Dive site rating:	■ Excellent	□ Very good	□ Fair	□ Photography
Management of resources:	■ Marine reserve	■ Protected species	■ Quotas	■ Collecting

Easy prey to spearfishermen, the long-snouted boarfish is becoming less familiar around inshore reefs.

PORT LINCOLN

Set on the foreshores of Boston Bay (Australia's largest natural harbour) on the southern tip of the Eyre Peninsula 650 kilometres west of Adelaide, is Port Lincoln. A city of 12,000 people, it is the traditional home of South Australia's tuna fishing industry and, more recently, centre of the abalone industry. Unfortunately Port Lincoln is perhaps best known as the base for white pointer shark feeding frenzy expeditions to Dangerous Reef, some 25 kilometres out into Spencer Gulf.

Port Lincoln has some very good shallow-water shore dives and some excellent boat diving country, especially around the many offshore islands such as Thistle, Wedge and the famous (or infamous) Neptunes. The islands at the mouth of Spencer Gulf are all subject

The firebrick sea star is more inclined to inhabit reefs below 20 metres.

to strong tidal movement and big seas though many are large enough to have a sheltered side. There is so much potential diving territory that it is advisable to check with local diving facilities to find out where to go for the best dives during the conditions present at the time of your visit.

Service:

PORT LINCOLN SKINDIVING & SURFING
PADI instruction, equipment sales, service, gear hire, air, local advice on dive sites.

Contact:
Port Lincoln Skindiving & Surfing
43 Mortlock Terrace, Port Lincoln SA 5606
Phone: (086) 82 4428

Remarks:

Yes, white pointer sharks exist and Port Lincoln is the closest dive site area to where they are lured in from the outer sea to be stars in the multi-million dollar profit making horror shows and the lucrative 'Dive with A Great White' shark cage sessions run for well-heeled diving tourists. What of the people in the area who just go diving because they enjoy it? What of the great whites that are left after all the filming is over and the boats have gone home? What of the future growth of diving as a sport in places where great whites have taken snorkellers? These questions remain unanswered.

GENERAL INFORMATION

Best times of the year:	■ Summer	■ Winter	□ Spring	◪ Autumn
Typical weather:	■ Excellent	□	□	□
	□ Very good	■	□	■
	□ Average	□	■	□
	□ Fair	□	□	□
Accommodation available:	■ Camping	□ Hostel	■ Hotel	■ Motel
Airport:	■ Light aircraft	□ Jet	□ International	□ Helicopter

DIVE SITE GUIDE

Access:	■ Boat ramp	■ Charter boat	■ Air	
Dive methods:	■ Scuba	■ Hookah	■ Snorkel	■ Snorkel diving
Types of diving:	■ Boat	■ Jetty	■ Shore	
Description of dive site:	■ Island	■ Submerged reef	■ Shore	
	□ Wreck	■ Shallow water	■ Deep water	
Conditions at site:	■ Current	■ Swell	■ Wind chop	
	■ Tide changes	□ Boat traffic	■ Good visibility	
	□ Fair visibility	□ Poor visibility		
Dive time:	■ In-coming tide	■ Out-going tide		
	■ Spring tide	■ Neap tide	■ Slack tide	
Underwater terrain:	■ Drop offs	■ Gutters	■ Patch reefs	
	■ Sand & rubble	■ Rocky reef	■ Flat bottom	
	■ Low profile reef	□ Coral reef	■ Slope	
	■ Caves	□ Swim-throughs	□ Silty bottom	
Marine life:	■ Kelp	■ Sea grass	■ Sponges	■ Corals
	■ Sea whips	■ Sea fans	■ Black coral	■ Soft corals
	■ Anemones	■ Fan worms	■ Bryozoans	□ Brachiopods
	■ Crays	■ Crabs	■ Shells	□ Commensal shrimps
	■ Nudibranchs	■ Cuttles	□ Scallops	■ Abalone
	■ Sea stars	■ Basket stars	■ Sea urchins	■ Feather stars
	■ Ascidians	■ Sea lions	■ Dolphins	■ Whales
	■ Sharks	■ Fish	□ Numerous fish	□ Abundant fish
Experience level:	■ Pupil	■ Beginner	■ Intermediate	■ Advanced
Dive site rating:	□ Excellent	■ Very good	□ Fair	□ Photography
Management of resources:	■ Marine reserve	■ Protected species	■ Quotas	■ Collecting

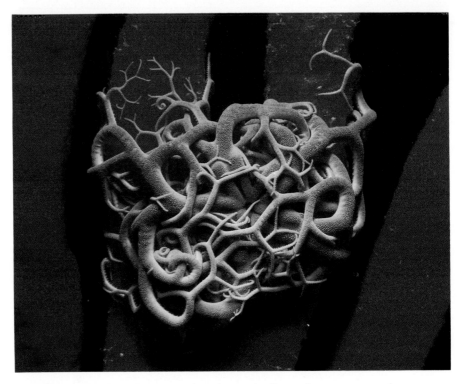

During the day Erna's basket star curls up in a protective pad on sponges and gorgonian sea fans.

GREAT AUSTRALIAN BIGHT

Between Port Lincoln and the Western Australian border (some 1200 kilometres) there are no air services, dive services, or charter boat services. Shore diving is possible in many areas, and boats can be launched at Elliston, Port Kenny, Streaky Bay, Smokey Bay and Ceduna. The majority of the diving around this part of the country is done by professional spearfishermen, amateur spearfishermen and abalone divers who dare to enter the inhospitable offshore reefs for the ocean's riches. Names like Avoid Bay, Coffin Bay and Anxious Bay don't give you much confidence, especially if you stand on the rugged limestone cliffs looking down into the clear water and realize that you are going to be the only diver underwater for hundreds of kilometres.

The Investigator group of islands off Elliston has some good diving but the weather must be right, as for most of the year the islands are pounded by huge seas and it is deep. Further up the coast off Ceduna, the Nuyts Archipelago has a number of interesting dive locations; Isles of St Francis, West Island, Egg Island, Masilon Island and Fenelon Island are all diveable, with underwater terrain and conditions ranging from 20 metre visibility in dense meadows of sea grass shallows, down to giant boulder seascapes at 64 metres where carpets of red algae, sea fans, huge rock lobsters and strong currents are all part of the dim, shadowless underwater depths.

Service: None.

Remarks: From Ceduna onwards to the Western Australian border, it's dry, semi-arid country, which then gives way to the Nullabor (without trees), and the 130 metre high limestone cliffs of the diver's no man's land.

GENERAL INFORMATION

Best times of the year:	□ Summer	■ Winter	□ Spring	■ Autumn
Typical weather:	□ Excellent	□	□	□
	□ Very good	■	□	■
	■ Average	□	■	□
	□ Fair	□	□	□
Accommodation available:	■ Camping	□ Hostel	■ Hotel	■ Motel
Airport:	■ Light aircraft	□ Jet	□ International	□ Helicopter

DIVE SITE GUIDE

Access:	■ Boat ramp	□ Charter boat	□ Air	
Dive methods:	■ Scuba	■ Hookah	■ Snorkel	■ Snorkel diving
Types of diving:	■ Boat	□ Jetty	■ Shore	
Description of dive site:	■ Island	■ Submerged reef	■ Shore	
	□ Wreck	■ Shallow water	■ Deep water	
Conditions at site:	■ Current	■ Swell	■ Wind chop	
	■ Tide changes	□ Boat traffic	□ Good visibility	
	■ Fair visibility	■ Poor visibility		
Dive time:	■ In-coming tide	■ Out-going tide		
	■ Spring tide	■ Neap tide	■ Slack tide	
Underwater terrain:	■ Drop offs	■ Gutters	■ Patch reefs	
	■ Sand & rubble	■ Rocky reef	■ Flat bottom	
	■ Low profile reef	□ Coral reef	■ Slope	
	□ Caves	□ Swim-throughs	□ Silty bottom	
Marine life:	■ Kelp	■ Sea grass	■ Sponges	□ Corals
	□ Sea whips	■ Sea fans	□ Black coral	■ Soft corals
	■ Anemones	■ Fan worms	■ Bryozoans	□ Brachiopods
	■ Crays	■ Crabs	■ Shells	□ Commensal shrimps
	■ Nudibranchs	□ Cuttles	■ Scallops	■ Abalone
	■ Sea stars	□ Basket stars	■ Sea urchins	■ Feather stars
	■ Ascidians	■ Sea lions	■ Dolphins	□ Turtles
	■ Sharks	■ Fish	□ Numerous fish	□ Abundant fish
Experience level:	□ Pupil	□ Beginner	■ Intermediate	■ Advanced
Dive site rating:	□ Excellent	□ Very good	■ Fair	□ Photography
Management of resources:	■ Marine reserve	■ Protected species	■ Quotas	■ Collecting

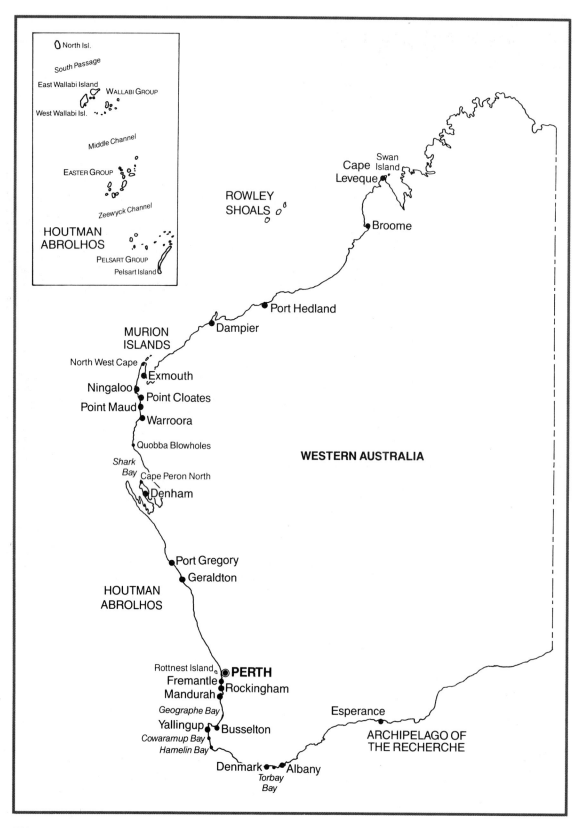

North Isl.

South Passage

East Wallabi Island

West Wallabi Isl.

WALLABI GROUP

Middle Channel

EASTER GROUP

Zeewyck Channel

HOUTMAN
ABROLHOS

PELSART GROUP

Pelsart Island

ROWLEY
SHOALS

Swan
Island

Cape
Leveque

Broome

Port Hedland

Dampier

MURION
ISLANDS

North West Cape

Exmouth

Ningaloo

Point Cloates

Point Maud

Warroora

Quobba Blowholes

*Shark
Bay* Cape Peron North

Denham

WESTERN AUSTRALIA

Port Gregory

Geraldton

HOUTMAN
ABROLHOS

Rottnest Island

PERTH

Fremantle

Rockingham

Mandurah

Geographe Bay

Esperance

Yallingup

Busselton

ARCHIPELAGO OF
THE RECHERCHE

Cowaramup Bay

Hamelin Bay

Denmark

Albany

*Torbay
Bay*

Diving
WESTERN AUSTRALIA

The town jetty at Esperance sports hundreds of pylons covered in rich growths of sessile marine life.

ESPERANCE

The present prosperity of Esperance was brought about by American foresight and ingenuity which has, by agronomist techniques, transformed millions of hectares of worthless farmland into a pastoral paradise. Esperance's 11,000 inhabitants also depend on wet fishing and on abalone and rock lobster fisheries.

Large tracts of land around Esperance are national parks. Cape le Grande National Park, Cape Arid National Park and Stoke's National Park have extensive intertidal zones that are also designated marine reserves.

Service: As of the time of this book's publication there are no professional dive facilities set up at Esperance, though air is available from locals with compressors. The nearest diving facility is at Albany, 479 kilometres west.

Charter Boat: *Flying Fish*
Twin hulled shark catamaran, half day and full day diving trips.

GENERAL INFORMATION

Best times of the year: ■ Summer ☐ Winter ☐ Spring ■ Autumn

Typical weather:
☐ Excellent ☐ ☐ ☐
■ Very good ☐ ☐ ■
☐ Average ☐ ☐ ☐
☐ Fair ■ ■ ☐

Accommodation available: ■ Camping ☐ Hostel ■ Hotel ■ Motel

Airport: ■ Light aircraft ■ Jet ☐ International ☐ Helicopter

DIVE SITE GUIDE

Access: ■ Boat ramp ■ Charter boat ■ Air

Dive methods: ■ Scuba ■ Hookah ☐ Snorkel ■ Snorkel diving

Types of diving: ■ Boat ■ Jetty ■ Shore

Description of dive site:
■ Island ■ Submerged reef ■ Shore
☐ Wreck ■ Shallow water ■ Deep water

Conditions at site:
■ Current ■ Swell ■ Wind chop
☐ Tide changes ☐ Boat traffic ■ Good visibility
■ Fair visibility ☐ Poor visibility

Dive time:
■ In-coming tide ■ Out-going tide
■ Spring tide ■ Neap tide ■ Slack tide

Underwater terrain:
■ Drop offs ■ Gutters ☐ Patch reefs
■ Sand & rubble ■ Rocky reef ☐ Flat bottom
■ Low profile reef ☐ Coral reef ■ Slope
☐ Caves ☐ Swim-throughs ☐ Silty bottom

Marine life:
■ Kelp ■ Sea grass ■ Sponges ■ Corals
☐ Sea whips ■ Sea fans ■ Black coral ■ Soft corals
■ Anemones ■ Fan worms ■ Bryozoans ☐ Brachiopods
■ Crays ■ Crabs ■ Shells ☐ Commensal shrimps
■ Nudibranchs ■ Cuttles ■ Scallops ■ Abalone
■ Sea stars ■ Basket stars ■ Sea urchins ■ Feather stars
■ Ascidians ■ Sea lions ■ Dolphins ☐ Turtles
■ Sharks ■ Fish ■ Numerous fish ☐ Abundant fish

Experience level: ☐ Pupil ■ Beginner ■ Intermediate ■ Advanced

Dive site rating: ■ Excellent ☐ Very good ☐ Fair ■ Photography

Management of resources: ☐ Marine reserve ■ Protected species ■ Quotas ■ Collecting

Contact:
Flying Fish Boat Charter
Phone: (090) 71 2940, A/H (090) 71 1924 for full details.

Remarks:

Gateway to the fabulous Recherche Archipelago, as a diving destination Esperance has been greatly underestimated. The diving around the Recherche islands may be scary at times, but it's spectacular country – granite gray and gorgeous underwater. The town jetty has a thousand pylons covered with a kaleidoscope of sea life. The last thing I ever expected to see in south Western Australia was 3 metre high coral bommies, but at Esperance they exist.

Black coral trees may grow up to 2 metres high, their branches entwined with predatory snake stars.

ALBANY – TORBAY – DENMARK

Situated in a saddle on the northern side of Princess Royal Harbour within King George Sound, Albany is the oldest settlement in Western Australia. In its early days it flourished, first as a coaling station and then as a whaling centre. The legacy of this whaling past can be seen today at the Whale-world Museum, and by divers who visit

Plate corals 2 metres across grow in the waters of southern Australia. Here a large plate coral has grown around a living sponge.

the 52 metre whale chaser *Cheynes III* which lies in 21 metres of sheltered water off the west end of Michaelmas Island, 12 kilometres out from the town of Albany.

Denmark, 53 kilometres west of Albany on Wilson Inlet, is the launching place for boats going out to such memorable dive sites as William Bay, and to fantastic Stanley Island. What a place! Stanley Island has drop offs, huge clouds of swallowtail nannygai, giant 2 metre high gorgonians, coral dishes you can sit in, black coral trees, sponges and giant blue groper wrasse. There is *never* enough bottom time.

At Torbay Head, 35 kilometres west of Albany, the scene is different. Reminiscent of the granite boulder formations which stud the entire southwest shorelines, giant boulders covered in encrusting lithothamnion algae lie all over the bottom. There are huge crevasse-like swim-throughs where sea fan gorgonians sweep out into the current, with sponges, corals and many species of fish.

Service:

SOUTH COAST DIVERS SUPPLIES
A complete dive shop operation with the only air available in the area. FAUI instruction, open 6 days a week for equipment sales, service and gear hire. Local dives organised, mostly small boat diving.

Contact:
South Coast Divers Supplies
115 Stead Road, Albany WA 6330
Phone: (098) 41 5068, A/H (098) 44 4042

Remarks: The entire southwest remains virtually unknown underwater, few surveys have been undertaken and, due to limited access and services and the wild, wild country, it is liable to stay that way for years to come. However, if you have a bit of 'go' and pick your times, it can be magnificent diving and offers superb water for underwater photography, with species galore.

GENERAL INFORMATION

Best times of the year:	■ Summer	□ Winter	□ Spring	□ Autumn
Typical weather:	■ Excellent	□	□	□
	□ Very good	□	□	□
	□ Average	■	■	□
	□ Fair	□	□	■
Accommodation available:	■ Camping	■ Hostel	■ Hotel	■ Motel
Airport:	■ Light aircraft	■ Jet	□ International	□ Helicopter

DIVE SITE GUIDE

Access:	■ Boat ramp	□ Charter boat	■ Air	
Dive methods:	■ Scuba	■ Hookah	■ Snorkel	■ Snorkel diving
Types of diving:	■ Boat	■ Jetty	■ Shore	
Description of dive site:	■ Island	■ Submerged reef	■ Shore	
	■ Wreck	■ Shallow water	■ Deep water	
Conditions at site:	■ Current	■ Swell	■ Wind chop	
	■ Tide changes	□ Boat traffic	■ Good visibility	
	□ Fair visibility	□ Poor visibility		
Dive time:	■ In-coming tide	■ Out-going tide		
	■ Spring tide	■ Neap tide	■ Slack tide	
Underwater terrain:	■ Drop offs	■ Gutters	□ Patch reefs	
	■ Sand & rubble	■ Rocky reef	□ Flat bottom	
	■ Low profile reef	□ Coral reef	■ Slope	
	■ Caves	■ Swim-throughs	□ Silty bottom	
Marine life:	■ Kelp	■ Sea grass	■ Sponges	■ Corals
	□ Sea whips	■ Sea fans	■ Black coral	■ Soft corals
	□ Anemones	□ Fan worms	■ Bryozoans	□ Brachiopods
	■ Crays	■ Crabs	■ Shells	□ Commensal shrimps
	■ Nudibranchs	■ Cuttles	■ Scallops	■ Abalone
	■ Sea stars	■ Basket stars	■ Sea urchins	■ Feather stars
	■ Ascidians	□ Sea lions	■ Dolphins	■ Whales
	■ Sharks	■ Fish	□ Numerous fish	■ Abundant fish
Experience level:	□ Pupil	□ Beginner	■ Intermediate	■ Advanced
Dive site rating:	■ Excellent	□ Very good	□ Fair	■ Photography
Management of resources:	■ Marine reserve	□ Protected species	□ Quotas	■ Collecting

Canal Rocks, some 50 kilometres south of Busselton near Yallingup, has a good launching ramp for trailer boats, providing access to a range of excellent dive sites.

HAMELIN BAY – COWARAMUP BAY – YALLINGUP

A good boat ramp exists at Hamelin Bay, in quite sheltered water. Hamelin Bay has a beautiful white sandy sea floor, patch reefs, great quantities of fish, a few abalone and crays. It's interesting to note that many divers in the south west of Australia use a look-box to

Big blue groper-wrasse, though not prevalent on inshore areas, are often observed on offshore reefs.

check over the side for reefs. The look-box originated with hand-line fishermen. Due to the clarity of the water, by using a look-box the reefs can be seen even 20 to 30 metres below. In the rest of Australia, divers just hang over the side with their masks on to see where a good reef is.

This coastline can produce very rough seas, remember: don't take chances. Rugged shoreline, surf beaches and cliffs are typical scenery on the way up the coast from Cape Leeuwin to Cape Naturaliste. Due to the nature of the terrain only a few places are suitable for diving.

Canal Rocks is a good snorkel and an enjoyable shallow-water dive, if the swells are down. The launching ramp is a good one and boat diving offshore is excellent. There is access for scuba diving and snorkelling at Yallingup and Cowaramup Bay. The entire sea is teeming with life: crays, abalone, big blue groper, wrasse and flathead with giant limpets on the rocks.

Service: No diving services exist in these areas.

GENERAL INFORMATION

Best times of the year:	■ Summer	☐ Winter	■ Spring	■ Autumn
Typical weather:	■ Excellent	☐	■	■
	☐ Very good	☐	☐	☐
	☐ Average	☐	☐	☐
	☐ Fair	■	☐	☐
Accommodation available:	■ Camping	☐ Hostel	☐ Hotel	☐ Motel
Airport:	☐ Light aircraft	☐ Jet	☐ International	☐ Helicopter

DIVE SITE GUIDE

Access:	■ Boat ramp	☐ Charter boat	☐ Air	
Dive methods:	■ Scuba	■ Hookah	■ Snorkel	■ Snorkel diving
Types of diving:	■ Boat	☐ Jetty	■ Shore	
Description of dive site:	☐ Island	■ Submerged reef	■ Shore	
	☐ Wreck	■ Shallow water	■ Deep water	
Conditions at site:	☐ Current	■ Swell	■ Wind chop	
	■ Tide changes	☐ Boat traffic	■ Good visibility	
	■ Fair visibility	☐ Poor visibility		
Dive time:	■ In-coming tide	■ Out-going tide		
	■ Spring tide	■ Neap tide	■ Slack tide	
Underwater terrain:	■ Drop offs	■ Gutters	■ Patch reefs	
	■ Sand & rubble	■ Rocky reef	■ Flat bottom	
	■ Low profile reef	☐ Coral reef	■ Slope	
	☐ Caves	☐ Swim-throughs	☐ Silty bottom	
Marine life:	■ Kelp	■ Sea grass	■ Sponges	■ Corals
	☐ Sea whips	■ Sea fans	☐ Black coral	■ Soft corals
	■ Anemones	☐ Fan worms	■ Bryozoans	☐ Brachiopods
	■ Crays	■ Crabs	■ Shells	☐ Commensal shrimps
	■ Nudibranchs	☐ Cuttles	■ Scallops	■ Abalone
	■ Sea stars	■ Basket stars	■ Sea urchins	■ Feather stars
	■ Ascidians	☐ Sea lions	■ Dolphins	☐ Turtles
	■ Sharks	■ Fish	☐ Numerous fish	■ Abundant fish
Experience level:	☐ Pupil	☐ Beginner	■ Intermediate	■ Advanced
Dive site rating:	☐ Excellent	■ Very good	■ Fair	■ Photography
Management of resources:	☐ Marine reserve	☐ Protected species	☐ Quotas	■ Collecting

Snorkelling for the very
beautiful Friend's cowry
off Busselton reefs.

BUSSELTON – GEOGRAPHE BAY

Founded in 1832, Busselton is a sleepy little seaside resort sheltering in the reaches of Geographe Bay. It's a beautiful piece of Australia: clean clear water teaming with life and boasting the longest wooden jetty in the Southern Hemisphere. The jetty was originally built to service the timber industry but has been disused for years. Go and see the Oceanarium and Bannamah Wildlife Park.

Service:

BUSSELTON DIVING SPECIALISTS
The only dive shop between Busselton and Mandurah, this facility is a complete service. It offers FAUI instruction, air 5½ days a week, equipment sales, service and gear hire. Dive trips can be organised through the shop and it also sells fishing, surfing and mixed sporting gear as well as having a hairdressing salon.

The sea grass meadows in Geographe Bay's sheltered crystal clear waters abound with life, like this Gurnard perch.

Contact:
Busselton Diving Specialists
99 Queen Street, Busselton WA 6280
Phone: (097) 52 2096, A/H (097) 52 3034

Remarks:

I'm sure I must have spent at least fifty per cent of the three months I took diving the Geographe Bay area under Busselton Jetty. Thousands of pylons drip with every coloured marine invertebrate you could imagine and are surrounded by schools of fish taking advantage of the jetty shadow; all in clear, clear water 4 to 7 metres deep.

The rest of Geographe Bay is just as good; calm and clear with hectares and hectares of bright-green sea grass meadows, giant red sponges bedecking the offshore reefs and, in Eagle Bay, 5 metre high coral bommies.

GENERAL INFORMATION

Best times of the year:	■ Summer	□ Winter	■ Spring	■ Autumn
Typical weather:	■ Excellent	□	■	■
	□ Very good	■	□	□
	□ Average	□	□	□
	□ Fair	□	□	□
Accommodation available:	■ Camping	■ Hostel	■ Hotel	■ Motel
Airport:	□ Light aircraft	□ Jet	□ International	□ Helicopter

DIVE SITE GUIDE

Access:	■ Boat ramp	■ Charter boat	■ Air	
Dive methods:	■ Scuba	■ Hookah	■ Snorkel	■ Snorkel diving
Types of diving:	■ Boat	■ Jetty	■ Shore	
Description of dive site:	□ Island	■ Submerged reef	■ Shore	
	□ Wreck	■ Shallow water	■ Deep water	
Conditions at site:	□ Current	□ Swell	■ Wind chop	
	□ Tide changes	□ Boat traffic	■ Good visibility	
	□ Fair visibility	□ Poor visibility		
Dive time:	■ In-coming tide	■ Out-going tide		
	■ Spring tide	■ Neap tide	■ Slack tide	
Underwater terrain:	□ Drop offs	□ Gutters	■ Patch reefs	
	■ Sand & rubble	■ Rocky reef	■ Flat bottom	
	■ Low profile reef	□ Coral reef	□ Slope	
	□ Caves	□ Swim-throughs	□ Silty bottom	
Marine life:	■ Kelp	■ Sea grass	■ Sponges	■ Corals
	□ Sea whips	■ Sea fans	□ Black coral	■ Soft corals
	■ Anemones	■ Fan worms	■ Bryozoans	□ Brachiopods
	■ Crays	■ Crabs	■ Shells	□ Commensal shrimps
	■ Nudibranchs	■ Cuttles	■ Scallops	■ Abalone
	■ Sea stars	■ Basket stars	■ Sea urchins	■ Feather stars
	■ Ascidians	□ Sea lions	■ Dolphins	□ Turtles
	■ Sharks	■ Fish	■ Numerous fish	□ Abundant fish
Experience level:	■ Pupil	■ Beginner	■ Intermediate	□ Advanced
Dive site rating:	■ Excellent	□ Very good	□ Fair	■ Photography
Management of resources:	□ Marine reserve	□ Protected species	□ Quotas	■ Collecting

Shore entries in the quiet waters off Woodman's Groyne make this area an excellent training site for underwater naturalist courses.

MANDURAH

Regarded today as Perth's holiday playground rather than the quiet seaside village it really is, Mandurah sits at the entrance to the Peel Inlet some 78 kilometres south of Perth.

Service:

DAVID BUDD WATERSPORTS
Full dive shop facility, FAUI/PADI instruction, open 7 days a week for air, equipment sales, service and gear hire. Underwater photography specialists. Local and overseas dive trips, charter boat *Toucan*.

Contact:
David Budd Watersports
3 The Plaza, Mandurah WA 6210
Phone: (095) 35 1520

Remarks:

Mandurah offers some good diving offshore on the Five Fathom Bank, Murray Reef, Bouvard Reef and the *James Service* wreck site. Boat dives are recommended, as the area is open to the Indian Ocean swells, which can make diving from shore somewhat hazardous. Peel Inlet is suitable for snorkelling. For general information on Mandurah see the guide to Fremantle – Rockhampton on page 189.

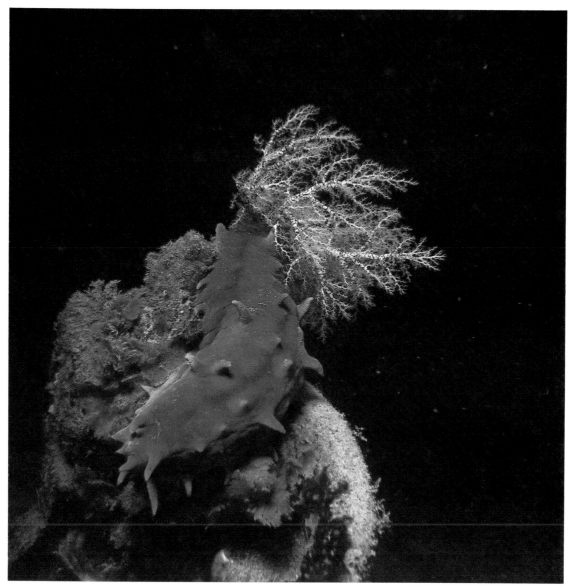

A common resident of Cockburn Sound is the four-sided sea cucumber, seen here with its feeding tentacles extended.

FREMANTLE – ROCKINGHAM

Until recently downtown Fremantle looked as though it had seen better days, despite being the chief port in Western Australia. But with Alan Bond (Bondy) bringing back the America's Cup and mounting the subsequent challenge, Fremantle has changed into a modern-looking up-to-date city with a skyline reaching for the stars. Neverthe-less it still retains a lot of old-world charm. Centre for the Western

Australian Museum's Maritime Archaeological Division, Fremantle Museum has a maritime display that is a credit to all who have contributed.

Service:

DIVERS HIRE AND SUPPLY
Open for air 7 days a week, complete dive shop facilities, FAUI instruction and hire services which include cameras and metal detectors. Recompression chamber, dive club, boat trips and charters arranged.

Contact:
Divers Hire and Supply
71A Sterling Highway, North Fremantle WA 6159
Phone: (09) 335 9097

Service:

DIVER'S EMPORIUM
Complete dive shop, equipment sales, service, gear hire, air, boat dives and charters arranged. Fully qualified instructors.

Contact:
Diver's Emporium
33 Canning Highway, East Fremantle WA 6158
Phone: (09) 339 5344

Service:

MALIBU DIVING
Regular dive trips to local wrecks and reefs; FAUI/PADI instruction to all levels, fully catered dive shop, air 7 days a week, equipment sales, gear hire and test station.

Contact:
Malibu Diving
43 Rockingham Road, Rockingham WA 6168
Phone: (095) 27 5842

Charter Boat:

Talma

Contact:
Phone: (095) 27 5842, A/H(095) 27 5892

Remarks:

I was very impressed with the diving in and around the Cockburn Sound area: fantastic limestone caverns, swim-throughs, and acres of sponges in colours and shapes the like of which I'd never seen before. From Sorrento reefs down to Carnac Island and to Garden Island are caves, caves and more caves, with stacks of invertebrates. Hall's Bank, City Beach, even Palm Beach Jetty with its silt-covered bottom, offer incredible fan worms and sea cucumbers. The Sound is sometimes scary in a small boat, especially when the sea breeze comes in early and the swell is up, but underwater it is diving at its best. Whether it's snorkelling with the sea lions at Carnac Island or with the seahorses at the Rockingham Jetty, it's all amazingly good stuff! Remember, all the islands in Shoalwater Bay are wildlife sanctuaries, observe the privacy of the inhabitants and take care.

GENERAL INFORMATION

Best times of the year:	■ Summer	□ Winter	■ Spring	■ Autumn
Typical weather:	■ Excellent	□	■	□
	□ Very good	□	□	□
	□ Average	■	□	□
	□ Fair	□	□	□
Accommodation available:	■ Camping	■ Hostel	■ Hotel	■ Motel
Airport:	□ Light aircraft	□ Jet	□ International	□ Helicopter

DIVE SITE GUIDE

Access:	■ Boat ramp	■ Charter boat	■ Air	
Dive methods:	■ Scuba	■ Hookah	■ Snorkel	■ Snorkel diving
Types of diving:	■ Boat	■ Jetty	■ Shore	
Description of dive site:	■ Island	■ Submerged reef	■ Shore	
	■ Wreck	■ Shallow water	■ Deep water	
Conditions at site:	□ Current	■ Swell	■ Wind chop	
	□ Tide changes	■ Boat traffic	■ Good visibility	
	■ Fair visibility	■ Poor visibility		
Dive time:	■ In-coming tide	■ Out-going tide		
	■ Spring tide	■ Neap tide	■ Slack tide	
Underwater terrain:	□ Drop offs	■ Gutters	■ Patch reefs	
	■ Sand & rubble	■ Rocky reef	■ Flat bottom	
	■ Low profile reef	□ Coral reef	■ Slope	
	■ Caves	■ Swim-throughs	■ Silty bottom	
Marine life:	■ Kelp	■ Sea grass	■ Sponges	■ Corals
	□ Sea whips	■ Sea fans	□ Black coral	■ Soft corals
	■ Anemones	■ Fan worms	■ Bryozoans	□ Brachiopods
	■ Crays	■ Crabs	■ Shells	□ Commensal shrimps
	■ Nudibranchs	■ Cuttles	■ Scallops	■ Abalone
	■ Sea stars	□ Basket stars	■ Sea urchins	■ Feather stars
	■ Ascidians	■ Sea lions	■ Dolphins	■ Turtles
	■ Sharks	■ Fish	■ Numerous fish	□ Abundant fish
Experience level:	■ Pupil	■ Beginner	■ Intermediate	■ Advanced
Dive site rating:	□ Excellent	■ Very good	■ Fair	■ Photography
Management of resources:	■ Marine reserve	■ Protected species	■ Quotas	■ Collecting

The reef platform at Fishhook Bay, Rottnest Island, is a perfect place for snorkelling.

PERTH – ROTTNEST ISLAND

With a population close to 850,000, Perth is situated on the Swan River at the base of Mt. Eliza and is the capital of Western Australia. Perth is not actually on the coast; the closest port is Fremantle some 19 kilometres away.

One of Australia's most beautiful and unhurried cities, Perth supports a fairly strong diving contingent and a number of facilities.

Brightly coloured sponges are a feature of the reefs off Rottnest Island.

Service: AUSTRALASIAN DIVING CENTRE
Complete dive shop, FAUI/PADI dive instruction, equipment sales, service, gear hire, air 6 days a week, local and overseas dive trips.

Contact:
Australasian Diving Centre
259 Stirling Highway, Claremont WA 6010
Phone: (09) 384 3552

Service: SCUBA 2
PADI 5 star facility and a PADI 5 star instruction centre. Equipment sales, service, gear hire, complete scuba services, air, local and overseas dive trips. Can arrange charter boats.

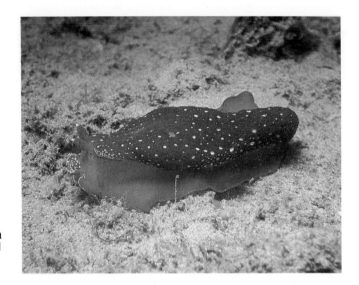

Inhabiting areas of soft bottom the variable armina is a burrowing species and as such is rarely seen by divers.

Contact:
Scuba 2
2 O'Beirne Street, Claremont WA 6010
Phone: (09) 384 8638, *or*

Contact:
Scuba 2 (Second Hand Gear Division)
Unit 102/396 Scarborough Beach, Osborne Park WA 6017
Phone: (09) 444 9442

Service:

PERTH DIVING ACADEMY
Full dive shop services, air, test station, open 7 days a week, FAUI instruction to all levels. Dive trips and charters available.

Contact:
Perth Diving Academy
281 Wanneroo Road, Nollamara WA 6061
Phone: (09) 344 1562

Remarks:

Rottnest Island is about 18 kilometres out of the Swan River and, with the modern high-speed 'ferry' services, divers can carry their gear over and dive off the rocks. However, it is much more rewarding going by one of the many dive charter vessels available. From the inshore reefs to the offshore reefs and wrecks, Rottnest offers all the diving you could wish for. Good visibility, caves, swim-throughs, sponge gardens filled with shapes and colours of every hue, plate corals, fish life and more, including big gorgonian fans, bright yellow bunches of zoanthids, and plenty of nudibranchs. The area is a marine reserve and care must be taken to comply with regulations.

GENERAL INFORMATION

Best times of the year: ■ Summer ☐ Winter ■ Spring ■ Autumn

Typical weather:

	Summer	Winter	Spring	Autumn
Excellent	■	☐	■	☐
Very good	☐	☐	☐	■
Average	☐	■	☐	☐
Fair	☐	☐	☐	☐

Accommodation available: ■ Camping ■ Hostel ■ Hotel ■ Motel

Airport: ■ Light aircraft ■ Jet ■ International ■ Helicopter

DIVE SITE GUIDE

Access: ■ Boat ramp ■ Charter boat ■ Air

Dive methods: ■ Scuba ■ Hookah ■ Snorkel ■ Snorkel diving

Types of diving: ■ Boat ☐ Jetty ■ Shore

Description of dive site: ■ Island ■ Submerged reef ■ Shore
■ Wreck ■ Shallow water ■ Deep water

Conditions at site: ☐ Current ■ Swell ■ Wind chop
☐ Tide changes ■ Boat traffic ■ Good visibility
■ Fair visibility ☐ Poor visibility

Dive time: ■ In-coming tide ☐ Out-going tide
■ Spring tide ■ Neap tide ■ Slack tide

Underwater terrain: ■ Drop offs ■ Gutters ■ Patch reefs
■ Sand & rubble ■ Rocky reef ■ Flat bottom
■ Low profile reef ☐ Coral reef ■ Slope
■ Caves ■ Swim-throughs ☐ Silty bottom

Marine life: ■ Kelp ■ Sea grass ■ Sponges ■ Corals
■ Sea whips ■ Sea fans ☐ Black coral ■ Soft corals
■ Anemones ■ Fan worms ■ Bryozoans ☐ Brachiopods
■ Crays ■ Crabs ■ Shells ■ Commensal shrimps

■ Nudibranchs ■ Cuttles ■ Scallops ■ Abalone
■ Sea stars ■ Basket stars ■ Sea urchins ■ Feather stars
■ Ascidians ■ Sea lions ■ Dolphins ■ Turtles
■ Sharks ■ Fish ■ Numerous fish ☐ Abundant fish

Experience level: ■ Pupil ■ Beginner ■ Intermediate ■ Advanced

Dive site rating: ■ Excellent ■ Very good ☐ Fair ■ Photography

Management of resources: ■ Marine reserve ■ Protected species ■ Quotas ■ Collecting

Snorkelling on a cannon from the 17th-century Dutch ship, the *Zeewyck*, wrecked at Gun Island in the Houtman Abrolhos, off Geraldton.

GERALDTON – HOUTMAN ABROLHOS

Geraldton is situated 400 kilometres north of Perth and, with an enterprising community bordering on 20,000, is one of the largest coastal towns in Western Australia. Centre of the rock lobster fishing industry of south western Australia, the 'Sun City', as it is sometimes called, is the point of departure to the Houtman Abrolhos. There are some quite good dive sites around Geraldton along with clear shallow areas for snorkelling. Check with services for local advice.

Service:

SCUBAQUATIC DIVING SCHOOL
FAUI instruction, air, local diving, dive trips organised.

Contact:
Scubaquatic Diving School
PO Box 42, Dongara WA 6525
Phone: (099) 55 2055

Service:

GERALDTON SPORTS
Air 7 days a week, dive equipment sales.

Contact:
Phone: (099) 21 3664

Service:

P.A.C.E. SPORTS
FAUI instruction, air, equipment sales; charter trips can be arranged
for groups.

Contact:
P.A.C.E. Sports
188 Marine Terrace, Geraldton WA 6530
Phone: (099) 21 4229

Remarks:

Names like *Batavia* and *Zeewyck* are now well entrenched in the
archaeology of maritime Australia. These early Dutch ships and
many others were wrecked on the Houtman Abrolhos.

Although I am more interested in the preservation of our living
underwater riches for the future than in studying our dead past,
I must admit I found it thrilling the first time I dived on a real
cannon off the *Zeewyck*.

The Houtman Abrolhos is comprised of three separate island reef
complexes: the Wallabi group is the most northern, with the Easter
group in the middle and then the Pelsart Island group to the south.
All these islands are wildlife sanctuaries and permission must be
obtained to land on them or to camp. The reason for doing so must
be in writing and a good one, unless you are accompanying a scheduled dive trip from an authorized diving facility or recognised organisation. Most of the wrecks themselves have now been removed
and are preserved in the Maritime Museum at Fremantle, but this
certainly does not detract from the diving.

The underwater scenery is magnificent, hectares and hectares
of coral formations, drop offs, slopes and terraces, lots of fish and
rock lobsters (which may not be taken by diving), 30 metres plus
visibility – the perfect place for underwater photography. There
are no services available on the islands whatsoever.

GENERAL INFORMATION

Best times of the year: ■ Summer ☑ Winter ☑ Spring ■ Autumn

Typical weather:

	Summer	Winter	Spring	Autumn
Excellent	□	□	□	□
Very good	■	□	□	■
Average	□	□	□	□
Fair	□	■	■	□

Accommodation available: ■ Camping ■ Hostel ■ Hotel ■ Motel

Airport: ■ Light aircraft ■ Jet □ International □ Helicopter

DIVE SITE GUIDE

Access: ■ Boat ramp □ Charter boat ■ Air

Dive methods: ■ Scuba ■ Hookah ■ Snorkel ■ Snorkel diving

Types of diving: ■ Boat □ Jetty □ Shore

Description of dive site: ■ Island ■ Submerged reef □ Shore
■ Wreck ■ Shallow water ■ Deep water

Conditions at site: ■ Current ■ Swell ■ Wind chop
■ Tide changes □ Boat traffic ■ Good visibility
■ Fair visibility □ Poor visibility

Dive time: ■ In-coming tide ■ Out-going tide
■ Spring tide ■ Neap tide ■ Slack tide

Underwater terrain: ■ Drop offs ■ Gutters ■ Patch reefs
■ Sand & rubble ■ Rocky reef ■ Flat bottom
■ Low profile reef ■ Coral reef ■ Slope
■ Caves ■ Swim-throughs □ Silty bottom

Marine life: ■ Kelp ■ Sea grass ■ Sponges ■ Corals
□ Sea whips ■ Sea fans □ Black coral ■ Soft corals
■ Anemones ■ Fan worms ■ Bryozoans □ Brachiopods
■ Crays ■ Crabs ■ Shells ■ Commensal shrimps

■ Nudibranchs ■ Cuttles □ Scallops ■ Abalone
■ Sea stars □ Basket stars ■ Sea urchins ■ Feather stars
■ Ascidians □ Sea lions ■ Dolphins ■ Turtles
■ Sharks ■ Fish □ Numerous fish □ Abundant fish

Experience level: ■ Pupil ■ Beginner ■ Intermediate ■ Advanced

Dive site rating: ■ Excellent □ Very good □ Fair ■ Photography

Management of resources: ■ Marine reserve ■ Protected species ■ Quotas ■ Collecting

The exquisite nudibranch lives in the sheltered waters within the Port Gregory lagoon.

PORT GREGORY

Nestled on the coast some 80 kilometres north of Geraldton is the sleepy little lagoon township of Port Gregory, with only caravan park or camping conveniences on location.

Service:

None (see Geraldton).

Remarks:

The remarkable thing about Port Gregory as far as the diver is concerned is that it has good safe, clear, shallow water for snorkellers, while out in the lagoon it is deep enough for scuba diving.

The other striking aspect of this place is the ease with which you can see two marine environments working in natural harmony side by side. In the warmer protected lagoon waters the fauna is tropical, with the corals, fishes and marine invertebrates having coral reef affinities, while on top of the outer barrier and on the surf side, the fauna and flora are of temperate origins.

To stand on the causeway separating the two and look from one side to the other makes you wonder if perhaps black is not really as very far away from white as we are led to believe. The entire area here is excellent for underwater photography.

197

The Western Australian jewfish inhabits the reefs in the more temperate waters outside the lagoon.

GENERAL INFORMATION

Best times of the year:	■ Summer	■ Winter	■ Spring	■ Autumn
Typical weather:	■ Excellent	■	■	■
	□ Very good	□	□	□
	□ Average	□	□	□
	□ Fair	□	□	□
Accommodation available:	■ Camping	□ Hostel	□ Hotel	□ Motel
Airport:	□ Light aircraft	□ Jet	□ International	□ Helicopter

DIVE SITE GUIDE

Access:	■ Boat ramp	□ Charter boat	□ Air	
Dive methods:	■ Scuba	■ Hookah	■ Snorkel	■ Snorkel diving
Types of diving:	■ Boat	□ Jetty	■ Shore	
Description of dive site:	□ Island	■ Submerged reef	■ Shore	
	□ Wreck	■ Shallow water	□ Deep water	
Conditions at site:	□ Current	□ Swell	■ Wind chop	
	□ Tide changes	■ Boat traffic	■ Good visibility	
	□ Fair visibility	□ Poor visibility		
Dive time:	■ In-coming tide	■ Out-going tide		
	■ Spring tide	■ Neap tide	■ Slack tide	
Underwater terrain:	□ Drop offs	□ Gutters	■ Patch reefs	
	■ Sand & rubble	■ Rocky reef	■ Flat bottom	
	■ Low profile reef	■ Coral reef	□ Slope	
	□ Caves	□ Swim-throughs	□ Silty bottom	
Marine life:	□ Kelp	■ Sea grass	■ Sponges	■ Corals
	□ Sea whips	□ Sea fans	□ Black coral	■ Soft corals
	■ Anemones	■ Fan worms	■ Bryozoans	□ Brachiopods
	■ Crays	■ Crabs	■ Shells	■ Commensal shrimps
	■ Nudibranchs	□ Cuttles	□ Scallops	□ Abalone
	■ Sea stars	□ Basket stars	■ Sea urchins	■ Feather stars
	■ Ascidians	□ Sea lions	■ Dolphins	■ Turtles
	□ Sharks	■ Fish	□ Numerous fish	□ Abundant fish
Experience level:	■ Pupil	■ Beginner	■ Intermediate	■ Advanced
Dive site rating:	■ Excellent	□ Very good	□ Fair	■ Photography
Management of resources:	□ Marine reserve	■ Protected species	□ Quotas	■ Collecting

The red sand cliffs of Point Gregory on Cape Peron Peninsula are a vivid contrast to the blue sky and shell grit beaches.

SHARK BAY

Denham on the western side of the Peron Peninsula is the only settlement in the area and has the distinction of being the western-most township in Australia.

Service: No services at present.

199

Scribbled angelfishes are common in the waters of Shark Bay.

Remarks:

Due to the sheltered embayments and extensive sea grass meadows, Shark Bay is the central area for the Western Australian dugong populations. Dolphins can be hand-fed with fish in the shallows at Monkey Mia, but the water is almost always too dirty to enable photographs to be taken. Snorkelling in the sea grass beds around Denham Jetty is good fun and the water in Denham Sound is much clearer than on the eastern side of Peron Peninsula.

Out at the tip of Peron Peninsula where the dirt road ends is a maze of boggy salt pans and red dust sandhills; the diving there is reasonable. Big cod, giant groper, heaps of snapper, emperors, big coral bommies, stonefish, lionfish, butterflyfish, angels.

This is big, big country with big, big fish, so take big, big care. Out here at the end of nowhere survival takes on a whole new meaning. On land or in the sea, you are on your own (regardless of whether you dive with buddies) and you must plan each event, taking every known experience into consideration. Never underestimate nature, or overestimate your ability; dare is dare, but dead is dead.

GENERAL INFORMATION

Best times of the year:	□ Summer	■ Winter	■ Spring	□ Autumn
Typical weather:	□ Excellent	■	■	□
	□ Very good	□	□	□
	■ Average	□	□	■
	□ Fair	□	□	□
Accommodation available:	■ Camping	□ Hostel	■ Hotel	■ Motel
Airport:	■ Light aircraft	□ Jet	□ International	□ Helicopter

DIVE SITE GUIDE

Access:	■ Boat ramp	□ Charter boat	□ Air	
Dive methods:	■ Scuba	■ Hookah	■ Snorkel	■ Snorkel diving
Types of diving:	■ Boat	■ Jetty	■ Shore	
Description of dive site:	■ Island	■ Submerged reef	■ Shore	
	□ Wreck	■ Shallow water	□ Deep water	
Conditions at site:	■ Current	□ Swell	□ Wind chop	
	■ Tide changes	□ Boat traffic	□ Good visibility	
	■ Fair visibility	■ Poor visibility		
Dive time:	■ In-coming tide	■ Out-going tide		
	■ Spring tide	■ Neap tide	■ Slack tide	
Underwater terrain:	□ Drop offs	□ Gutters	■ Patch reefs	
	■ Sand & rubble	■ Rocky reef	■ Flat bottom	
	■ Low profile reef	■ Coral reef	■ Slope	
	□ Caves	□ Swim-throughs	■ Silty bottom	
Marine life:	□ Kelp	■ Sea grass	■ Sponges	■ Corals
	□ Sea whips	□ Sea fans	□ Black coral	■ Soft corals
	■ Anemones	■ Fan worms	■ Bryozoans	□ Brachiopods
	■ Crays	■ Crabs	■ Shells	■ Commensal shrimps
	■ Nudibranchs	□ Cuttles	□ Scallops	□ Abalone
	■ Sea stars	□ Basket stars	■ Sea urchins	■ Feather stars
	■ Ascidians	■ Dugong	■ Dolphins	■ Turtles
	■ Sharks	■ Fish	■ Numerous fish	□ Abundant fish
Experience level:	■ Pupil	■ Beginner	■ Intermediate	■ Advanced
Dive site rating:	□ Excellent	□ Very good	■ Fair	■ Photography
Management of resources:	□ Marine reserve	■ Protected species	□ Quotas	■ Collecting

Nowhere in Australia does coral reef grow as close to the shoreline as it does at The Blows, on Quobba Station. The entire area is a marine reserve.

QUOBBA BLOWHOLES

Quobba is approximately 40 kilometres north of Carnarvon. It's a beautiful little place rimmed by grassy sandhills where coral reefs almost touch the shoreline.

Service:

No services or settlement exists.

Nudibranchs like this undescribed species of *Phyllodesmium* abound in the shallow waters at The Blows.

Remarks:

This is the only place I know of where true coral reef formations grow close to the coast in nice clear water and are completely accessible to people. The entire area around Point Quobba (approximately 38 hectares) is a declared marine reserve. Unfortunately, due to the out-of-the-way location in Quobba, the one little rusty sign explaining this often goes unnoticed, or is ignored.

Perfect for snorkelling, Quobba reefs at high or medium tide are just the place to introduce a beginner to the joys of underwater. In clear shallow water and with fairly calm conditions (depending on the sea), the low profile coral reef labyrinths and small sand patches in between beckon to be seen.

When snorkelling, snorkel diving or scuba diving in and around coral reefs, always remember to wear some means of protection to stop cuts, scratches and sunburn. Lycra suits, lightweight wetsuits, even old jeans and sloppy joes will do. When in the water for any length of time the skin becomes very soft, and coral is very sharp and can cause severe wounds and infection. So can sunburn, so cover up.

GENERAL INFORMATION

Best times of the year:	☐ Summer	■ Winter	■ Spring	☐ Autumn
Typical weather:	☐ Excellent	■	■	☐
	☐ Very good	☐	☐	☐
	■ Average	☐	☐	■
	☐ Fair	☐	☐	☐
Accommodation available:	■ Camping	☐ Hostel	☐ Hotel	☐ Motel
Airport:	☐ Light aircraft	☐ Jet	☐ International	☐ Helicopter

DIVE SITE GUIDE

Access:	☐ Boat ramp	☐ Charter boat	☐ Air	
Dive methods:	■ Scuba	☐ Hookah	■ Snorkel	■ Snorkel diving
Types of diving:	☐ Boat	☐ Jetty	■ Shore	
Description of dive site:	☐ Island	■ Submerged reef	■ Shore	
	☐ Wreck	■ Shallow water	☐ Deep water	
Conditions at site:	☐ Current	■ Swell	■ Wind chop	
	☐ Tide changes	☐ Boat traffic	■ Good visibility	
	☐ Fair visibility	☐ Poor visibility		
Dive time:	■ In-coming tide	■ Out-going tide		
	■ Spring tide	■ Neap tide	■ Slack tide	
Underwater terrain:	☐ Drop offs	☐ Gutters	■ Patch reefs	
	■ Sand & rubble	☐ Rocky reef	■ Flat bottom	
	■ Low profile reef	■ Coral reef	☐ Slope	
	☐ Caves	☐ Swim-throughs	☐ Silty bottom	
Marine life:	☐ Kelp	☐ Sea grass	■ Sponges	■ Corals
	☐ Sea whips	☐ Sea fans	☐ Black coral	■ Soft corals
	■ Anemones	■ Fan worms	■ Bryozoans	☐ Brachiopods
	■ Crays	■ Crabs	■ Shells	■ Commensal shrimps
	■ Nudibranchs	☐ Cuttles	☐ Scallops	☐ Abalone
	■ Sea stars	☐ Basket stars	■ Sea urchins	■ Feather stars
	■ Ascidians	☐ Sea lions	☐ Dolphins	■ Turtles
	■ Sharks	■ Fish	☐ Numerous fish	☐ Abundant fish
Experience level:	■ Pupil	■ Beginner	■ Intermediate	■ Advanced
Dive site rating:	■ Excellent	☐ Very good	☐ Fair	■ Photography
Management of resources:	■ Marine reserve	■ Protected species	☐ Quotas	☐ Collecting

Creating a new record for Western Australia when it was discovered at Warroora in 1971, the dancing shrimp is a voracious predator of small sea stars.

WARROORA (Alison Point) – CORAL BAY (Point Maud) – NINGALOO (Point Cloates)

As both Warroora and Ningaloo are sheep stations and to get through to the coast requires crossing private property, there are no facilities.

Coral Bay on the other hand has an enterprising tourist development with a hotel and a couple of caravan parks, glass-bottomed boats, etc. All fresh water must be tankered in from Exmouth, 100 kilometres to the north.

Service: No diving services exist at present.

Turtles are regularly seen within the lagoon area behind the reef, feeding on brown algae.

Remarks:

At one time Coral Bay was the mecca for the West's professional spearfishermen who worked these reefs for over twenty years. Today the area is a marine reserve (there are no professional spearfishermen) but those who know of its past can recognize the signs. Compared to waters 50 kilometres south and 50 kilometres north, there is a significant thing missing on the reefs around Coral Bay – *Fish*! The reefs off Ningaloo have been surveyed and are about to become a part of Western Australia's largest marine reserve, which will include the area from Amherst Point (south of Warroora) and right up the cape, around to Bundegi Reef in Exmouth Gulf and out to sea a distance of 10 nautical miles. And deservedly so, before they too go by way of the trigger.

Warroora, Coral Bay and Ningaloo are an underwater photographer's paradise, both inside the shallow waters of the protective reef ramparts, and outside the reef on the slopes and bommies in the real action of the ocean.

GENERAL INFORMATION

Best times of the year:	□ Summer	■ Winter	■ Spring	□ Autumn
Typical weather:	□ Excellent	■	■	□
	■ Very good	□	□	■
	□ Average	□	□	□
	□ Fair	□	□	□
Accommodation available:	■ Camping	□ Hostel	■ Hotel	□ Motel
Airport:	□ Light aircraft	□ Jet	□ International	□ Helicopter

DIVE SITE GUIDE

Access:	■ Boat ramp	□ Charter boat	□ Air	
Dive methods:	■ Scuba	■ Hookah	■ Snorkel	■ Snorkel diving
Types of diving:	■ Boat	□ Jetty	■ Shore	
Description of dive site:	□ Island	■ Submerged reef	■ Shore	
	□ Wreck	■ Shallow water	■ Deep water	
Conditions at site:	□ Current	■ Swell	■ Wind chop	
	□ Tide changes	□ Boat traffic	■ Good visibility	
	□ Fair visibility	□ Poor visibility		
Dive time:	■ In-coming tide	■ Out-going tide		
	■ Spring tide	■ Neap tide	■ Slack tide	
Underwater terrain:	■ Drop offs	■ Gutters	■ Patch reefs	
	■ Sand & rubble	□ Rocky reef	■ Flat bottom	
	■ Low profile reef	□ Coral reef	■ Slope	
	□ Caves	□ Swim-throughs	□ Silty bottom	
Marine life:	□ Kelp	□ Sea grass	■ Sponges	■ Corals
	□ Sea whips	□ Sea fans	□ Black coral	■ Soft corals
	■ Anemones	■ Fan worms	□ Bryozoans	□ Brachiopods
	■ Crays	■ Crabs	■ Shells	■ Commensal shrimps
	■ Nudibranchs	□ Cuttles	□ Scallops	□ Abalone
	■ Sea stars	□ Basket stars	■ Sea urchins	■ Feather stars
	■ Ascidians	□ Sea lions	□ Dolphins	■ Turtles
	■ Sharks	■ Fish	□ Numerous fish	□ Abundant fish
Experience level:	■ Pupil	■ Beginner	■ Intermediate	■ Advanced
Dive site rating:	■ Excellent	□ Very good	□ Fair	■ Photography
Management of resources:	■ Marine reserve	■ Protected species	□ Quotas	□ Collecting

Large, well-developed stands of the bladed soft coral inhabit the reefs off Exmouth Gulf.

EXMOUTH

Despite the fact that the Dutch and French have frequented the northwest cape area since 1618, Exmouth is one of Australia's newest towns. The American Navy communication station has certainly contributed to its growth and in more recent years its game fishing and prawn trawling industries have been added to by oil and gas exploration activities. Exmouth Gulf itself has a very rich underwater fauna, but due to the extensive trawling in the area visibility has closed in over the last two decades and now rarely exceeds 3 metres. However, the Murion Islands provide quite good diving (if you can get out there), with a good selection of big fish and invertebrates, especially sea fans and brilliantly coloured soft corals, lots of turtles and feather stars.

Service: No professional service exists but there are a number of divers that have compressors or hookahs and boats who may be willing to take a dive buddy out on a share cost basis. If you get there, ask around.

Remarks: Some excellent diving can be done around Point Murat, Vlaming Head and Bundegi Reef, and the offshore barrier reef which runs from False Island Point right down the coast to just north off Red Bluff (some 200 kilometres) can only be described as a pioneer diver's paradise. It is only accessible by boat from the sea or boat launched by trailer and four wheel drive from the beaches.

Regal angelfish seem to prefer the cleaner waters around the offshore islands and reefs.

GENERAL INFORMATION

Best times of the year:	☐ Summer	■ Winter	■ Spring	■ Autumn
Typical weather:	☐ Excellent	☐	☐	☐
	■ Very good	■	■	☐
	☐ Average	☐	☐	■
	☐ Fair	☐	☐	☐
Accommodation available:	■ Camping	☐ Hostel	■ Hotel	■ Motel
Airport: (Learmonth)	■ Light aircraft	■ Jet	☐ International	☐ Helicopter

DIVE SITE GUIDE

Access:	■ Boat ramp	☐ Charter boat	☐ Air	
Dive methods:	■ Scuba	■ Hookah	■ Snorkel	■ Snorkel diving
Types of diving:	■ Boat	■ Jetty	■ Shore	
Description of dive site:	■ Island	■ Submerged reef	■ Shore	
	☐ Wreck	■ Shallow water	☐ Deep water	
Conditions at site:	■ Current	■ Swell	■ Wind chop	
	■ Tide changes	☐ Boat traffic	■ Good visibility	
	■ Fair visibility	■ Poor visibility		
Dive time:	■ In-coming tide	■ Out-going tide		
	■ Spring tide	■ Neap tide	■ Slack tide	
Underwater terrain:	■ Drop offs	■ Gutters	■ Patch reefs	
	■ Sand & rubble	■ Rocky reef	■ Flat bottom	
	■ Low profile reef	■ Coral reef	■ Slope	
	☐ Caves	☐ Swim-throughs	■ Silty bottom	
Marine life:	☐ Kelp	☐ Sea grass	■ Sponges	■ Corals
	■ Sea whips	■ Sea fans	■ Black coral	■ Soft corals
	■ Anemones	■ Fan worms	■ Bryozoans	☐ Brachiopods
	■ Crays	■ Crabs	■ Shells	■ Commensal shrimps
	■ Nudibranchs	☐ Cuttles	☐ Scallops	☐ Abalone
	■ Sea stars	☐ Basket stars	■ Sea urchins	■ Feather stars
	■ Ascidians	☐ Sea lions	■ Dolphins	■ Turtles
	■ Sharks	■ Fish	■ Numerous fish	☐ Abundant fish
Experience level:	■ Pupil	■ Beginner	■ Intermediate	■ Advanced
Dive site rating:	☐ Excellent	■ Very good	☐ Fair	■ Photography
Management of resources:	☐ Marine reserve	■ Protected species	☐ Quotas	■ Collecting

Ribbon sweetlips are found only in north Western Australia and the Northern Territory.

DAMPIER

A typical mining town, Dampier is a green oasis in a sea of red. It is situated at King Bay, a shallow-water mangrove-fringed mud-covered shoreline that has one of the richest coastline marine invertebrate faunas anywhere. Iron ore and salt are the mainstays of the area.

Service:

INNERSPACE DIVING
Run on a part-time basis this service can supply air, has PADI instruction and will arrange day trips.

Contact:
Innerspace Diving
281 Stuart Crescent, Dampier WA 6713
Phone: (091) 83 1761

Remarks:

The outer islands of the Dampier Archipelago are certainly the most extensive accessible coral reef dives on the northwest coast. The outer islands of Rosemary, Legendre, C. Bruguieres, Goodwyn and Delambre have fairly good visibility and abound with fish, excellent coral coverage, giant groper, turtles, sharks, sea snakes, and lots of other sea life. However, in many places the fish are very skittish (as are the crays) due to their having been shot on hookah, scuba, snorkel, etc.

The inshore islands are also good dives but the visibility rarely exceeds 5 metres even on neap tides. Sharks and sea snakes are no problem. I did the first photographic underwater survey of these reefs in 1971 and found the tidal rips and strong Western Australian seabreezes to be the most difficult factors to work with.

GENERAL INFORMATION

Best times of the year: □ Summer ■ Winter ■ Spring □ Autumn

Typical weather:
- □ Excellent □ □ □
- □ Very good ■ ■ □
- ■ Average □ □ ■
- □ Fair □ □ □

Accommodation available: ■ Camping □ Hostel ■ Hotel □ Motel

Airport: ■ Light aircraft ■ Jet □ International □ Helicopter
(Karratha)

DIVE SITE GUIDE

Access: □ Boat ramp □ Charter boat ■ Air

Dive methods: □ Scuba □ Hookah □ Snorkel □ Snorkel diving

Types of diving: □ Boat ■ Jetty □ Shore

Description of dive site:
- ■ Island ■ Submerged reef □ Shore
- □ Wreck ■ Shallow water □ Deep water

Conditions at site:
- ■ Current ■ Swell ■ Wind chop
- ■ Tide changes □ Boat traffic □ Good visibility
- ■ Fair visibility □ Poor visibility

Dive time:
- ■ In-coming tide ■ Out-going tide
- ■ Spring tide ■ Neap tide ■ Slack tide

Underwater terrain:
- ■ Drop offs ■ Gutters ■ Patch reefs
- ■ Sand & rubble □ Rocky reef ■ Flat bottom
- ■ Low profile reef ■ Coral reef ■ Slope
- □ Caves □ Swim-throughs ■ Silty bottom

Marine life:
- □ Kelp □ Sea grass ■ Sponges ■ Corals
- □ Sea whips ■ Sea fans □ Black coral ■ Soft corals
- ■ Anemones ■ Fan worms ■ Bryozoans □ Brachiopods
- ■ Crays ■ Crabs ■ Shells ■ Commensal shrimps
- ■ Nudibranchs □ Cuttles □ Scallops □ Abalone
- ■ Sea stars □ Basket stars ■ Sea urchins ■ Feather stars
- ■ Ascidians □ Sea lions ■ Dolphins ■ Turtles
- ■ Sharks ■ Fish ■ Numerous fish □ Abundant fish

Experience level: □ Pupil ■ Beginner ■ Intermediate ■ Advanced

Dive site rating: □ Excellent □ Very good ■ Fair ■ Photography

Management of resources: □ Marine reserve ■ Protected species □ Quotas ■ Collecting

Huge schools of fish gather around the shipping channel markers off Port Hedland.

PORT HEDLAND

Regarded as one of Western Australia's fastest growing towns and with a population of over 12,000, Port Hedland is the centre for the entire Pilbara mining region. Primarily concerned with the iron ore export trade, its man-made channel leading far out to sea assures easy entry for the world's largest iron ore carriers. The second largest industry is salt production. Huge glaring white mountains scraped from thousands of hectares of salt farm ponds stud the skyline.

Service:

PORT HEDLAND DIVE SUPPLIES
and
COOPER MARINE
Run in conjunction with each other, both these dive shops can supply air, equipment sales, service, FAUI instruction and can organise dive trips.

Contact:
Port Hedland Dive Supplies
3 Richardson Street, Port Headland WA 6721
Phone: (091) 73 1304

Contact:
Cooper Marine
17 Anderson Street, Port Hedland WA 6721
Phone: (091) 73 1304 (both shops)

Remarks:

Flying into Port Hedland and looking down into a sea which is red with iron ore dust inshore and like green soup offshore, you wouldn't give Buckley's chance of a dive, let alone a good one. (Buckley's chance is Australian idiom for a very slim chance or forlorn hope. According to folklore Buckley was an Australian highwayman who, when cornered by the police, jumped off a cliff rather than be caught.) The visibility mightn't be that wonderful and the dives sites (channel marker buoys and low profile reef) mightn't be your idea of adventure, but let me enlighten you. By the time you have crashed your way out through the swells and wave chop whipped up by the Western Australian trade winds and the tide rips, got a line on a channel marker buoy (while the boat's playing Yo-Yos in the swell), got your gear on in one piece and fallen over the side hanging onto the mermaid line, you've already had your adventure.

To dive Port Hedland you have to be keen, but the rewards are exceptional: huge schools of fish, new species everywhere, every type of invertebrate you can think of in every colour imaginable. A close-up photographer's paradise and hardly anybody knows about it.

GENERAL INFORMATION

Best times of the year:	□ Summer	■ Winter	■ Spring	□ Autumn
Typical weather:	□ Excellent	□	□	□
	□ Very good	■	■	□
	■ Average	□	□	■
	□ Fair	□	□	□
Accommodation available:	■ Camping	□ Hostel	■ Hotel	■ Motel
Airport:	■ Light aircraft	■ Jet	□ International	□ Helicopter

DIVE SITE GUIDE

Access:	■ Boat ramp	■ Charter boat	■ Air	
Dive methods:	■ Scuba	■ Hookah	□ Snorkel	□ Snorkel diving
Types of diving:	■ Boat	■ Jetty	□ Shore	
Description of dive site:	□ Island	■ Submerged reef	□ Shore	
	□ Wreck	■ Shallow water	□ Deep water	
Conditions at site:	■ Current	■ Swell	■ Wind chop	
	■ Tide changes	■ Boat traffic	□ Good visibility	
	□ Fair visibility	■ Poor visibility		
Dive time:	■ In-coming tide	■ Out-going tide		
	■ Spring tide	■ Neap tide	■ Slack tide	
Underwater terrain:	□ Drop offs	□ Gutters	■ Patch reefs	
	■ Sand & rubble	■ Rocky reef	■ Flat bottom	
	■ Low profile reef	□ Coral reef	□ Slope	
	□ Caves	□ Swim-throughs	■ Silty bottom	
Marine life:	□ Kelp	□ Sea grass	■ Sponges	■ Corals
	□ Sea whips	■ Sea fans	■ Black coral	■ Soft corals
	■ Anemones	■ Fan worms	■ Bryozoans	□ Brachiopods
	□ Crays	■ Crabs	■ Shells	■ Commensal shrimps
	■ Nudibranchs	□ Cuttles	□ Scallops	□ Abalone
	■ Sea stars	□ Basket stars	■ Sea urchins	■ Feather stars
	■ Ascidians	□ Sea lions	■ Dolphins	■ Turtles
	■ Sharks	■ Fish	■ Numerous fish	□ Abundant fish
Experience level:	□ Pupil	□ Beginner	■ Intermediate	■ Advanced
Dive site rating:	□ Excellent	□ Very good	■ Fair	■ Photography
Management of resources:	□ Marine reserve	■ Protected species	□ Quotas	■ Collecting

The altar at the Beagle Bay mission church is made out of gold-lip pearl shells.

BROOME

A thriving pearl and pearl shell centre for over a century, Broome is situated on Roebuck Bay, a large muddy-shored embayment fringed with mangroves, where miles of sandbanks lie exposed at low water. Pearling is still carried out in Broome in conjunction with supplying the cultured pearl industry with seed oysters, but beef has taken over as the main industry.

Due to poor visibility (almost none) and the 11 metre tidal range, diving is not a popular pastime in Broome itself. In fact the only thing I could tell about the piles on the town jetty was that they had quite a bit of growth on them (by touch). All my recording and photographing at Broome was done in tide pools in the rocky reef and in sea caves left high and dry by the receding tide.

Service: None.

Remarks: One hundred and fifty kilometres north of Broome is Cape Leveque, guarding the entrance to King Sound where there are several pearl culture farms. I found diving was possible at Cape Leveque, but with knot currents, whirlpools and only 2 metre visibility, I didn't take too many photographs.

However, like all coastal environments, the marine life was rich and interesting. Permission is required to visit the Aboriginal Mission in the area, but not to visit the fantastic pearl shell church altar at Beagle Bay.

GENERAL INFORMATION

Best times of the year:	☐ Summer	■ Winter	■ Spring	☐ Autumn
Typical weather:	☐ Excellent	■	■	☐
	☐ Very good	☐	☐	☐
	■ Average	☐	☐	■
	☐ Fair	☐	☐	☐
Accommodation available:	■ Camping	☐ Hostel	■ Hotel	■ Motel
Airport:	■ Light aircraft	■ Jet	☐ International	☐ Helicopter

DIVE SITE GUIDE

Access:	■ Boat ramp	☐ Charter boat	☐ Air	
Dive methods:	■ Scuba	■ Hookah	■ Snorkel	■ Snorkel diving
Types of diving:	☐ Boat	■ Jetty	☐ Shore	
Description of dive site:	☐ Island	☐ Submerged reef	■ Shore	
	☐ Wreck	■ Shallow water	☐ Deep water	
Conditions at site:	■ Current	☐ Swell	☐ Wind chop	
	■ Tide changes	☐ Boat traffic	☐ Good visibility	
	☐ Fair visibility	■ Poor visibility		
Dive time:	■ In-coming tide	☐ Out-going tide		
	☐ Spring tide	■ Neap tide	■ Slack tide	
Underwater terrain:	☐ Drop offs	☐ Gutters	☐ Patch reefs	
	☐ Sand & rubble	☐ Rocky reef	■ Flat bottom	
	☐ Low profile reef	☐ Coral reef	☐ Slope	
	☐ Caves	☐ Swim-throughs	■ Silty bottom	
Marine life:	☐ Kelp	☐ Sea grass	■ Sponges	■ Corals
	☐ Sea whips	☐ Sea fans	☐ Black coral	■ Soft corals
	■ Anemones	■ Fan worms	☐ Bryozoans	☐ Brachiopods
	☐ Crays	■ Crabs	■ Shells	■ Commensal shrimps
	■ Nudibranchs	☐ Cuttles	☐ Scallops	☐ Abalone
	■ Sea stars	☐ Basket stars	■ Sea urchins	☐ Feather stars
	■ Ascidians	☐ Sea lions	☐ Dolphins	■ Turtles
	■ Sharks	■ Fish	☐ Numerous fish	☐ Abundant fish
Experience level:	☐ Pupil	☐ Beginner	■ Intermediate	■ Advanced
Dive site rating:	☐ Excellent	☐ Very good	☐ Fair	☐ Photography
Management of resources:	☐ Marine reserve	■ Protected species	☐ Quotas	■ Collecting

Giant cods, which grow up to almost 3 metres in length, were thought to be more dangerous than sharks by the early pearl shell divers. This specimen, over 2 metres long, seemed to be saying 'Get out of my territory' — so I got! But at least I also got its picture!

ROWLEY SHOALS

Situated some 300 kilometres west of Broome, Rowley Shoals represents the most significant geological example of coral atoll to be seen in Australia. The complex is made up of three independent atolls – Clarke Reef, Imperieuse Reef and Mermaid Reef; the latter two having sand cays.

Although through the years there have been excursions out to these magnificent diving areas, it is only in the last decade that

A recent addition to the marine fauna lists of northern Australia is the very beautiful Navarchus angelfish.

fauna surveys and maritime archaeological expeditions by the Western Australian Museum have put it on the diving map. One of the last great unexplored territories, Rowley Shoals surrendered up dozens of new species and hundreds of new marine life records for the Australian marine faunal checklists compiled by the museum.

Rising some 440 metres from the sea bed, the atolls provide no safe anchorages, and due to their being only half a metre or so above sea level, protection from the weather is limited, even inside the lagoons. Visibility can vary from 10 metres to 60 metres and the marine life is rich and diverse.

Service:

None at present. All the charter boats that used to make regular trips have been disposed of or are no longer running. I believe that one dive trip per year may run in the future, but no viable information is currently available.

GENERAL INFORMATION

Best times of the year:	☐ Summer	■ Winter	■ Spring	☐ Autumn
Typical weather:	☐ Excellent	■	■	☐
	☐ Very good	☐	☐	☐
	■ Average	☐	☐	■
	☐ Fair	☐	☐	☐
Accommodation available:	☐ Camping	☐ Hostel	☐ Hotel	☐ Motel
Airport:	☐ Light aircraft	☐ Jet	☐ International	☐ Helicopter

DIVE SITE GUIDE

Access:	☐ Boat ramp	■ Charter boat	☐ Air	
Dive methods:	■ Scuba	■ Hookah	■ Snorkel	■ Snorkel diving
Types of diving:	■ Boat	☐ Jetty	☐ Shore	
Description of dive site:	☐ Island	■ Submerged reef	☐ Shore	
	■ Wreck	■ Shallow water	■ Deep water	
Conditions at site:	■ Current	■ Swell	■ Wind chop	
	■ Tide changes	☐ Boat traffic	■ Good visibility	
	■ Fair visibility	☐ Poor visibility		
Dive time:	■ In-coming tide	■ Out-going tide		
	■ Spring tide	■ Neap tide	■ Slack tide	
Underwater terrain:	■ Drop offs	■ Gutters	☐ Patch reefs	
	■ Sand & rubble	☐ Rocky reef	■ Flat bottom	
	☐ Low profile reef	■ Coral reef	■ Slope	
	■ Caves	■ Swim-throughs	☐ Silty bottom	
Marine life:	☐ Kelp	☐ Sea grass	■ Sponges	■ Corals
	☐ Sea whips	■ Sea fans	■ Black coral	■ Soft corals
	■ Anemones	■ Fan worms	■ Bryozoans	☐ Brachiopods
	■ Crays	■ Crabs	■ Shells	■ Commensal shrimps
	■ Nudibranchs	☐ Cuttles	☐ Scallops	☐ Abalone
	■ Sea stars	☐ Basket stars	■ Sea urchins	■ Feather stars
	■ Ascidians	☐ Sea lions	■ Dolphins	■ Turtles
	■ Sharks	■ Fish	☐ Numerous fish	■ Abundant fish
Experience level:	☐ Pupil	☐ Beginner	■ Intermediate	■ Advanced
Dive site rating:	■ Excellent	☐ Very good	☐ Fair	■ Photography
Management of resources:	☐ Marine reserve	■ Protected species	☐ Quotas	■ Collecting

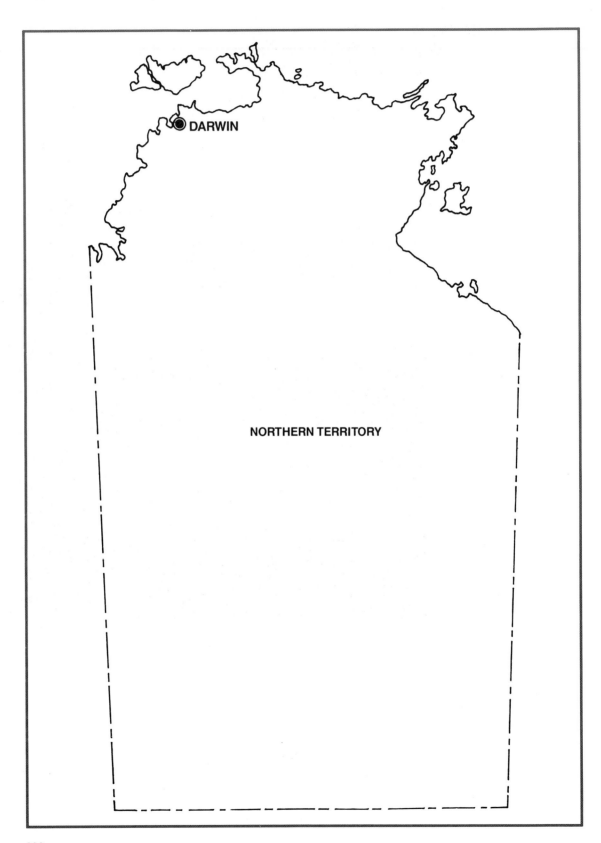

DARWIN

NORTHERN TERRITORY

Diving
THE NORTHERN TERRITORY

When sunrise coincides with tide-rise, many interesting animals can be found in intertidal areas – but diving is unnecessary.

DARWIN

As the northern gateway to Australia and capital of the Northern Territory, Darwin, with a population of 70,000, is one of our most rapidly expanding cities. However, during the wet season (November to April) many things are restricted, including the diving to some extent.

Diving off Darwin is quite an experience. There are a number of wrecks as a result of the Second World War and Cyclone Tracey, ranging in depths from 9 to 30 metres. The waters abound with butterfly fish and angels in most areas and the invertebrate life is

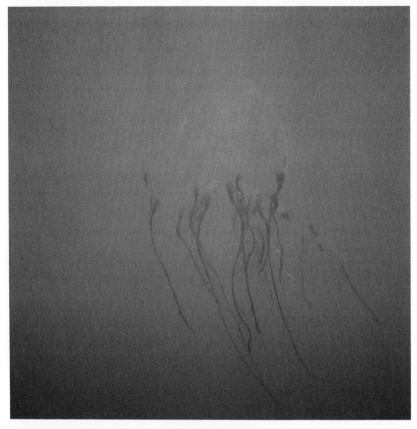

Due to the poor visibility in coastal areas box jellies are almost impossible to see underwater. Protective clothing must be worn for any entry into the water during the spring and summer months.

rich and prolific. Large fish may be present but I didn't see any.

Soft corals and sea fans cover the bottom and during the summer the sea is so hot that even at 25 metres the scuba tank air comes out the same temperature as the inside of the mouth, resulting in no feeling of breathing. The temperature in the air (around 30°C) and the temperature in the water also feel pretty much the same.

Service:

DIVE NORTH
PADI instruction, equipment sales, service, gear hire, air 7 days a week, boat dives (8 metre *Reef Runner*).

Contact:
Dive North
Shop 15 Wingate Complex,
Cnr Sadgrove & Stuart Highway, Winnellie, Darwin NT 5789
Phone: (089) 84 5197

Service:

TERRITORY DIVE SERVICES
Full dive shop and training facilities, and dive boat.

Contact:
Territory Dive Services
Fannie Bay Shopping Centre, Fannie Bay NT 5790
Phone: (089) 81 7665

Charter Boat:

Pacific Adventurer
15 metre luxury cruiser

Contact:
Pacific Adventurer
PO Box 39530, Winnellie 5789
Phone: (089) 88 1202

Although its bright red patterns contrast vividly against the green tentacles of its anemone home, the spotted procellanid crab is a resident commensal.

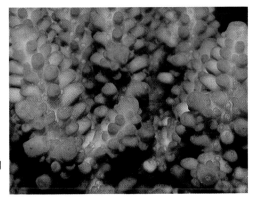

Shallow-water dwelling corals like this staghorn have special compounds that filter out the damaging ultra-violet rays.

Remarks:

Although comprising one sixth of the Australian continent, the Northern Territory can only be considered fair as a diving destination due to much of its coastline being bordered with dense mangrove forests. The shallow inshore reefs are influenced by strong tides and local knowledge should be sought from the local dive facility before diving them.

Around the offshore islands visibility may get to 20 metres during calm weather neaps in the dry season. Photography is generally restricted to close ups or wide angle.

The inshore waters around Darwin are inhabited by box jellies or 'sea wasps'. These deadly stingers have been responsible for more deaths than any other marine animal in Australia's tropical north (see page 232). Although the box jelly may be seen at various times of the year, it is especially prolific during the wet season. No diver or snorkeller or wader or swimmer should enter any inshore waters whatsoever unless completely covered by protective clothing: lycra

223

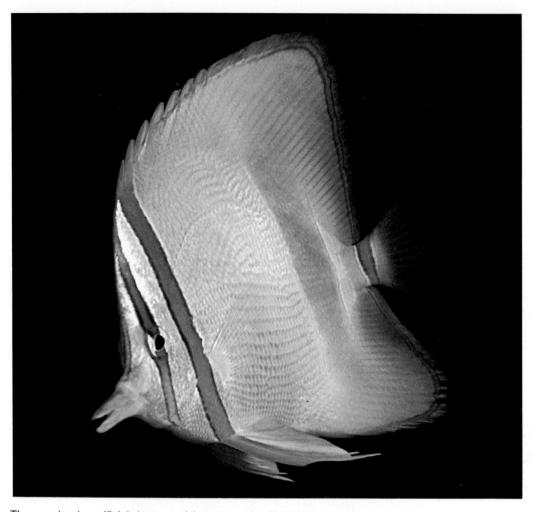

The margined coralfish is just one of the many colourful fish that inhabit Darwin Harbour.

suit, pantihose, lightweight wetsuit – anything to cover up. Box jellies are not to be taken lightly. The deaths of over sixty people vouch for that. Crocodile and shark stories may be exaggerated, but the dangers of box jellies are real.

Well-known dive sites include Darwin Harbour reefs, the harbour jetty, Fannie Bay, Nightcliff Reef, East Point Coral Gardens, the wrecks *U.S.S. Meigs*, *U.S.S. Peary*, the *Zealandia* and the *Catalinas*. Mandorah Jetty, No. 6 Buoy and Plater's Rocks can also provide a good dive. Visibility ranges from 2 to 20 metres, the best dives being on neap tides.

In the dry season there are some interesting sideline dives at the freshwater sites of Berry Springs, Edith Falls and Rum Jungle. Take care: diving here may be deep and visibility rarely exceeds 3 metres, though some smaller pools may be clearer. Other attractions around

Darwin include feeding fish by hand at the Doctor's Gully Fishery Reserve, and Cobourg Peninsula Marine National Park, some 200 kilometres northeast of Darwin, where coral fringed reefs, mangroves, dugong, turtles and crocodiles may be seen.

GENERAL INFORMATION

Best times of the year:	☐ Summer	■ Winter	■ Spring	☐ Autumn
Typical weather:	☐ Excellent	☐	☐	☐
	☐ Very good	■	■	☐
	■ Average	☐	☐	■
	☐ Fair	☐	☐	☐
Accommodation available:	■ Camping	■ Hostel	■ Hotel	■ Motel
Airport:	■ Light aircraft	■ Jet	■ International	■ Helicopter

DIVE SITE GUIDE

Access:	■ Boat ramp	☐ Charter boat	■ Air	
Dive methods:	■ Scuba	■ Hookah	■ Snorkel	■ Snorkel diving
Types of diving:	■ Boat	■ Jetty	■ Shore	
Description of dive site:	☐ Island	■ Submerged reef	■ Shore	
	■ Wreck	■ Shallow water	☐ Deep water	
Conditions at site:	■ Current	☐ Swell	☐ Wind chop	
	■ Tide changes	☐ Boat traffic	☐ Good visibility	
	■ Fair visibility	■ Poor visibility		
Dive time:	■ In-coming tide	☐ Out-going tide		
	☐ Spring tide	■ Neap tide	■ Slack tide	
Underwater terrain:	✓ Drop offs	☐ Gutters	■ Patch reefs	
	■ Sand & rubble	☐ Rocky reef	■ Flat bottom	
	■ Low profile reef	■ Coral reef	☐ Slope	
	☐ Caves	☐ Swim-throughs	■ Silty bottom	
Marine life:	☐ Kelp	☐ Sea grass	■ Sponges	■ Corals
	■ Sea whips	■ Sea fans	■ Black coral	■ Soft corals
	■ Anemones	■ Fan worms	■ Bryozoans	☐ Brachiopods
	■ Crays	■ Crabs	■ Shells	■ Commensal shrimps
	■ Nudibranchs	■ Cuttles	☐ Scallops	☐ Abalone
	■ Sea stars	☐ Basket stars	■ Sea urchins	■ Feather stars
	■ Ascidians	☐ Sea lions	☐ Dolphins	☐ Turtles
	■ Sharks	■ Fish	■ Numerous fish	☐ Abundant fish
Experience level:	☐ Pupil	☐ Beginner	■ Intermediate	■ Advanced
Dive site rating:	☐ Excellent	☐ Very good	■ Fair	☐ Photography
Management of resources:	■ Marine reserve	■ Protected species	☐ Quotas	■ Collecting

UNDERWATER WILDLIFE

Whale sharks generally inhabit the offshore areas of the Coral Sea, but on occasion visit inshore areas from southern New South Wales to northern Queensland.

To many people the words 'marine biology' conjure up an image of scientists engaged in all kinds of academic brainbending research, far above and beyond the understanding of ordinary people. This attitude is as unrealistic today as outdated attitudes on the dangers of sharks.

In fact, divers have a greater opportunity to observe and understand wildlife than participants in any other sport. Ninety-nine per cent of what divers see underwater are animals and plants. In Australia the recording of our underwater wildlife has only just started; hundreds, maybe even thousands of species are still awaiting discovery.

Real *exploration* still takes place in Underwater Australia. Most dive sites have never been surveyed, and it remains a mystery as to what animals can be found in many areas because only a few underwater fauna surveys have ever been carried out.

Even in, by Australian standards, popular areas (forty divers a day), new species can be found on almost every dive and are recorded continuously.

It has only been over the last few years that underwater naturalists have succeeded in having visual identification guides published on Australia's living marine fauna. Much of the work in photographing and recording the fauna is still going on and expeditions to special locations to carry out fauna surveys and establish checklists for future marine parks are run on a regular basis throughout the Indo-Pacific and Indian Ocean areas, particularly in areas like Lord Howe Island and Papua New Guinea.

Animals inhabiting the waters in the tropical areas of Australia, such as the Great Barrier Reef, are very similar to species found in other tropical seas.

Although we do have a number of species unique to the tropical Australian waters bordering Queensland, the Northern Territory and Western Australia, it is in the southern waters that the truly fascinating Australian underwater endemic species can be seen.

A marvellous diversity of Australian species exists (numbering over 20,000), and in only two decades we have advanced to where we can now recognise some 6000 species in the wild (some 3000 species are reproduced in colour in my different books; see references and further reading).

The animal kingdom has been classified into a hierarchy of categories, of which species is the lowest. From single-celled animals to the structurally complex human, over one million species having already been described and named.

Animals illustrated in this book belong to the vertebrate and invertebrate groups, although there are far more species of invertebrates than vertebrates living underwater. Vertebrates have skeletons and invertebrates are without skeletons; each group is separated into their own phylum. Each phylum is divided into classes, the classes into orders, the orders into families, and the families into smaller units called genera, which are comprised of one or more closely related species.

Of the vertebrates, the bony fishes belong to one class in the chordata phylum and the cartilaginous sharks and rays belong to another. Underwater, members of the invertebrate phyla are not always as easy to recognise as the vertebrates and to accurately identify underwater invertebrates it is necessary to study them or to attend one of the excellent underwater marine biology courses available in most states (see pages 256–7).

The major underwater invertebrate phyla includes sponges, cnidarians or coelenterates (corals, sea jellies), worms (annelids, flatworms), bryozoans (lace corals), brachiopods (lamp shells), molluscs (shells, etc), crustaceans (crabs, rocklobsters), and echinoderms (sea stars, sea urchins). The tunicates or ascidians are a subphylum of the phylum chordata, for when they are in the larval stages they have a notochord, or backbone-like supporting rod.

Little is known about the behaviour of underwater animals. Publications that can assist with information are listed under Further Reading, or refer to my journal, published quarterly by Sea Australia Productions Pty Ltd, *Underwater, The Diver's Journal*.

PHYLA CHART (numbers refer to species world wide)

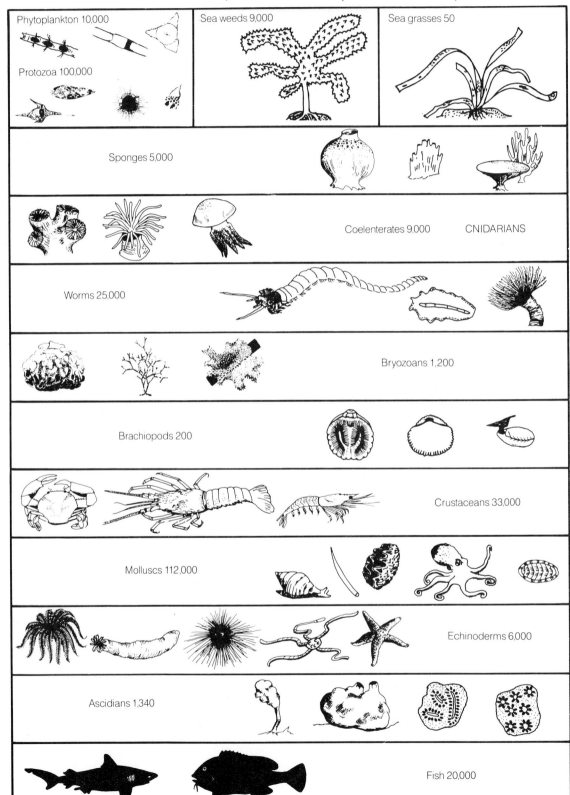

Phytoplankton 10,000

Protozoa 100,000

Sea weeds 9,000

Sea grasses 50

Sponges 5,000

Coelenterates 9,000   CNIDARIANS

Worms 25,000

Bryozoans 1,200

Brachiopods 200

Crustaceans 33,000

Molluscs 112,000

Echinoderms 6,000

Ascidians 1,340

Fish 20,000

SIMPLE PHYLOGENETIC CLASSIFICATION OF AQUATIC ANIMALS		
PHYLUM	PROTOZOA	Single celled animals
PHYLUM	PORIFERA	Sponges
PHYLUM	COELENTERATA (CNIDARIA)	Corals, soft corals, black corals, hydroids, sea jellies, gorgonians, sea whips, sea pens, sea anemones, zoanthids.
PHYLUM	CTENOPHORA	Combjellies, sessile ctenophores.
PHYLUM	PLATYHELMINTHES	Flatworms
PHYLUM	NEMERTINEA	Ribbon worms
PHYLUM	ACANTHOCEPHALA	Thorny headed worms
PHYLUM	BRYOZOA (polyzoa)	Moss animals
PHYLUM	PHORONIDA	Horseshoe worms
PHYLUM	BRACHIOPODA	Lampshells
PHYLUM	SIPUNCULA	Peanut worms
PHYLUM	ECHIURA	Spoon worms
PHYLUM	ANNELIDA	Segmented worms
PHYLUM	ARTHROPODA	Insects, crustaceans, sea spiders
PHYLUM	TARDIGRADA	Water bears
PHYLUM	MOLLUSCA	Chitons, tusk shells, univalves, bivalves, cephalopods
PHYLUM	CHAETOGNATHA	Arrow worms
PHYLUM	ECHINODERMATA	Sea stars, brittle stars, feather stars, sea urchins, sea cucumbers
PHYLUM	HEMICHORDATA	Acorn worms
PHYLUM	CHORDATA	Vertebrates
Subphylum	CEPHALOCHORDATA	Ascidians or tunicates
Subphylum	VERTEBRATA	Lampreys, sharks, rays, bony fishes, reptiles, mammals

UNDERWATER HAZARDS

One of Australia's most venomous species, the armed sea anemone will kill this captured toadfish in seconds.

Common sense is a most important factor in dealing with the underwater environment, whether in Australian seas or any other. Think before you act; plan ahead. There is every chance you will suffer more from sunburn (because you forgot your hat) than you will ever suffer from a potentially harmful sea creature. Ninety-nine per cent of all my experiences on the receiving end of nematocysts, spines, tentacles, teeth, bristles and barbs have all been experiments, so I could learn from my experience and teach others how to avoid similar unpleasantries.

Underwater animals have all sorts of defence mechanisms for survival. It is simply a matter of divers knowing such animals exist, accepting their roles in nature, recognising them in their natural habitat and understanding their behaviour.

We are learning more and more about the roles and temperaments of so many species and discovering that very few underwater animals are as aggressive as 'armchair authors' would have us believe. Rather than waste time thinking about fantasy encounters with man-eating monsters, it is much more practical to come to terms with the real danger in the sea: ourselves and our clumsy, ignorant ways.

For this reason I have included information on those animals about which people ask the most questions or appear to have the greatest concern.

HYDROIDS

The hydroids, or stinging sea ferns, are colonies of animals that are related to corals. They possess minute stinging cells by which they immobilise their planktonic food.

Although the venom cells are microscopic in size, they are quite potent and when the colonies brush against bare skin, the resulting stings can be severe. Initially the sting is a little painful, but it is not normally very dangerous. Secondary problems may occur because of the intense itching that the stings cause for up to several weeks afterwards. Scratching the stings leads to open wounds and, particularly with continued immersion in saltwater, infections may develop. As with all cnidarian stings, vinegar should be applied to the initial sting and calamine lotion used to subdue the itching in the recovery period afterwards.

SEA ANEMONES

There are only twelve Australian sea anemones so far recorded as being harmful to humans. Many of these occur on the Great Barrier Reef and on the coast of Queensland, some in New South Wales and Victoria, and three in Western Australia. Although the majority of these anemones are found below tide level, there are a couple of intertidal species that are capable of dealing a severe sting.

The armed anemone *Dofleina armata* of Queensland is a fairly large, solitary anemone found at low tide on sand or sandy mud-flats. Records have so far shown this intertidal species occurs as far south as Yeppoon, where it is not regarded as common.

Pain is felt immediately on contact with the tentacles. Pods of nematocyst batteries adhere to the flesh when the affected part is removed from the anemone. Wherever tentacles have touched the skin, distinct white patterns of dead skin are left that match their pattern. Several hours later the stinging is still persistent, having the same sensation as an open burn, with red inflamed swelling appearing around affected parts. The skin is very sore to touch with deep blisters appearing within five hours. Healing and skin peeling continue for one and a half weeks and scars are still visible a month later.

Treatment
There have been no fatalities from sea anemones in Australian waters. For divers and snorkellers there appears little danger if adequate

commonsense precautions are taken, e.g. protective clothing, gloves.

As with any cnidarian sting, the affected part should be flooded with vinegar to deactivate any nematocysts on the skin, and a flat compressive bandage applied to the wound. The patient should be kept quiet until any shock wears off, as nausea may be present.

It's best to avoid touching any larger sea anemones, especially those growing in sandy, muddy or rubble bottomed areas.

BOX JELLIES

Although there are a number of sea jellies in Australian waters which sting, none are as deadly as the box jellies. The two largest species are *Chiropsalmus quadrigatus* and *Chironex fleckeri*. They occur along the northern coast in a regular time cycle, appearing mainly between November and May. Although both of these species have caused the deaths of many people, *C. fleckeri* is considered to be the more dangerous of the two.

Amongst the factors which contribute to the severity of the sting are: the size of the sea jelly; the sex; the quantity of venom injected; the health and age of the victim; and the proximity of the sting to vital organs. A victim's individual sensitivity to the venom is also a factor. While some victims have died within minutes of being stung and others have prominent scars still visible ten to fourteen years later, there are those who have suffered no extensive damage or lasting visual reminders.

The majority of people who have been stung were swimming or wading in creeks, rivers or coastal waters along the north coast of Australia. Fatalities were always during the summer months — the wet season in the north. At this time of year the air is heavy with humidity and the rain turns the rivers muddy brown. Suspended sediment pours into the ocean and the coastal waters become murky. The consequent lack of visibility keeps the deadly box jellies from being seen.

Treatment

Immediate treatment for victims of the box jelly should first be directed to maintaining respiration. Vinegar splashed on the attacked area disarms the nematocysts (4–6 per cent acetic acid will do as well). The tentacles may also be gently removed with a knife or stick. Sand should *not* be rubbed on the wound, as this will cause any undischarged nematocysts to be activated and so discharge their poison. Apply firm compressive bandages over the stung areas or as high as possible on the limb.

An antitoxin is available but, because of the potency of the venom and the often short period between attack and death, it cannot always be used. The Commonwealth Serum Laboratories have produced a 'sea wasp' antivenene, but, like all antivenenes, it requires a trained medical person to administer it. Pain killing sprays such as Stingose may give some partial relief on box jelly stings; they certainly work on other cnidarian injuries.

BLUE-RINGED OCTOPUSES

Octopuses are bottom-dwelling creatures that feed mostly on crustaceans and other molluscs. Hiding away by day in holes, caves and beneath rocks, they venture out at night in search of food. With long, suckered arms and a body that can squeeze through the smallest hole or crack, they give their prey little chance of escape. Once snared in the enmeshing web of their suckered arms, the prey is quickly brought to the mouth. Here the octopus uses its sharp, horny beak (somewhat like that of a parrot) to break its prey into pieces.

Octopuses have salivary glands at the rear of their beak. These glands produce various toxic substances that are injected onto the wound as the prey is bitten. In some cases, for instance when the prey is a crustacean, the toxin not only paralyses, but also breaks down the tissue and allows the octopus to suck out the almost liquid flesh.

Three species of blue-ringed octopus occur in Australian waters, but only the north-western *Hapalochaena lunulata*, which is the largest, and its southern counterpart *H. maculosa*, have been implicated in human deaths.

Under normal conditions, the colour of the blue-ringed octopus varies between yellow, brown and grey on its body, with dark brown or black bands on the arms. Superimposed on these darker bands

Blue-ringed octopuses are small and totally harmless unless picked up or otherwise disturbed by inquisitive humans. Leave them alone!

are fine blue circles. Even when its hiding place has been exposed, a blue-ringed octopus will still make every effort to escape. It is not until it is angered by being poked, picked up or otherwise disturbed that the octopus turns darker and the circles expand. It is during this period that the blue-ringed octopus is at its most dangerous. Instead of being a small, unobtrusive sea creature, it is transformed into a brilliantly coloured miniature that would attract the attention of any seaside explorer.

Few people have ever felt the actual bite of a blue-ringed octopus. In most cases the beak of the octopus has only produced a small break in the skin. Only a very small amount of venom entering the bloodstream results in the immediate symptoms of weakness, loss of breath, a choking feeling in the throat, nausea and collapse. The toxin of *Hapalochaena*, called tetrotoxin, is more potent, at least for humans, than that of any other species of octopus.

Treatment

Keep patient still, immobilize bite area and apply a compressive bandage to the bite.

Observe for signs of respiratory difficulties; should these occur, immediately start Expired Air Resuscitation and carry this on until normal breathing takes over — this could take anything from 3 to 6 hours. If possible, seek medical attention.

CONE SHELLS

Almost all cone shells can be regarded with suspicion, for there are several species that are known to deliver a fatal sting. Fish-eating cones have venom glands that produce a toxin affecting most vertebrates, including human beings. Cones that feed on worms and other molluscs have similar venom glands and apparatus for injection, but the potency of their venom is not as great.

However, very few experiments have been conducted on human beings, so it is better to handle all cone shells cautiously. *Never*, under any circumstances, place a live cone in your pocket or allow its shell aperture to come in contact with your body.

A number of venomous harpoons (modified radular teeth) are carried in the radular sac. They can be shot out through an extensible proboscis, which appears at the top (anterior) end of the shell. The following species are considered to be dangerous: *Conus textile, C. striatus, C. marmoreus, C. geographus, C. aulicus, C. tulipa, C. cattus, C. segravei* and *C. magus*.

Treatment

As there has only been one death in Australia traced to cone shell envenomation, these molluscs are not considered a major threat to the lives of snorkellers or divers. There is no antivenene and experts advise treatment along the same lines as for the blue-ringed octopus.

In tropical areas where normal populations of crown-of-thorns sea stars occur, they are nocturnal and pose little risk to divers. However, when in plague proportions the crown-of-thorns feeds in the open, both day and night. Make no mistake – these are *real* underwater hazards!

SEA STARS

The crown-of-thorns sea star is the most venomous asteroid in Australian waters. Encountered on the offshore islands and reefs of the northwestern and the northeastern coasts of Australia and south to Lord Howe Island, these sea stars are easily avoided and present little problem, unless you come into contact with one accidentally while exploring or taking pictures or on night dives when they may be out feeding.

The pain and possibly serious aftermath of being badly spined is probably the best reason for taking extra precautions when you are in areas inhabited by this sea star. Seek medical attention as soon as possible should an incident occur.

SEA URCHINS

In many areas of Australia, sea urchins are amongst the most prolific of the moderate-sized, mobile invertebrates.

A number of species are venomous – all those with sharp spines should be avoided or treated carefully. The spines are comprised of bone-like material and are very brittle. Some species have reverse serrations on the spines. Upon penetrating flesh, the spines break off and can be extremely painful. Removing them is difficult and if the flesh is badly spined nothing short of minor surgery will suffice.

Several of the larger tropical sea urchins, such as *Echinothrix diadema*, *Diadema setosum* and *Asthenosoma intermedium*, are quite dangerous. They have caused serious wounds, leading to infection and even paralysis of the affected limb. Once the immediate reaction and subsequent symptoms have subsided, pain may be felt in the vicinity of the wound for some time after. However, the smaller, finer spines will eventually be dissolved by body fluids.

Few precautions can be taken, except to be careful when in areas where there are urchins. This warning is extended in particular to night divers and to those who dive in caves and between ledges that are lined with sea urchins.

MORAY EELS

Moray eels are slimy, snake-like animals that live in holes and crevices in rocky and coral reefs right around Australia. Their history is mixed with tales of sea serpents, but the fairy stories should no longer be taken seriously. Like so many other animals, the much-maligned Moray eel can only be regarded as potentially dangerous. Its fearsome countenance – which is exaggerated by jaws that are studded with three frightening arrays of needle-sharp teeth opening and closing alternately – has a less-than-sinister purpose. The eel is only breathing when it moves its jaw like this; it is not licking its 'chops' and thinking how good you will taste! Remember, a diver in the water is large and bulky and would usually be regarded by the eel as a threat.

So, unless stupidity or carelessness overrules reason and you intimidate the eel by placing your exposed fingers into its reefy retreat, there is remarkably little to fear. Again, the emphasis is on you – look where you place your hands.

SHARKS

There is little doubt that the carnivorous eating habits of sharks have resulted in their being feared to a greater extent than any other marine creature.

Because of their size, speed, shape, armament, accurate vibratory senses and teeth, sharks are probably the most efficient inhabitants of their environment. It is this efficiency that causes them to be hunted and slaughtered wherever they are found. But sharks are a vital link in the life cycle of the sea and their part in the overall plan must be appreciated. This, of course, does little to comfort the snorkeller, or diver who encounters a hungry shark – even if nine times out of ten the 'encounter' is imaginery.

There are probably about nine species of sharks that are capable of attacking and injuring a diver or wader in Australian waters. Yet, compared with the number of people who swim and dive in these waters every year, the number of shark attacks is relatively small.

With pectoral fins lowered, this Galapagos shark is obviously excited and should definitely be avoided.

The main two types of sharks that divers might encounter are free-swimming sharks and ground sharks. In general, it is the free-swimming species that tend to cause the greatest anxiety.

The behaviour of various free-swimming sharks throughout the world has been studied at length and, although many millions of dollars have been spent, there is still little about it that can be predicted. Most free-swimming sharks seem to feed during change-over times at dusk or twilight, and also at night. However, sharks do not strictly adhere to this pattern. They also feed when they are hungry, whenever the opportunity presents itself, or when they have been excited by the invitational behaviour of a prey or a potential prey.

Most wading, look-box diving and snorkelling is carried out in shallow areas around coral reefs. Since the water is moderately clear, there is little reason to fear a shark attack during daylight hours. By not making undue noise or disturbing the water (by excessive splashing of fins, for instance), vibrations can be kept to a minimum and the somewhat small risk greatly lessened.

In very cloudy or silty waters, the risk is a little higher. Movements and vibrations may attract small reef sharks. Because of the poor visibility they cannot see and must come closer, which usually results in both you and the shark getting a fright.

As yet, there has not been a serious shark attack by a free-swimming shark on a scuba diver. As almost every scuba diver has probably been seen by a shark at some time without his or her knowledge, it seems that – until proven otherwise – we can assume this type of diving to be the safest.

Bottom-dwelling sharks are capable of injuring a wader, snorkeller or diver, but they are not usually aggressive and prefer to sleep under caves and ledges during the day. Because of their camouflaged appearance, there is always the chance of standing or lying on a shark when photographing in weedbeds or on rocky reefs.

Sharks do not normally feed on humans. More often than not an attack is a mistake on the shark's part – a misinterpretation of human behaviour in the water as that of an injured or disabled prey species. Or you may unwittingly invade a territory and so set off behaviour that is aggressive. In these circumstances, it is best to move away or to get out of the water.

GIANT CODS

Residents of shallow, deep, clear and murky waters, giant cods are usually found around submerged reefs, shipwrecks and wharves along the coastal areas of the offshore islands of northern Australia. During the days of commercial pearl fishing in Australia they were feared even more than sharks. The giant cod is inquisitive, so much so that it may come right up to you. It may become aggressive when its territory is invaded. If aggressive tendencies are observed, it is in the diver's best interest to back off to a point outside the territory of the fish. Giant cods eat mud crabs, fish, reef crays and offal. As yet there has been no substantiated case of an attack on a diver in Australia.

FIRE FISH

Spectacularly coloured, the fire fish inhabits caves and ledges during the day. The juveniles may live beneath dead coral slabs and small coral heads and rocks.

Some fish collectors have, while turning over coral slabs, put their hands on the dorsal spines of these fish – because they often remain immobile, fire fish are not easily seen.

Fire fish is an apt name, as they can deliver a very painful sting. A relative of the stonefish, the fire fish has a venom which is not lethal, but its sting can end a day's diving in no uncertain manner due to the pain and after effects. Immersing the affected part in hot water does alleviate the pain. Be careful not to scald.

STONEFISH

There are three species of stonefish in Australian waters; at least two are thought capable of delivering a fatal sting. The reef stonefish *Synanceichthys verrucosus* generally inhabits offshore reefs and islands. The horrid stonefish *Synanceja horrida* is generally a mainland species, but has been recorded on the Great Barrier Reef coral cays.

Both fish are normally found in shallow, silty areas up to 10 metres deep, although the horrid stonefish has been recorded at a depth of 22 metres. To most people who are new to the reef and intertidal tropical waters, thongs may seem adequate footwear, but they are not. Without well-protected feet, there is a risk of cuts from coral, oysters, razor clams and many other invertebrates, not to mention being stung by stonefish. A good pair of thick soled sandshoes (sneakers, jogging shoes) must be regarded as minimal footwear anywhere on the reef.

The danger of being stung is minimal for the shallow-water snorkeller or diver, however, should a diver be stung accidentally, help

Horrid stonefish are generally so well camouflaged that they are rarely seen. However, accidental envenomations have occurred due to the fish's excellent ability to conceal itself.

would be required to stop any secondary results being brought on by shock.

The stonefish is the uncrowned king of camouflage in the underwater world. The very fact that only a very small percentage of people have ever seen one in its natural habitat proves this.

Concealed in the first thirteen spines of the dorsal fin are twenty-six of the most efficient injection systems to be found in any marine animal. Should the fish be trodden upon, the needle-sharp tip of each spine penetrates the foot. Penetration constricts the poison ducts and allows the venom to shoot up into the wound, causing immediate and intense pain.

Treatment

Immerse the affected area in a container of hot water as soon as possible, taking care that the heat is periodically checked by hand to ensure scalding does not occur. Due to the nature of the venom, the patient may want the water hotter and hotter to alleviate the pain.

Antivenene is available but must be administered by an experienced medical practitioner *only* after accurate identification of the fish is confirmed.

SEA SNAKES

In the past much has been written and filmed about the aggressive behaviour of sea snakes. In recent years irrational fears about these reptiles have given way to common sense. Sea snakes are now seen as inquisitive onlookers, rather than dealers of instant death.

This does not mean that they are not capable of killing a human – certainly their poison is amongst the most deadly of venoms. But sea snakes feed on fish, not on people.

When a sea snake approaches a diver it is only being curious, they are not normally aggressive and, if treated in the same fashion i.e. without aggression, they will go their own way. A sea snake uses its tongue to taste, so don't be worried if they taste your wetsuit, fins, or curl around your camera. They are not to be feared, just understood.

Sea snakes have very poor eyesight and must be quite close to an object in order to recognise it. They are attracted by movement and have a curious nature. If a diver does not see a snake and kneels or leans on it, there is a chance the snake will bite to get away. This is only an instinctive reaction, like that found in many frightened animals, including humans.

Treatment

There have been no diver deaths from sea snakes recorded in Australian waters. Even when a sea snake bites (which is rarely), it does not always envenomate. However, whether envenomation has taken place can hardly be checked at the time the bite occurs. When treating a bite the patient should be restrained from all movement and a compressive bandage applied immediately. Medical attention must be sought as soon as possible.

Antivenene is available from the Commonwealth Serum Laboratories, but, like all antivenenes, it must be administered by a doctor or trained medical person.

There are hundreds of dangerous or potentially dangerous species of marine animals. I suppose every fish with a spine might be judged so, as could every piece of sharp coral!

For the most part, coping with these animals in their own environment is a matter of common sense. If you leave them alone, they will generally do the same for you. Most problems are just accidents, caused by ignorance; understanding them is the best preventative measure.

MEDICAL SERVICES

RECOMPRESSION CHAMBERS

Throughout my twenty-four years of diving, I have been asked the same question innumerable times by both divers and non-divers: 'How many times have you been bent?'

It is almost as if people automatically expected an answer in the affirmative. Some found it hard to believe that I haven't been bent or rescued and have never finished up in hospital with a diver-related injury or disease. One person even boasted to me that he'd been in the chamber twice on two separate occasions, and he'd only been diving a year or so (enough said!).

Personally, I don't ever want to see the inside of a chamber and, apart from inspections on invitation to see how they operate, I could go through my next twenty years as a diver quite happily without feeling left out because I haven't been in one. Sure, I could have been bent on a hundred different occasions, if I had pushed my limits. I know dozens of divers who have been in the 'pot' for one reason or another; some with minor bends, others with serious brain bends.

To me any bend is serious. I dive to stay alive. Because I love diving I don't see a few minutes more or less as being of any consequence in my life. This dive plan has stood me in good stead for over 10,000 dives and I stick to it.

In the early years of diving, if you made a mistake no one was there to come and get you, so you made quite sure that you dived well inside the tables and ran a decompression stop on all dives.

However, I am increasingly worried about why so many divers have been bent over the last ten years. Perhaps it is just that many more are being trained. Perhaps, because of the mere fact that chambers exist now, people take more chances. I really don't know. I must admit that it is certainly reassuring to have available lists of diving doctors in each state, as well as a diver emergency service aimed at promoting a greater awareness of underwater safety and offering a number of chamber facilities. Regardless of these things, all divers should take care and remain aware that diving and alcohol or dope don't mix. Don't be a fool; dive on the right side and stay alive!

CHAMBER FACILITIES IN AUSTRALIA

Victoria

Prince Henry's Hospital
St Kilda Road, Melbourne Vic. 3000
Phone: (03) 62 0621
Contact: Dr Gavin Dawson, Director of Anaesthesia, *or* Dr Tronson
Chamber: 1 man, 1 compartment, 20 metres, O_2 therapy.

Peter McCallum Clinic
481 Little Lonsdale Street, Melbourne Vic. 3000
Phone: (03) 602 1333, extension 348
Contact: Dr Hurley
Chamber: 1 man, 1 compartment, 30 metres, O_2 therapy.

Abalone Fishermen's Co-Op. Ltd
Genoa Road, Mallacoota Vic. 3889
Phone: (051) 58 0388, (051) 58 0235
Contact: H. Stanistreet

Bource-Martech Pty Ltd
119 Rouse Street, Port Melbourne Vic. 3207
Phone: (03) 64 1724
Contact: H. Bource
Chamber: 6 man, 2 compartment, 198 metres, O_2 therapy.

Metropolitan Board of Works
Lower Dandenong Road, Braeside Vic. 3195
Phone: Head Office (03) 62 0221
After Hours (03) 792 1402, (03) 906 0448
Contact: Medical Officer-in-Charge
Chamber: 2 man, 2 compartment, 40 metres, O_2 therapy.

Melbourne Diving Services
144 Bell Street, Heidelberg Vic. 3081
Phone: (03) 459 4432
Chamber: 54 inch (138 cm), twin lock, skid-mounted chamber with 500 foot (152 m) operation. Medical lock, oxygen bibs, seats four people in main lock or one person reclining plus attendant. Quincy compressor, 120 cubic feet, 2 stage, diesel operated.

Melbourne Hyperbaric Centre
19 Rouse Street, Port Melbourne Vic. 3207
Phone: (03) 64 1724
Contact: Director of Operations: Henri Bource
Medical Director: Dr Ken Shepherd
Service: Hyperbaric medicine and decompression courses.

Offshore Diving Chambers (Sale, Eastern Victoria)
Comex Off-shore Australia Pty Ltd
7 McAllister Court, *or* 67 McAllister Street, Sale Vic. 3850
Phone: (051) 44 4248, (03) 420 5688, (03) 848 4973
Contact: P. Larment
Chamber: 4 man, 2 compartments, 90 metres, O_2 therapy.

J. Roy McDermott (Australia) Pty Ltd
398 Raymond Street, Sale Vic. 3850
Phone: (051) 44 1322
Contact: N. Clarke
Chamber: 4 bed, 2 compartment, 198 metres, O_2 therapy (can
        hold 20 men in an emergency).

Oceaneering Australia Pty Ltd
308 Raglin Street, Sale Vic. 3850
Phone: (051) 44 2487
Contact: P. Washington
After hours: C. Batten (051) 44 1727
            D. Rowe (051) 44 4073
Chamber: 2 x 4 bed, 2 compartments, 182 metres, O_2 therapy.

New South Wales

RAN School of Underwater Medicine
HMAS Penguin
Balmoral, Sydney NSW 2088
Phone: (02) 960 0321
Emergency: (02) 960 0321

Prince Henry Hospital
Anzac Parade, Little Bay Sydney NSW 2036
Phone: (02) 661 0111
Contact: Ask for the Director of Hyperbaric and Diving Medicine,
        or the Deputy Director on Duty if the Director is not
        available.

Tasmania

Royal Hobart Hospital
48 Liverpool Street, Hobart Tas. 7000
Phone: (002) 38 8308
Contact: Medical Superintendent
        Dial '000' for Emergency Service

South Australia

Royal Adelaide Hospital
Dequeteville Terrace, Kent Town SA 5067
Phone: (08) 244 5514
Contact: Intensive Care Unit: (08) 223 2330 or
        St John's Ambulance, phone '000'.
Chamber: 50 metres depth, 2 compartment, oxygen bibs, 3
        bunks.

Western Australia

Fremantle Hospital
Alma Street, Fremantle WA 6160
Phone: (09) 335 0111
Service: Hospital will refer cases to *HMAS Stirling*.

HMAS Stirling
Phone: (095) 27 0470

Queensland

Australian Institute of Marine Science
Clevedon, Townsville Qld 4810
Phone: (077) 78 9211, (007) 78 9221
Contact: Director

Aqua-Nautic Pty Ltd
12 Yeronga Street, Yeronga, Brisbane Qld 4000
Phone: (07) 48 5448
Contact: Joe Engwirda (proprietor)
Chamber: Large recompression chamber with one man
portable chamber which marries onto main
chamber. This is a privately owned facility and
arrangements have to be made with the proprietor
for its use. This chamber is not permanently
manned, as the proprietor is not always on the
premises.

Australia-wide

Diver Emergency Service (DES)
Phone: (008) 08 8200
Service: Connects to Hyperbaric Medicine Unit, Royal Adelaide
Hospital. A specialist advice service operates from
there, or calls may be transferred instantly to a unit
nearer the accident site.

DES GOES AUSTRALIA WIDE

The Diver Emergency Service (DES), introduced in 1986 after an agreement was reached between the Australian Underwater Federation (AUF) and the Department of Defence, has rapidly gained recognition and diver acceptance. It has, however, placed a very large strain on the School of Underwater Medicine at *HMAS Penguin*.

As a result, further negotiations are in progress to enlarge the DES scheme and reduce the load on the Navy. As from May 87 the newly established Hyperbaric Medicine Unit (HMU) at the Royal Adelaide Hospital has offered the Diver Emergency Service a toll free 008 telephone number. The number connects to a 24-hour Australia-wide advice service manned by specialists in hyperbaric medicine employed at HMU and at other establishments around Australia.

By means of a 'diverto phone', a call from an accident site to HMU can be transferred to a specialist on duty anywhere in Australia, who can then speak directly to the accident site.

Those medical units involved in the expanded DES scheme are: Royal Adelaide Hospital; Prince Henry Hospital, Sydney; Fremantle Hospital; Royal Hobart Hospital; Townsville General Hospital; Australian Institute of Marine Science, Townsville; The National Safety Council of Australia (Victorian Division) Morwell; and, of course, The Royal Australian Navy at Sydney (*HMAS Penguin*) and Perth (*HMAS Stirling*).

DOCTORS OF UNDERWATER MEDICINE

Included below is a listing of resident Australian doctors with training in underwater medicine, reproduced courtesy of South Pacific Underwater Medicine Society (SPUMS). They have completed at least the Royal Australian Navy School of Underwater Medicine introductory course, or have had equivalent training.

The list has been compiled with the cooperation of the School of Underwater Medicine (SUM) and includes all members that can be identified from the SUM records. As a result it may include doctors who no longer do diving medicals. The addresses given are those to where the *SPUMS Journal* is sent, and so may not be the actual doctor's professional rooms.

Australian Capital Territory

Dr G.D. Davies
28 Berne Crescent, Macgregor ACT 2615

New South Wales

Dr J.M. Anderson
105 Karalta Road, Erina NSW 2250

Dr T. Anderson
School of Underwater Medicine
HMAS Penguin, Balmoral Naval PO Box, NSW 2091

Dr G. Barry
Box 268, Newport Beach NSW 2106

Dr C. Edmonds
25 Battle Boulevard, Seaforth NSW 2092

Dr C. Finlay-Jones
165 Morgan Street, Merewether NSW 2291

Dr R. Gray
21 Coombar Close, Coffs Harbour NSW 2450

Dr R. Green
47 Shorter Avenue, Beverly Hills NSW 2209

Dr T.J. Horgan
232 Mona Vale Road, St Ives NSW 2075

Dr P. Kolisch
33 Mann Street, Nambucca Heads NSW 2248

Dr R. Lloyd-Williams
102 Yanko Road, West Pymble NSW 2073

Dr C. Lowrey
233 Raglan Street, Mosman NSW 2088

Lcdr C.J. McDonald
PO Box 875, Ballina NSW 2478

Dr W. Pettigrew
c/- Lidcombe Hospital, Lidcombe NSW 2141

Dr C.P. Pidcock
39 Stockton Road, Nelson Bay NSW 2315

Dr F. Summers
56 Hickson Street, Merewether NSW 2291

Dr A. Temperley ·
16 Normanhurst Road, Normanhurst NSW 2076

Dr I. Unsworth
Hyperbaric Unit, Prince Henry Hospital
PO Box 333, Matraville NSW 2036

Dr A. Vane
Police Medical Officer
NSW Police Headquarters
PO Box 45, Sydney NSW 2001

Dr D.G. Walker
1423 Pittwater Road, Narrabeen NSW 2101

Dr D.B. Wallace
1/26 Aubin Street, Neutral Bay NSW 2089

Dr K.J. Wishaw
5 Clearly Avenue, Cheltenham NSW 2119

Dr A.W. Swain
46 The Parade, Norwood SA 5067

Queensland

Dr Chris Acott
39 Oswald Street, Rockhampton Qld 4700

Dr J.W. Cairns
65 Potts Street, Belgian Gardens Qld 4810

Dr I. Gibbs
PO Box 131, Mackay Qld 4740

Dr J. Orton
Townsville General Hospital
Townsville Qld 4810

Dr D. Pashen
3 White Street, Ingham Qld 4850

Dr D. Richards
5/25 Ascot Terrace, Toowong Qld 4066

Dr P. Sullivan
33 Rutledge Street, Coolangatta Qld 4225

Dr R.L. Thomas
39 Kersley Road, Kenmore Qld 4069

Dr M. Unwin
8 Fulham Road, Pimlico Qld 4810

Dr R. M. Walker
Gold Coast Hospital, Nerang Street,
Southport Qld 4215

Dr J. Williamson
137 Wills Street, Townsville Qld 4810

Dr K Woodhead
Suite 9, Milton Shopping Centre
Baroona Road, Milton Qld 4064

South Australia

Dr D. Gorman
Hyperbaric Unit
Royal Adelaide Hospital, Adelaide SA 5000

Dr W. Heddle
19 Alexander Avenue, Ashford SA 5035

Dr G. Rawson
4 Brierbank Terrace, Stonyfell SA 5066

Tasmania

Dr D. Griffiths
9 Topham Street, Rosebay Tas. 7015

Dr V. Haller
12 Moirunna Road, Lindisfarne Tas. 7015

Dr M. Martin
Dept of Anaesthesia
Royal Hobart Hospital, Hobart Tas. 7000

Dr P. McCartney
PO Box 1317N, Hobart Tas. 7001

Victoria

Dr G. Broomhall
472 Belmore Road, North Box Hill Vic. 3129

Dr C.B.E. Davis
8 Ascot Street North, Ballarat Vic. 3350

Dr J. Knight
80 Wellington Parade,
East Melbourne Vic. 3002

Dr C. Lourey
25 Hastings Street, Frankston Vic. 3199

Dr J.E. Mannerheim
25 Wellard Street, Box Hill Vic. 3128

Dr I. Millar
National Safety Council of Australia
(Vic. Division)
1 Chickerell Street, Morwell Vic. 3840

Dr R. Moffitt
1170 Main Road, Eltham Vic. 3095

Dr L.J. Norton
44 Eleanor Street, Footscray Vic. 3011

Dr K. Shepherd
7 Young Street, Brighton Vic. 3186

Dr J. Silver
PO Box 140, Williamstown Vic. 3016

Dr G. Zimmerman
46 Begonia Road, Elsternwick Vic. 3185

Western Australia

Dr A.R. Adams
24 Gilford Road, Dunsborough WA 6281

Major P. Alexander
RAP Special Air Services Regiment
Campbell Barracks, Swanbourne WA 6010

Dr G. Carter
254 Canning Highway,
East Fremantle WA 6158

Dr D.E. Davies
Suite 6 Killowen House
St Anne's Hospital, Mount Lawley WA 6050

Dr G. Deleuil
135 Dunedin Street,
Mount Hawthorn WA 6016

Dr H. Oxer
331 Riverton Drive, Shelley WA 6155

Dr J. Rippon
764 Canning Highway, Applecross WA 6153

Dr A. Robertson
Sick Quarters, *HMAS Stirling*
PO Box 228, Garden Island WA 6168

Dr J. Taylor
PO Box 498, Exmouth WA 6707

Dr R. Wong
34 Loftus Street, Nedlands WA 6009

Errors in this list should be notified to the
Secretary of SPUMS:
Dr David Davies
Suite 6 Killowen House, St Anne's Hospital
Ellesmere Road, Mt. Lawley WA 6050

Project stickybeak

This project is an ongoing investigation seeking to document all types of diving-related incidents at all levels of severity. Information, all of which is treated as strictly *confidential*, about incidents and their identifying details, is utilised in reports and case reports on non-fatal occurrences. Such reports can be freely used by any interested person or organisation to increase diving safety through better awareness of critical factors. Information may be sent (in confidence) to:

Dr D. Walker
PO Box 120, Narrabeen NSW 2101

List of doctors and information on project stickybeak reprinted by permission *SPUMS Journal*, Vol. 16, 1986, issue No. 3, July/Sept.

INSTRUCTION AGENCIES

AUSTRALIAN UNDERWATER FEDERATION

The following information has been supplied by the Australian Underwater Federation:

The Australian Underwater Federation is the National Sporting Body for all underwater activities in Australia. It is the diver's own organisation, owing its existence to individuals who recognise the need to be represented in a variety of forms to protect the recreational and sporting environment.

Through the AUF, all divers have a voice in the setting of standards, competitions, conservation matters and representations to government. In return, the AUF provides divers with services of USE to them. Membership of the Australian Underwater Federation entitles you to:

- A voice to government (state and federal)
- Bi-monthly newsletter
- Lectures/seminars
- Regular social events
- Cheap air travel
- International recognition of your skills (CMAS)
- Participation in organised competitions
- Discount purchasing at some dive shops
- Discount accommodation
- Advice on technical matters
- Discount dive tours
- Help in control of standards
- Diver personal accident insurance (AUF Gold Diver Insurance)

Do you want to know about snorkelling, underwater hockey, marine biology, spear fishing competitions, underwater photography, archaeology, cave diving? — join the Australian Underwater Federation. Applications are available from: Australian Underwater Federation, PO Box 1006, Civic Square, ACT 2608.

BSAC

This information has been supplied by The British Sub-Aqua Club:

There is no other sport that offers the opportunities for exploration, knowledge and excitement that underwater swimming provides. It is a sport which is enjoyed in a different element, where humans can enjoy the exhilaration of weightlessness – an experience only shared by astronauts in space. Like many of the exploration sports, it is appealing to more and more people of all ages.

Although the first diving club was formed in Paris in 1926, it is really only since the marketing of the compressed air aqualung in 1950 that the sport has developed. The British Sub-Aqua Club was founded in London in 1953 and branches were very quickly formed in other parts of the country.

Training is essential

It is absolutely vital that the novice has a thorough training and the instructors in BSAC branches – which now exceed 1000 – all conform to a standard training programme. This training programme is the result of many years' experience and aims at producing competent, safe divers. Although the French have called aqualung diving 'the sport for active grandmothers', it is highly dangerous to merely put on the equipment and swim down to the depths. Properly taught, the risks are minimal and the BSAC, which is the governing body of the sport in the United Kingdom, is proud of its safely record.

Membership of the BSAC is obtained by the payment of an entry fee and annual subscription. The entrance fee provides each member with a copy of the BSAC Diving Manual which is a 584 page volume with numerous illustrations and is regarded as one of the most authoritative books on diving in the world. Every month, members receive a copy of Diver magazine – a colourful publication giving all the latest news and views on the sport.

Joining Procedure

When a member joins a branch, it is necessary to pass a medical and a simple swimming test before starting training. Initially, the new member learns the use of the 'basic' equipment – face mask, fins and snorkel tube – before graduating to the use of the aqualung in the swimming pool. Pool training usually takes between three to six months and once completed, the new diver will be ready to take part in open water dives with the branch either in the sea or an inland water sites. Dives are recorded in a Qualification Record Logbook which acts as an international passport to the underwater world. CMAS (World Underwater Federation) certificates and cards are available recognising the BSAC qualifications internationally.

Once diving skills have been mastered, either with a branch of the BSAC or with a recognised BSAC school, the amateur can decide what to do with the new-found skill which provides a means to explore and enjoy the new world of 'inner space'.

The main attraction for many newly-qualified divers is to explore wrecks and there are more of these around the coast of Britain than anywhere else in the world. BSAC members have discovered many of these and have researched and worked on them in conjunction with recognised nautical archaeologists. These wrecks include the *Mary Rose* – a unique Tudor man of war which sank in full view of Henry VIII; the *Trinidad Valencera* – an Armada galleon; and

HMS Dartmouth – a frigate which foundered in the Sound of Mull while extracting tribute from the rebellious clans for the new King William of Orange. Many more ancient wrecks are still to be found and each year brings news of more exciting finds.

Other groups of sport divers have specialised in researching and lifting the more modern wrecks left from World War II. Numerous aircraft and underwater craft, such as midget submarines, have been located, raised and brought ashore. The method generally employed is to use large numbers of oil drums or lifting bags filled with air to provide enough buoyancy to raise them to the surface. Marine biology is another interest which captures the imagination and the BSAC organise a number of courses specially for divers. Quite recently, an amateur diver on a marine biology course held on the Isle of Lundy in the Bristol Channel, pushed his arm into a long burrow in the sea-bed and pulled out a long and highly coloured eel-like fish (*Cepola*) which although known in British waters, had never been discovered close to the surface. Now, extensive studies of the fish in its natural burrows are under way and new knowledge will be gained. A great number of divers become keen underwater photographers. The problems are considerable even in clear water but equipment has progressed from primitive 'pressure cooker' cases for conventional cameras to easily manoeuverable amphibious ones that can be operated just as easily below the surface as above. The problems of underwater photography stem mainly from the lack of light, and for colour shots, an underwater flash unit is normally needed.

Underwater cine cameras are also popular and many film and photographic competitions are organised. Possibly one of the reasons that underwater photography is so popular is because it enables a diver to share some of the wonderful sights with those who have never learned to dive.

The BSAC run courses in underwater photography and in fact, for almost every underwater activity. They also represent divers and their interests on national and international bodies such as the World Underwater Federation.

Members of the BSAC are automatically covered with third party and liability insurance while diving. The Club also produces a range of publications on diving and these can be obtained from the BSAC Postal Shop. In addition, the shop sells a varied range of BSAC items such as T-shirts, sweater shirts, ties, scarves, badges, diving slates and wet suit badges.

Australian Branches

NSW	2 branches	**Training handbooks**	
SA	2 branches	Training Manual	
Vic.	5 branches	MDC Bulletin	
WA	1 branch	Diver magazine	
NT	1 branch		

Sport Diver Training
Novice – sport – dive leader – advanced – first class

Instructors
ITC – club instructor – advanced instructor – National instructor
Contact: PO Box 318, Noble Park, Vic. 3174

FEDERATION OF AUSTRALIAN UNDERWATER INSTRUCTORS

The following information has been supplied by FAUI:

The Federation of Australian Underwater Instructors (FAUI) is an organisation having as members scuba diving instructors from all states of Australia and Papua New Guinea. FAUI instructors and the levels of training of FAUI are through the recognition and support of the Australian Underwater Federation.

The aims of FAUI are to ensure that people are taught to dive by qualified instructors and that such tuition meets the requirements of FAUI, the Confederation Mondiale des Activities Sub-Aquatiques (CMAS — World Underwater Federation), Australian Underwater Federation, and the National Coaching Accreditation Scheme.

The Federation of Australian Underwater Instructors is recognised by the Australian Underwater Federation (AUF) – and, therefore by CMAS – and is able to qualify a diver for CMAS. FAUI is also recognised by the Scuba Divers Federation of Australia (SDFA).

FAUI membership includes representatives from both amateur and professional diving instruction fields – from service organisations (Army, Navy), and State Police Forces. The only criterion for instructor membership of FAUI is that the member reach a sufficient standard of diving and instructional ability to satisfy the requirements of FAUI and CMAS.

Associate membership of FAUI is open to any person interested in diving instruction, which allows the member access to all FAUI services. Anyone wishing to teach divers, however, must become a full member. This can only be achieved by succesfully completing an Instructor Certification Program, during which the candidate is examined in all areas of diving instruction to the highest standards of the World Underwater Federation (CMAS) – 2 and 3 Star instructor level. Each FAUI Instructor Certification Program is supervised by the National Examiner of the Federation and two other highly experienced members of the National Examining Panel, who come from other States to ensure that both standards and impartiality are maintained.

The FAUI Instructor standard is very similar to standards adopted in the United States of America and Britain. In fact, both basic and instructor level qualifications issued by FAUI are recognised by all major instructor groups affiliated to CMAS and are recognised in over 50 countries throughout the world.

Except in special cases, entry to an Instructor Certification

Program is conditional upon the candidate satisfying certain pre-requisites and upon successfully undergoing an accredited Instructor Training Program.

In addition to training and testing diving instructors and setting-up and maintaining standards for scuba diving courses in conjunction with diving bodies such as the AUF and SDFA, other activities of the Federation include regular publications of Technical Bulletins (covering advances in diving medicine, equipment and operations, advances in teaching theory and methods, etc), staging of the Annual Indo-Pacific Conference on Underwater Education, and the provision of text and reference material (books, films, audio-visual programs).

FAUI News: **The Official Journal of Australian Underwater Instructors.**

FAUI News is published quarterly and is available to subscribers at the rate of $10 per annual subscription. *FAUI News* is an entertaining, informative journal, recording topical events on the dive scene throughout Australia with particular emphasis on the activities of the Federation of Australia Underwater Instructors.

Contact: Dave Wilson, (09) 344 7882.

NAUI

The following information has been supplied by NAUI:

The National Association of Underwater Instructors (NAUI) is one of the two largest diver training agencies in the world. It was formed in the United States in 1960 (several years before any other similar agency) to serve the educational needs of scuba instructors and leaders and the safety needs of the public. NAUI AUSTRALIA, NAUI CANADA and NAUI JAPAN are autonomous associations affiliated with NAUI INTERNATIONAL. NAUI chapters also exist in many other areas – New Zealand, Papua New Guinea, South-east Asia and, of course, in Europe. The high levels of activity in these areas well illustrates the rapidly expanding international influence of NAUI.

Each NAUI national body is a professional, non-profit corporation involved solely in diver education. NAUI is not supported by government or outside corporate funding and so is completely independent. NAUI is owned by its Membership and the Membership elects the Board of Directors. Distribution of profits to these Directors is not possible under the NAUI Constitution. This democratic organisational structure of NAUI is unique in the world's diving industry.

'SAFETY THROUGH EDUCATION' is NAUI's motto and Continuing Education is NAUI's goal. The whole NAUI international organisation evolves and grows in order to achieve that goal through quality programs and services.

NAUI Instructors are fully accredited under the Australian Government sponsored National Coaching Accreditation Scheme (NCAS). This has also resulted in NAUI Members in Australia having full access to the World Underwater Federation (CMAS) certification system through the Australia Underwater Federation – the administrators of the NCAS and the national CMAS authority.

Also unique to NAUI are the eye-catching positive identification cards issued to divers of all levels graduating from NAUI certification courses. As well as bearing a photograph of the diver on the reverse for ID purposes, the face of each card is based on a full colour underwater photo relevant to the certification level involved.

In Australia, NAUI operations are handled by a fulltime professional staff from a spacious office in one of the fastest growing business areas of Brisbane. Brisbane is the geographical centre between the diving areas of the Great Barrier Reef and the population centres of the southern states. This puts NAUI in an ideal position to provide quality support services at very competitive prices to the scuba diving instructors operating in the resort areas of Queensland as well as the numerous dive shops in the other states. There are active NAUI Instructors in all the states of Australia.

NAUI AUSTRALIA is continuing to build upon an already enviable reputation for not only rapid service and extremely competitive prices, but also solid support for the interests of its members in the face of ever increasing calls for more regulation of diving.

If you are seeking the 'Quality Difference' in diver education, ask for the local NAUI Instructor when next you want to go 'down-under'. If you are already a diver and feel that it is about time you took the next step, then step up to NAUI and once again experience that 'Quality Difference'.

For further information, contact the NAUI AUSTRALIA Office, PO Box 183, Capalaba QLD 4157, Australia. Phone: (07) 390 3113.

PADI

AUSTRALIAN HEADQUARTERS: PADI Australia, 8th Floor, 181 Elizabeth Street, Sydney, 2000.
Phone: (02) 267 8020 (4 lines) Fax: (02) 267 1357

Director of Training: Terry Cummins
Projects Manager: Bruce Jameson
Standards Co-ordinator: Nancy Cummins
Office Manager: Lorraine Strutt
Executive Secretary: Julie Duncan
Membership Services: Jenny Balzan
Certifications: Paul Jolliffe

PADI College of Australia, 3rd Floor, 181 Elizabeth Street, Sydney, 2000.
Phone: (02) 267 8600 (2 lines)
Manager: John Storey

INTERNATIONAL HEADQUARTRERS:
PADI International, 1243 East Warner Avenue Santa Ana, California, 92705.
Phone: (714) 540 7234

The following information has been supplied by PADI:

The Professional Association of Diving Instructors was initially conceived during 1966, in an effort to provide safe instructional techniques and training for divers in the United States.

Established as a non-profit, educational organisation, PADI quickly grew nationally within the United States whilst at an international level, PADI emerged as a guiding force.

PADI has over 18,000 instructors and more than 1050 Training Facilities, with a Headquarters staff of 150 full-time professionals, branch offices in many major cities throughout the world, including Australia, Japan, Canada, Sweden, Norway, New Zealand and Europe. Courses are conducted in over 90 countries. In 1986 PADI certified 310,000 divers worldwide, 4,000 of those in Australia.

The PADI training program was introduced into Australia in 1969 by visiting US instructors. After this initial contact, a small nucleus of local instructors was established. In 1973 the first Australian PADI Instructor Training Course (ITC) was convened and since then a steady stream of instructor graduates has been maintained. Now regular programs are convened all over Australia and at PADI's College in Sydney.

There are currently over 1600 PADI members in Australia.

PADI Instructor Development programs are developed along the concept of the professional instructor, including instructor training in the classroom, pool and open water. This is necessary to properly prepare an individual to cope with student problems and to effectively develop the ability to communicate and control class training.

All phases of course operation, training schools and professional scuba facilities are covered during Instructor Training. The final Instructor Evaluation Course for candidates (IEC) is held by PADI full time staff professionals.

Instructors of recognised agencies with a willingness to adopt modern training methods and philosophies have always been welcomed by PADI. Their contributions have added considerably to PADI's growth and development.

Due to the rapid advancement in PADI teaching methodology in recent years, these individuals have, since 1979, been required to attend special PADI Instructor Orientation Course (IOC's) in order to qualify for PADI membership.

PADI believes that a professional educator never stops learning. To keep members up-to-date, PADI Headquarters staff regularly conduct a variety of instructor developments seminars at locations throughout the world. These programs cover such topics as new methods for conducting entry-level diver training and how to promote and conduct continuing education courses. The annual Australian Development Seminar is usually held in September in conjunction with Oceans.

Within two years of its birth PADI had created one of many products which would have major impact on the entire diving industry. The PADI Positive Identification Card (PIC), introduced in 1968, was the first certification credential to include the diver's picture and personal identification information. The PIC card is used to recognise divers who have participated in the PADI system of diver education.

PADI's continuing education programs are based on the concept that divers cannot be taught everything they need to know in a single course. Continuing education provides a step-to-step series of courses which result in a competent, safe and enthusiastic diver. The steps in PADI's educational system included Open Water, Advanced Open Water, Rescue Diver, Specialty, Divemaster and Master Scuba Diver ratings.

In 1977, the Open Water Diver program was further enhanced by the creation of the PADI Modular Scuba Course. This totally co-ordinated program, consisting of an instructor manual, student test, dive tables, standardised quizzes and exams, A/V program and aquatic cue cards made teaching a consistent, high-quality diver training program easy. Today, the PADI Modular Scuba Course components are the most widely used diver training materials in the world.

In addition to diving texts such as the PADI Dive Manual, PADI Advance Dive Manual, PADI Rescue Manual, PADI Divemaster Manual and Scuba review workbook, PADI publishes three quarterly magazines.

The Undersea Journal is devoted to diver training and instructor information. It is distributed to all active PADI Instructors, Assistant Instructors and Divemaster members, as well as to all PADI Training Facilities.

Dive Industry News is mailed without charge to all dive stores, manufacturers, resorts and other businesses within the diving industry. It is recognised as the industry's most informative trade publication.

Diving Ventures is a unique consumer publication, which lists local diving activities and describes resort destinations worldwide. Diving Ventures magazine is sent to all members of Diving Ventures International – The PADI Diving Society.

In addition to these magazines PADI Australia publishes *PADI Newsline* to keep local instructors up to date on local issues and items of interest.

PADI publishes a number of other support materials, including the *PADI Instructor Training Manual* and the *Retail Dive Store: Management and Operations Manual*. The *Instructor Manual* functions as the professional educator's guide to offering the entire PADI educational system, including how to use all the components of the PADI Modular Scuba Course. The *Retail Dive Store: Management and Operations Manual* covers all aspects of running a dive store, including financial management, promotion and marketing.

It is recognised as the most comprehensive management guide available to diving retailers.

INDEPENDENT EDUCATION COURSES

UNDERWATER PHOTOGRAPHY COURSES (ALL STATES)

Nikon School of Underwater Photography

Principal:
Neville Coleman, member Australian Institute of Professional Photography. Awarded the Australian Photographic Society's highest award, the 1984 Commonwealth Medal for the Advancement of Photographic Technology.

Courses conducted through dive shop facilities or by special arrangement. Complete full colour course brochure available on request. Certificates issued. Weekend workshops, introductory courses. Accredited NAUI, AUF/FAUI, PADI instruction by arrangement.

Contact:
Nikon School of Underwater Photography
PO Box 702, Springwood Qld 4127
Phone: (07) 341 8931 for the next course near you.

LIVING MARINE BIOLOGY & UNDERWATER NATURALIST COURSES (ALL STATES)

Principal:
Neville Coleman, Associate Australian Museum;
Curator, Australasian Marine Photographic Index;
Director, Sea Australia Resource Centre.

Courses conducted through dive shop facilities or by special arrangement. Complete full colour course brochure available on request. Certificates issued. Weekend workshops, introductory courses, free course folder and course book included in costs. Accredited NAUI, AUF/FAUI, PADI instruction by arrangement.

Contact:
The Director: Sea Australia Resource Centre
PO Box 702, Springwood Qld 4127
Phone: (07) 341 8931

MARINE BIOLOGY COURSES

Vic., SA, Tas.
Reg and Kay Lipson
NAUI, PADI & FAUI, AUF
Certificates issued, brochure available on request.

Contact:
Sea Studies Services
70 Railway Parade, South Chadstone Vic. 3148
Phone: (03) 277 0773 anytime.

ACT
Dr Angela Ivanovici
FAUI, AUF instruction. Certificates issued, brochure available on request.

Contact:
Dr A Ivanovici
61 Erlduna Circuit, Hawker ACT 2614
Phone: (062) 54 6001 (home)

AUSTRALIAN ASSOCIATIONS AND SOCIETIES

GREAT BARRIER REEF MARINE PARK AUTHORITY
PO Box 1379, Townsville Qld 4810, *or*
94 Denham Street
Townsville Qld 4180
Phone: (077) 81 8811

MARINE AQUARIUM SOCIETY OF VICTORIA
PO Box 286, Moorabbin Vic. 3189

WORLD WILDLIFE FUND AUSTRALIA
Level 17, St Martins Tower
31 Market Street, Sydney NSW 2000, *or*
PO Box 528, Sydney NSW 2001
Phone: (02) 29 7572

AUSTRALIAN CONSERVATION FOUNDATION
672B Glenferrie Road, Hawthorn Vic. 3122
Phone: (03) 819 2888

CAVE DIVERS ASSOCIATION OF AUSTRALIA
PO Box 290, North Adelaide SA 5006

MARINE AQUARIUM RESEARCH INSTITUTE OF AUSTRALIA (MARIA)
PO Box 279, Coogee NSW 2034

GREENPEACE AUSTRALIA (INC.)
787 George Street, Sydney NSW 2000

ORGANIZATION FOR THE RESUSCITATION AND RESEARCH OF CETACEANS IN AUSTRALIA (ORRCA)
PO Box E293, St James NSW 2001
Phone: (02) 969 5784

PROJECT JONAH QLD INC.
PO Box 238, North Quay Qld 4000
Phone: (07) 221 0188

AUSTRALIAN SOCIETY FOR FISH BIOLOGY
Hon. Sec.: NSW Dept of Agriculture Fisheries Research Institute
PO Box 21, Cronulla NSW 2230
Phone: (02) 523 6222

COAST AND WETLANDS SOCIETY
PO Box A225, Sydney South NSW 2000

AUSTRALIAN MARINE SCIENCES ASSOCIATION
Hon. Sec./Treasurer AMSA
20/8 Waratah Street, Cronulla NSW 2230

SOUTH PACIFIC UNDERWATER MEDICAL SOCIETY
Suite 6, Killowen House, St Anne's Hospital
Ellesmere Road, Mt. Lawley WA 6050

AUSTRALIAN INSTITUTE OF PROFESSIONAL PHOTOGRAPHY
Federal Secretary
PO Box 665, Blackwood SA 5051
Phone: (08) 278 8662

MALACOLOGICAL SOCIETY OF AUSTRALIA
Hon. Sec. c/- Department of Zoology
University of Queensland, St Lucia Qld 4067

FUND FOR ANIMALS LTD AUSTRALIA
PO Box 371, Manly NSW 2095
Phone: (02) 77 1557

AUSTRALIAN PHOTOGRAPHIC SOCIETY INC.
PO Box 17, Surrey Hills Vic 3127

MARINE EDUCATION SOCIETY OF AUSTRALASIA
Hon. Sec. MESA Marine Studies Centre
Queenscliff Vic. 3225
Phone: (052) 52 0375

AUSTRALIAN LITTORAL SOCIETY
PO Box 49, Moorooka Qld 4105
Phone: (07) 848 5235

FURTHER READING

Beilby, Dick, *Perth Diveguide*, Creative Research, Perth, 1981.

Byron, Tom, *Scuba Diving the New South Wales Coast*, 3rd edn, Aqua Sports Publications, Sydney, 1986.

Coleman, Neville, *Australian Sea Fishes North of 30 degrees*, Doubleday, Lane Cove, 1982.

Coleman, Neville, *Australian Sea Fishes South of 30 degrees*, Doubleday, Lane Cove, 1980.

Coleman, Neville, *Australian Sea Life South of 30 degrees*, Doubleday, Lane Cove, 1987.

Coleman, Neville, *Beginner's Guide to Underwater Marine Biology*, Australasian Marine Photographic Index, Sydney, 1985.

Coleman, Neville, *Nudibranchs of Australasia*, Australasian Marine Photographic Index, Sydney, 1984.

Coleman, Neville, *Shells Alive*, Rigby, Adelaide, 1981.

Coleman, Neville, *What Shell Is That?*, Landsdowne Press, Sydney, 1985.

Coleman, Neville, *Underwater, The Diver's Journal*, Nos 1–20, Sea Australia Productions Pty Ltd, 1981–87.

Daniel, Michael & Cohen, Shlomo, *Red Sea Diver's Guide*, Red Sea Divers (Publications) Ltd, Israel, 1975.

Ivanovici, Angela M. (ed.), *Inventory of Declared Marine and Estuarine Protected Areas in Australian Waters: Vols 1 & 2*, Australian National Parks and Wildlife, Canberra, 1984.

Kelley, Kate, & Shobe, John, *Diver's Guide to Underwater America*, Divesports Publishing, Texas, 1982.

Marsh, Loisette & Slack-Smith, Shirley, *Sea Stingers*, Western Australian Museum, Perth, 1987.

National Roads and Motorists' Association, *NRMA Accommodation Directory*, NRMA, Sydney, 1986–87.

_____ NRMA Camping Guide, NRMA, Sydney, 1986–87.

Reader's Digest, *Reader's Digest Complete Atlas of Australia*, Reader's Digest, Sydney, 1968.

Smith, David & Westlake, Michael, with Castaneda, Por Firio, *The Diver's Guide to the Philippines*, International Diving Guides.

South Pacific Underwater Medicine Society, *SPUMS Journal*, SPUMS.

INDEX OF SCIENTIFIC AND COMMON NAMES

Horrid stonefish	*Synanceia horrida*
Kelp	*Ecklonia radiata*
Kent's flatworm	*Pseudoceros kenti*
Leafy sea dragon	*Phycodurus eques*
Lightning volute	*Ericusa fulgetra*
Long-nosed coralfish	*Chelmon rostratus*
Long-snouted boarfish	*Pentaceropsis recurvirostris*
Magnificent biscuit star	*Tosia magnifica*
Magnificent volute	*Cymbiolena magnifica*
Manta ray	*Manta alfreda*
Margined coralfish	*Chelmon marginalis*
Margined flatworm	*Callioplana marginata*
Mosaic sea star	*Plectaster decanus*
Multi-pored sea star	*Linckia multiflora*
Multi-spined sea star	*Nectia multispina*
Navarchus angelfish	*Pomacanthus navarchus*
Noble feather star	*Comanthina nobilis*
Old wife	*Enoplosus armatus*
Opalescent nudibranch	*Pterolidia ianthina*
Ornate wobbegong	*Orectolobus ornatus*
Paper nautilus	*Argonauta nodosa*
Pearly nautilus	*Nautilus pompilius*
Plumed ovulid	*Pseudosimnia* sp.
Potato cod	*Epinephelus tuka*
Red gurnard scorpionfish	*Helicolenus papillosus*
Red-lined aeolid nudibranch	*Flabellina rubrolineata*
Red-margined casella nudibranch	*Casella* sp.
Red-striped fairy basslet	*Anthais fasciatus*
Regal angelfish	*Pygoplites diacanthus*
Ribbon sweetlips	*Plectorhychus polytaenia*
Round-armed sea star	*Echinaster glomeratus*
Scribbled angelfish	*Chaetodontoplus duboulayi*
Short dragonfish	*Eurypegasus draconis*
Slipper lobster	*Scyllarides* sp.
Southern basket star	*Conocladus australis*
Southern jewel anemone	*Corynactis australis*
Southern melibe	*Melibe australis*
Southern rock lobster	*Jasus novaehollandiae*
Spanish dancer nudibranch	*Hexabranchus sanguineus*
Spotted procellanid crab	*Neopetrolisthes maculatus*
Sweet dorid	*Chromodoris amoena*
Tassel-snouted flathead	*Platycephalus cirronasus*
Tiera batfish	*Ephippium tiera*
Undulate volute	*Amoria undulata*
Variable armina	*Armina varilosa*
Variable dorid	*Aphelodoris varia*
Varicose nudibranch	*Phyllidia varicosa*
Verco's nudibranch	*Tambja verconis*
Vermilion biscuit star	*Pentagonaster dubeni*
Watanabei's angelfish	*Genicanthus watanabei*
Weedy sea dragon	*Phyllopteryx taeniolatus*
Western Australian jewfish	*Glaucosoma hebraicum*
Whale shark	*Rhineodon typus*
Yellow zoanthid	*Parazoanthus* sp.
Zimmer's sea fan	*Mopsella zimmeri*

INDEX TO FLORA AND FAUNA

INDEX TO REGIONAL DIVING CENTRES

INDEX TO ORGANISATIONS

(Includes commercial services, government agencies, professional associations, and other interest groups mentioned in this guide)

SUBJECT
INDEX

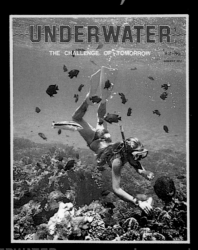
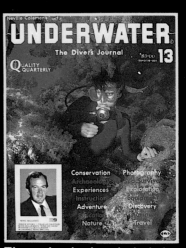

HERON ISLAND.
JUST A MINUTE'S SWIM FROM THE GREAT BARRIER REEF.

Many resorts promise you fantastic diving on the Great Barrier Reef. Trouble is, those resorts aren't right on the reef. That means a lot of travelling time just getting to the dive spot.

The solution is Heron Island.

Heron Island is actually right on the Great Barrier Reef. So you'll find dozens of famous dives only minutes away. And Heron is in a Marine National Park.

So you get some of the most colourful coral and fish in the world, and more time to see it in.

If you want to see more, send for our free brochure.

If Heron wasn't right on the Great Barrier Reef, it would be just another Island Resort.

Heron Island. A P&O Resort.

WHAT CAN YOU BUY FOR YOUR AUSSIE $$...

A HOLIDAY WONDERLAND...
A SCUBA DIVER'S DREAM.

ONLY we have an Island so unspoilt, so untouched, it's been declared a "World Heritage Area". An Island so perfect that only your Australian Dollar will get you there!

Your Aussie $ won't buy you the world's largest swimming pool — but it will get you the biggest crystal clear lagoon, trimmed by white sandy beaches and coral seas.

It won't get you a 5 Star Hotel — but you will feel just as spoilt.

It won't get you crowded out by tourists — but it will get you good times with travellers.

...and best of all, you'll never get bored because our warm waters teem with exotic marine life, and our tropical Island is a paradise.

LORD HOWE ISLAND...

A SPECIAL PLACE FOR SPECIAL PEOPLE — A PLACE WHERE REAL DIVERS DIVE AND THOSE WHO CAN'T, CAN LEARN TO!

For BARGAINS ON YOUR AUSSIE $ contact Pat at Sea Life International Travel, 27 Alfreda Street, Coogee. Phone (02) 665 6333 or send for Our FREE BROCHURE.

t.a.r.b. B1452   **P.L.**

**27 ALFREDA STREET, COOGEE, N.S.W. 2034
TELEPHONE No. (02) 665 6333 TELEX: AA70111
FAX 664 2623**

DIVE

H₂O SPORTZ

Hamilton Island
Great Barrier Reef, Australia

Hamilton Island Resort *Private Mail Bag, Mackay Q. 4740 Australia Phone (079) 46 9144 Telex AA48516*
...dney Suite 609, Eastpoint, 180 Ocean Street, Edgecliff NSW 2027 Australia Phone (02) 327 1899 Telex AA176359 Fax (02) 327 5124

TUSA

COLOURS THE DEEP

TABATA AUSTRALIA PTY. LTD. (Incorporated in N.S.W.) West Ryde Industrial Estate. P.O. Box 117, 86 Falconer Street, West Ryde N.S.W. 2114. Tel: (02) 807 4177 Fax: G3-61-2-808-1638.